A Handbook on the Conduct of Public Inquiries in Canada

A Handbook on the Conduct of Public Inquiries in Canada

Russell J. Anthony
B.A., LL.B., LL.M.
and
Alastair R. Lucas
B.A., LL.B., LL.M.

Butterworths
Toronto

A Handbook on the Conduct of Public Inquiries in Canada

© 1985 Butterworth & Co. (Canada) Ltd.

Printed and bound in Canada

The Butterworth Group of Companies
Canada:
Butterworth & Co. (Canada) Ltd., Toronto and Vancouver
United Kingdom:
Butterworth & Co. (Publishers) Ltd., London
Australia:
Butterworths Pty. Ltd., Sydney, Melbourne, Brisbane, Adelaide and Perth
New Zealand:
Butterworths (New Zealand) Ltd., Wellington and Auckland
Singapore:
Butterworth & Co. (Asia) Pte. Ltd., Singapore
South Africa:
Butterworth Publishers (SA) (Pty) Ltd., Durban and Pretoria
United States:
Butterworth Legal Publishers, Boston, Seattle, Austin and St. Paul
D&S Publishers, Clearwater

Canadian Cataloguing in Publication Data

Anthony, Russell J.
A handbook on the conduct of public inquiries in Canada

Includes index.
ISBN 0-409-84673-2

1. Governmental investigations — Canada. 2. Judicial review of administrative acts — Canada. I. Lucas, Alastair R. II. Title. III. Title: The conduct of public inquiries in Canada.

KE4765.A57 1985   354.7109'3   C85-099210-9

Sponsoring Editor: Derek Lundy
Managing Editor: Linda Kee
Supervisory Editor: Marie Graham
Freelance Projects Co-ordinator/Cover Design: Joan Chaplin
Editor: Susan Gaitskell

Preface

This book is not strictly a law text. While we hope it will prove useful to lawyers advising or appearing before public inquiries, the book will be of more assistance to non-lawyers appointed commissioners of inquiry, to inquiry staff persons and to participants in the inquiry process.

The intention is not to deal with every issue relevant to the establishment and operation of an inquiry. Rather we have focused on those issues or decisions, many apparently insignificant, that stamp the inquiry and affect its credibility and ability to carry out its responsibilities. These issues are discussed in a non-technical way to provide a mental checklist against which organizational decisions may be taken. In areas where there has been significant judicial comment, such as the nature of public inquiries and judicial review, leading decisions and commentaries have been cited.

Nor is it our intention to present a comprehensive legal advice handbook on participation in public inquiries. Detailed information is available from public interest advocacy centres, legal advice clinics and publications prepared by various law associations and public interest organizations. Reference to leading judicial cases has been limited to the sections designed for those interested in reviewing the law. The other chapters also deal with many questions of legal rights and duties, but these issues are discussed in an organizational way.

We have tended to concentrate on information-gathering and project type inquiries, as opposed to inquiries established to investigate suspected wrong-doing. One reason is that formal court-like procedures have traditionally been used, and seem appropriate, for investigative inquiries where the main object is to determine whether criminal proceedings should be initiated. However, formal judicial-style procedures are often patently inappropriate for information-gathering inquiries, where commissioners may find themselves in relatively uncharted procedural territory, faced with a range of uncertain alternatives. A second reason is that the authors' experience has been largely in the context of information-gathering and assessment inquiries. We have not attempted to directly incorporate this basic distinction between types of inquiries into the organization of the book. While differences have been noted where appropriate, generally issues have been discussed in a manner applicable in greater or lesser degree to both types of public inquiry.

The over all organization is roughly chronological, beginning with the establishment of a public inquiry and moving through the various stages to reporting and termination of the inquiry. There are brief historical and constitutional chapters at the beginning to set the proper context and the more technical judical review chapter, which will be of interest primarily to lawyers, at the end. The Appendices are in keeping with the handbook format, and include basic precedents needed to formalize authority, define relationships or help structure the inquiry process.

Clearly there are many forms of public inquiry. Some are quite formal and highly organized; others are informal and personal. The handbook covers the issues and concerns of a more formal hearing process, not because it is the recommended form of procedure, but as a means of presenting a comprehensive list of procedural and organizational options. From this procedural menu the inquiry participants can promote those that best advance their interests and the commissioner can pick and choose those most appropriate for the type of inquiry he considers necessary and for his own personal style. Through this process of selection and combination it is hoped new techniques and forms of inquiry will develop.

Generally we hope that this handbook will be of help to all those involved in the public inquiry process, whether directly as participants, as observers in the media, or as members of the public evaluating the effectiveness of the public inquiry process.

Our debts are numerous. Professor Lucas' work was done at the University of Calgary Law Faculty and while on sabbatical leave in France with a leave fellowship from the Social Sciences and Humanities Research Council of Canada. He benefited from discussions of the work with colleagues, particularly, Nigel D. Bankes, Constance D. Hunt, J. Owen Saunders, and John P. S. McLaren. Russell Anthony searched for documents and recalled personal experiences while taking on new responsibilities, first in constitutional reform while in Ottawa and then with Expo 86 in Vancouver. We both relied heavily on the understanding and co-operation of our colleagues.

The manuscript was prepared in Ottawa by Jeannine Cornellier and in Vancouver by Debra Thompson and at the University of Calgary Law Faculty by Maureen Mahony, Colleen Irwin and Bev Hawkins. Special thanks is due to Bev Hawkins who keyed the manuscript and often had to cope with the well-known problem of two authors, both bent on apparently unending changes and additions. Thanks is also due to the Butterworths people, particularly Linda Kee, who kept us on the job, and our project co-ordinator Joan Chaplin.

Most importantly, we acknowledge and thank our wives and families who tolerated this work and gave up family time for meetings in Calgary, Vancouver, Ottawa, and even Aix-en-Provence. To Lee Anthony, and daughters Catherine and Susan, and Sandra Lucas, son Tony and daughter Katy our heartfelt thanks. Your support and encouragement was essential to the successful completion of this project.

Vancouver,   Russell J. Anthony
Calgary,   Alastair R. Lucas
July, 1985

Table of Contents

I

History and Legal Nature of Commissions of Inquiry

I. HISTORY

Commissions of inquiry in England date from the later Middle Ages and have been traced back as far as the Doomsday Book. These were royal commissions, originally appointed by the Crown, first, by virtue of the royal prerogative, and later under the authority of parliament. The particular prerogative was simply the kings' authority to appoint officials under the royal seal to carry out prescribed duties on behalf of the Crown. It has been pointed out (T.J. Lockwood, "A History of Royal Commissions" (1967), 5 Osgoode Hall L.J. 172, 179) that, even in early times, commissions were subject to controversy concerning their powers and procedures because their appointment was often associated with constitutional disputes concerning the royal prerogative.

Examples from the Tudor period include the commissions on enclosures, monastaries, and operation of the navy. Later, in the Victorian period, before development of an efficient public service, royal commissions were used as a means of initiating legislation. Commissions thoroughly documented needs for legislative reform, particularly for a wide range of social reforms. Thus, until about 1870, commissions functioned as a government bureaucracy, and it has been suggested that they constitute part of the beginnings of modern governmental regulatory bodies (see C.T. Carr, *Concerning English Administrative Law* (1941), 1-14).

Canada's first royal commissions of inquiry were English commissions pertaining to Canada appointed during the colonial period. These ranged from a statutory commission authorized after 1759 to investigate losses and compensation of United Empire Loyalists, to the 1838 commission of Lord Durham to investigate the causes of the 1837–38 rebellions which produced the famous

Durham Report. Beginning about 1825, royal commissions were also appointed by the Canadian colonial governments.

After Confederation federal commissions investigated the Northwest rebellions, alleged railway scandals, transportation, banking, and various complaints against the judiciary. Noteworthy is the landmark nation-building Rowell–Sirois Commission on Dominion Provincial Relations, which reported in 1939. Numerous provincial commissions were also appointed. Recent commissions include the policy development commissions on corporate concentration, taxation, bilingualism and biculturalism, and the "economic union and development prospects for Canada" (Macdonald Royal Commission on the Economy); the commissions to investigate alleged wrongdoing, such as the Quebec crime commissions and the McDonald Commission on the RCMP; and the major project assessment inquiries, such as the Mackenzie Valley Pipeline Inquiry, the West Coast Oil Ports Inquiry, the Saskatchewan Cluff Lake Uranium Mining Board of Inquiry, and the British Columbia Uranium Mining Inquiry.

In Canada, as in England, royal commissions appointed under prerogative powers eventually gave way to statutory commissions appointed under provisions of public inquiry acts. The first Inquiries Act was enacted as a temporary measure by the Assembly of the United Provinces of Canada in 1846, extended, and finally permanently enacted in 1867. This Act is the forerunner of Part I of the present Inquiries Act. Subsequent amendments added the Part II provisions dealing with departmental inquiries in 1880, and the Part III powers to summon and examine witnesses and retain counsel in 1912 (see Watson Sellar, "A Century of Commissions of Inquiry" (1947), 25 Can. Bar Rev. 1, 3–7).

The numbers of inquiries have been subject to peaks and valleys over the decades, the result of a variety of political and economic factors. But it appears that there were nearly four hundred Canadian inquiries of all types between 1867 and 1947. Time and again commissions have been assailed as costly and inefficient. But their obvious political value ensures that commissions continue to be appointed today and are likely to continue to be appointed in the future.

II. LEGAL CHARACTER

Modern commissions of inquiry owe their existence to executive powers conferred on the Governor and Lieutenant Governors in Council by the federal and provincial inquiry acts, and to other specific powers contained in a variety of statutes. (The Law Reform Commission of Canada has compiled a list of federal statutes that contain powers to establish inquiries: *Commissions of Inquiry, Working Paper 17* (1977), 77–86.) There may still be scope for establishment of royal commissions in the traditional manner under the residue of royal prerogative power. However, in practice governments are likely to continue to use the well-tested statutory powers for appointment of commissions of inquiry.

It is clear that inquiries are not courts; nor are they a branch of the judiciary (*Re Commission of Inquiry Concerning Certain Activities of the RCMP* (*RCMP Commission*) (1978), 94 D.L.R. (3d) 365, 370 (ruling of the commission *per* McDonald J.)). Rather, they carry out executive or administrative functions notwithstanding that they usually adopt the judicial procedure of holding hearings (*Re Copeland and McDonald*, [1978] 2 F.C. 815; 88 D.L.R. (3d) 724 (T.D.); *RCMP Commission, supra*). In the rulings of the *RCMP Commission*, Mr. Justice D.C. McDonald described investigative inquiries, such as his, as specially created units of the executive branch of government designed to examine some particular aspect of executive government. "The Executive Branch," according to McDonald J., "through its chosen Executive instrument, is examining itself" (*supra*, at 370). Inquiries are, therefore, creations of government and, unless the empowering statute provides otherwise (see B.C., Inquiry Act, s. 14; Quebec, Public Inquiry Commissions Act, s. 6; New Brunswick, Inquiries Act, s. 10), they can be abolished or their terms of reference can be altered by the executive at any time by means of an amending order in council (see Chapter VII, Terminating the Inquiry, "Government Intervention").

However, government cannot treat inquiries like ordinary government departments. Apart from clear direction by order in council, inquiries cannot be required by ministers or by Cabinet to interpret their terms of reference in a particular way or to follow a particular procedure. Thus, the RCMP Commission ruled that it alone had the power to determine whether or not to receive evidence *in camera*. It would hear and consider submissions on behalf of the Solicitor General or any other Minister, but would not be bound by those views (*supra*, at 327–73).

Information-gathering inquiries are similar in form to investigative inquiries. However, the essential purpose usually differs. It is not so much a matter of the executive examining itself; rather, it is the executive, through the inquiry, examining matters either outside government or outside the traditional government structure. The inquiry's task is to inquire and report to a Minister or to Cabinet so that ultimate policy determinations can be made by government. However, inevitably the inquiry's report goes beyond mere compilation of facts and includes analyses and conclusions on the ultimate policy issues.

II

Constitutional Position of
Public Inquiries

I. DIVISION OF POWERS

Powers of commissions to inquire are limited by the division of legislative powers under the Canadian Constitution. The idea that an inquiry is simply an investigative undertaking analogous to private or university-based research, and therefore without limit as to subject matter, was firmly rejected by the Supreme Court of Canada in *A.G. Quebec v. A.G. Canada*, [1979] 1 S.C.R. 218, 24 N.R. 1 (*sub nom. Keable v. A.G. Canada*). Mr. Justice Pigeon reasoned that a public inquiry is fundamentally different from an ordinary research undertaking. It is conducted not only by means of standard research techniques but also by means of testimony given under oath by witnesses compelled to testify and to produce documents. His Lordship noted that these powers are not available to an inquiry set up under royal prerogative; rather, they depend on statutory authority, particularly the various inquiry acts. The mandate of commissions of inquiry is, consequently, limited to matters within the legislative authority of the level of government by which they are appointed.

Such limitation is confirmed by the result in *A.G. Quebec v. A.G. Canada, supra*. It was held that a provincially appointed inquiry (Keable Commission) could validly inquire into criminal acts allegedly committed by members of the federal Royal Canadian Mounted Police since these matters are in relation to "the administration of justice in the province" (Constitution Act, 1867 (U.K.), c. 3, s. 92(15)). However, the jurisdiction of the inquiry did not extend to an examination of the administration and management of the Royal Canadian Mounted Police. The latter was clearly a matter within the federal criminal law power (s. 91 (27)) and within the residual peace order and good government jurisdiction (opening and concluding words of s. 91).

Provincial authority to establish crime inquiries was also upheld in *Bisaillon v. Keable*, [1983] 2 S.C.R. 60, 51 N.R. 81 at 102-103, and *Saulnier v. Quebec Police Commission*, [1976] 1 S.C.R. 572.

These decisions are consistent with the result of earlier cases, including decisions that a provincial inquiry may validly be empowered to investigate matters related to the construction of a new legislative building (*Kelly v. Mathers* (1915), 25 Man. R. 580, 23 D.L.R. 225 (C.A.); *Re Public Inquiries Act* (1919), 48 D.L.R. 237 (B.C.C.A.)); that a federal commission under the federal Inquiries Act is limited to matters falling within the subjects enumerated in s. 91 of the Constitution Act, 1867 (*North West Grain Dealers' Ass'n. v. Hyndman* (1921), 61 D.L.R. 548 (Man. C.A.)); and that a provincial inquiry has authority to investigate alleged wrong-doing related to federal wartime prohibitory orders with respect to the liquor traffic (*Re Public Inquiries Act* (1919), 48 D.L.R. 237 (B.C.C.A.)).

The Supreme Court of Canada held that consideration by the Keable Commission of events surrounding the 1970 October Crisis did not take the inquiry beyond provincial jurisdiction into exclusive federal national security and criminal law matters. The inquiry was justified in considering these matters, not through systematic investigation, but as necessary background events clearly connected with the specific police activities set out in its terms of reference.

It also appears that provincial commissions of inquiry will exceed provincial legislative jurisdiction if they express conclusions as to criminal responsibility. These powers would carry the inquiry into investigation of specific alleged offences — criminal investigation activities normally carried out by police. This is a matter in substance in relation to criminal law (s. 91(27)), even though it may also relate to the investigation of offences and thus appear to fall within s. 92(15), the administration of justice (*R. v. Hoffman–La Roche Ltd. (Nos. 1 & 2)* (1981), 125 D.L.R. (3d) 607 at 637-38, 62 C.C.C. (2d) 118 at 147-49 (Ont. C.A.); *A.G. Canada v. Canadian National Transportation Ltd.*, [1983] 2 S.C.R. 206, 3 D.L.R. (4th) 16 at 42, 7 C.C.C. (3d) 449 at 475; *Re Nelles and Grange* (1984), 9 D.L.R. (4th) 79 at 85-86 (Ont. C.A.); *A.G. Quebec v. A.G. Canada*, [1979] 1 S.C.R. 218, at 257).

Mere apprehension that an inquiry will attempt to deal with matters outside the constitutionally defined scope of its authority is not sufficient to justify an injunction restraining the entire inquiry. However, an injunction may be obtained where it is relatively clear that an inquiry proposes to investigate matters outside the scope of its authority (*Black Diamond Oil Fields v. Carpenter* (1915), 24 D.L.R. 515 (Alta. S.C.)).

In *Di Iorio v. Montreal Jail Warden*, [1978] 1 S.C.R. 152, 8 N.R. 361 at 392, Mr. Justice Dickson (now Chief Justice) stated that "a provincial commission of inquiry inquiring into *any* subject, might submit a report in which it appeared that changes in federal laws would be desirable." This dictum was explained by Mr. Justice Pigeon in *A.G. Quebec v. A.G. Canada, supra,* to mean, not that a provincial inquiry may validly inquire into any subject, but that "any inquiry into a matter within provincial competence may reveal the desirability of changes in federal laws" (at 29 N.R.).

Generally then, what a provincial inquiry cannot do is directly inquire into a matter related to its terms of reference that is within federal legislative jurisdiction. However, where federal and provincial aspects of a matter are closely related, some incidental consideration of relevant federal laws is appropriate. The limits will be a question of degree in each case.

There might, for example, be reason to question the interpretation placed upon its terms of reference by the Saskatchewan Cluff Lake Uranium Mining Inquiry (Final Report of the Cluff Lake Board of Inquiry, 1978, pp. 6, 121–26). The inquiry decided that the issues to be addressed included: (1) whether the requirements of Canadian and Saskatchewan health and safety law and policies are adequate in terms of the fixing and enforcement of standards; and (2) whether the requirements of Canadian and Saskatchewan uranium mining law and policies designed to protect the physical and living environment are adequate, also in terms of standards and enforcement.

Investigation by a provincial inquiry of health, safety, and environment protection issues related to proposed provincial uranium mining activity is constitutionally unobjectionable even if this inquiry should reveal the necessity for changes in federal laws. However, if the inquiry explicitly undertakes assessment of the effectiveness of federal laws, even as they relate to what are essentially provincial matters, and clearly designates this as a task of the inquiry, this may take the provincial inquiry beyond the scope of its constitutional authority.

Self-incrimination protection has (apart from the Canadian Charter of Rights and Freedoms. See, *infra*.) been held to be legislation in relation to criminal law and procedure and, consequently, a matter within exclusive federal constitutional authority. Thus, federal statutory protection against self-incrimination is available even in relation to wholly provincial inquiries (*Di Iorio v. Montreal Jail Warden, supra,* at 402–403 N.R.). It has been held that s. 5 of the Canada Evidence Act, R.S.C. 1970, c. E-10, extends to questions put to a witness by a provincial inquiry where the witness was subpoenaed by the inquiry (*Di Iorio*, at 403 (N.R.)). Similarly, the common law rule against judicial disclosure of the identity of police informers is essentially a matter of criminal law, so that inquiry into identity of informers lies beyond the powers of a provincial inquiry, and the province lacks authority to modify or abrogate the rule (*Bisaillon v. Keable*, [1983] 2 S.C.R. 60; 51 N.R. 81, 124 at 138-141; *Solicitor General of Canada v. Royal Commission of Inquiry into the Confidentiality of Health Records in Ontario*, [1981] 2 S.C.R. 494).

There is no constitutional restriction on a provincial commission of inquiry exercising powers to punish for contempt in the case of a refusal to testify (*Di Iorio* at 403 (N.R.)). The rationale is that provincial power to punish for violations of provincial laws is unrestricted. Commitment of the witness is valid since it is an act that is merely coercive. It is not punitive in nature and, therefore, it is not an essentially criminal matter within federal criminal law jurisdiction (*Di Iorio* at 380 N.R.).

It was held in *A.G. Quebec v. A.G. Canada*, [1979] 1 S.C.R. 218, 24 N.R. 1 (*sub nom. Keable v. A.G. Canada*) that provincial inquiries lack the authority to compel federal ministers or officials to testify as witnesses. Any jurisdiction to compel attendance of witnesses or to require production of documents depends on statutory authority, and provincial legislation is not constitutionally effective to confer such jurisdiction in relation to the federal Crown (*A.G. Quebec v. A.G. Canada* at 24 N.R.).

The Supreme Court of Canada refused to grant a motion for a stay of a provincial court order to suspend a provincial inquiry (*Keable v. A.G. Canada*, [1978] 2 S.C.R. 135, 20 N.R. 243). The Supreme Court concluded that, if granted, the motion would have the effect of disposing, at least in part, of serious constitutional and jurisdictional questions in an interlocutory motion.

II. CANADIAN CHARTER OF RIGHTS AND FREEDOMS

Another potential basis for constitutional attack on the jurisdiction of public inquiries is the Canadian Charter of Rights and Freedoms. It is possible that the very terms of reference of an inquiry, as well as action taken by the inquiry under this authority, such as preliminary rulings, could have the effect of infringing any of the fundamental freedoms, such as freedom of religion and freedom of expression, enumerated in s. 2 of the Charter. These rights are guaranteed, according to section 1, "subject only to such reasonable limits prescribed by law as can be demonstrably justified in a free and democratic society." The Charter came into effect in 1982, and Canadian courts have now begun to develop the analytical principles, particularly the balancing of interests required by s. 1, necessary to apply the Charter.

For example, it may be asserted that the terms of reference of an inquiry established to investigate the activities of a particular religious sect infringe the affected persons' guarantee of freedom of religion. Similarly, it is possible that recommendations of an inquiry in relation to particular persons that adversely affect the public character or reputation of those persons may be declared to infringe protected rights, such as the s. 7 right to "security of the person."

Section 7 has the potential to substantially extend the "fairness" rights of persons involved in public inquiries. This section reads as follows:

> 7. Everyone has the right to life, liberty and security of the person and the right not to be deprived thereof except in accordance with the principles of fundamental justice.

It appears to enlarge existing statute and common-law-based natural justice and procedural fairness rights of inquiry participants. (See *Singh v. Minister of Manpower and Immigration*, not yet reported (May 9, 1985 S.C.C.). It may also have the substantive effect of invalidating "unfair" inquiring powers.

For example, a provision of the Federal Combines Investigation Act which authorizes the Director of Research and Investigation when conducting an inquiry, to compel any person to testify, was held to be inconsistent with s. 7 and consequently of no force and effect. (*R.L. Crain Inc. v. Couture* (1983), 30 Sask. R. 191, 6 D.L.R. (4th) 478 (Q.B.)). The court noted that there was no requirement that a person compelled to testify be advised of any allegations against him. It concluded that the provision is an integral step in the eventual criminal prosecution of a suspected person, that it authorizes the arbitrary compulsion of a person to assist in his own prosecution, and that there are no compelling factors to justify the result dictated. This decision suggests that the Inquiry Act provisions empowering commissioners to compel witnesses to testify may be of no force and effect, to the extent that the proceedings are aimed at investigating suspected wrongdoing of the very persons summoned.

Section 11 provides specific fair procedure rights to persons charged with an offence, as well as a general right to a "fair and public hearing by an independent and impartial tribunal." This may be relevant to investigative inquiries, since many inquiry acts use the same "persons charged" language in providing procedural fairness rights (see Chapter VIII, Judicial Review of Inquiries).

A protection for witnesses against the use of their incriminating evidence in subsequent proceedings is provided by s. 13 of the Charter. This appears to be a constitutionalization of the self-incrimination protection found in s. 5 of the Canada Evidence Act and in provincial evidence acts (*R.L. Crain Inc. v. Couture*). However unlike the Evidence Act provisions, s. 13 does not require the person claiming the protection to have specifically invoked the privilege against self-incrimination in the earlier proceedings.

According to s. 24(2) of the Charter, in any judicial proceedings to obtain a remedy for infringement of charter-protected rights or freedoms, evidence obtained in a manner that infringes any of the Charter rights or freedoms, must be excluded if a court concludes that in the circumstances admission of the evidence would bring the administration of justice into disrepute. This protection has been held not to preclude admission by an inquiry of illegally obtained evidence not obtained in a manner that involved infringement of the Charter rights (*Smallwood v. A.G. Can.* (1983), 3 **D.L.R.** (4th) 301, 122 **A.P.R.** 278 (Nfld S.C.)). It may, as the court suggested in the *Smallwood* case, be largely or exclusively limited to evidence obtained in consequence of activities held to be unreasonable searches or seizures under s. 8 of the Charter.

III

Establishing the Inquiry

I. DOCUMENTS OF CREATION

Canadian commissions of inquiry are usually established by order in council of either the federal Cabinet or a provincial Cabinet under inquiry statutes. These general inquiry statutes authorize the establishment of inquiries into matters within the respective federal and provincial constitutional jurisdiction. The federal Act is entitled the Inquiries Act. Provincially, titles differ somewhat, but "Public Inquiries Act" is the term most commonly used. The statutes from various Canadian jurisdictions are cited in Appendix A-1. The complete text of the federal Inquiries Act is reproduced in Appendix A-2.

This handbook is concerned mainly with inquiries established under the various Inquiry Acts. But is must be remembered that, in addition to the inquiry acts, many other statutes authorize the establishment of inquiries. It has been estimated that, at the federal level alone, there are over forty-seven statutes that confer powers of inquiry and incorporate specific powers from the Inquiries Act concerning such matters as the summoning of witnesses (Law Reform Commission of Canada, *Commissions of Inquiry*, Working Paper 17, (1977)). At least forty other federal statutes authorize inquiries without reference to the Inquiries Act. An example of an inquiry of this latter type is the Mackenzie Valley Pipeline Inquiry, which drew its authority from a provision of the Territorial Lands Act. Many of these statutes directly confer specific powers to inquire on persons or agencies, while other statutes merely contain general inquiry powers that may be more particularly defined by the Governor in Council. A similar array of empowering statutes exists at the provincial level.

A careful reading of the authorizing legislation is important before embarking on any inquiry. While most inquiry acts are generally similar, there are important differences. Some statutes require the hearing officer (the "commissioner") to report to the government; others require that the report be made to the Legislature by initially providing it to the government, which must table it in the Legislature within a specified time. This distinction is important since it determines whether public release of the inquiry's report is a matter of discretion left to the government or whether it is required by statute. In some cases the legislation requires the commissioner to "investigate and report." This statutory directive arguably affects the government's authority to curtail the inquiry before it has reported (see Chapter VII, Terminating the Inquiry).

It is also important that the commissioner be satisfied that the scope of the issues on which he is to report falls within the constitutional jurisdiction of the level of government that appointed him. If the inquiry is established under specific legislation, rather than a general inquiry Act, a second jurisdictional concern arises. In this latter case, the inquiry may be limited in the scope of its investigation by the very legislation under which it is created.

Most enabling statutes that authorize the establishment of inquiries provide that the inquiry shall be created by the Lieutenant Governor in Council (provincial) or the Governor in Council (federal). It is, therefore, the Cabinet of the particular level of government that establishes an inquiry. Generally, evidence of creation of an inquiry is in the form of an order in council.

Individuals approached to undertake the conduct of an inquiry should immediately inquire as to whether or not the authorizing order in council has been prepared. If not, the proposed hearing officer should be prepared to play a creative role in drafting the order in council for submission to Cabinet to ensure it meets the commissioner's needs as well as those of the government. So that there are no questions concerning the authority and jurisdiction of the commissioner and the ability of the inquiry to carry out its responsibilities as perceived, not only by Cabinet but by the commissioner and those who will play a role in the inquiry process, the proposed commissioner should request a copy of the draft terms of reference order in council before it is submitted to Cabinet and take an active role in determining the form the order in council should take. Depending on the nature of the inquiry, the issues the proposed Commissioner may wish to consider include:

1. The commissioner or commissioners should be personally and correctly named. If there are to be a number of commissioners, the chairman should be specifically designated. Identification of the commissioner by current position or title should be avoided in the event that, during the course of the inquiry, the incumbent ceases to hold that position.

2. Commissioners who are not employees of the government, and particularly part-time commissioners, require authority for payment of living, travel, and *per diem* compensation. Rather than specifically setting out the commissioner's remuneration, it is suggested that the order in council merely authorize such payment as may be agreed from time to time. In that case a separate written agreement setting out the remuneration should be prepared and executed at the time the order in council is approved.

3. If possible, the inquiry should be funded by the general revenue of the government rather than from the budgetary allotment of any particular ministry (see Chapter III, Establishing the Inquiry, "Financing the Inquiry").

4. The order in council should identify a reporting ministry of the government for purposes of the day-to-day conduct of the inquiry, even when the inquiry is to report to the government or the Legislature as a whole.

5. The commissioner should be given the authority to retain staff and consultative or administrative services, including professional service such as legal counsel, and generally to incur the expenses necessary to fulfil the mandate of the inquiry. Terms such as, "within the guidelines for government audit" are appropriate, but terms such as "within limits prescribed by the government" and other such general controls on rates of remuneration or other expenditures should be avoided (see Chapter III, Establishing the Inquiry).

6. Any preamble to the order in council should be worded so that it cannot be used as a matter of interpretation to create ambiguities in the terms of reference of the inquiry stated in the substantive portion of the order in council. It also should be free of potentially embarrassing assumptions or conclusions that may be in the government's mind, yet may be the subject of controversy in the inquiry itself.

7. The commissioner must be satisfied that he has sufficient authority to inquire into and report on the issues referred to him for investigation. Some orders in council suggest that the commissioner is merely to report on information that currently exists and is not authorized to undertake his own additional studies to round out the available information. If the commissioner wishes to have the authority to undertake such additional studies, it is best to ensure that the powers given the commissioner are sufficiently broad and clear to give that authority. The authority to travel, hire consultants, and hire professional staff, if properly worded, may be sufficient to imply the authority to undertake independent study.

8. The terms of reference of the inquiry should be defined broadly

enough to allow the commissioner the scope to define the issues as events unfold. For example, authority to conduct an inquiry into construction of a specific oil port should be stated as a general authority to investigate the question of construction of an oil port on the coast. This would ensure that, should the existing proposal be withdrawn and a competing proposal presented during the course of the inquiry, the commissioner would have authority to proceed with the investigation. Where possible, the inquiry should be generically defined rather than tied directly to a named project or event.

9. The terms of reference should be sufficiently wide to allow consideration of alternatives to any specific project that may have been the genesis of the inquiry and to ensure that the inquiry is not bound to accept particular assumptions. For example, an order in council that provides: "assuming the stated project is constructed, the commissioner is to investigate what are the potential impacts," may prevent the inquiry from examining the question of whether the project, in its entirety, should go ahead. An inquiry to determine the impact of a project that is assumed to proceed in the form presented merely considers ameliorating effects; it is much more limited than an inquiry authorized to examine a range of alternatives, including the option of determining that the project, as proposed, should not proceed at all (see Chapter IV, The Inquiry Structure, "Preliminary Hearings").

10. Unless authority to compel the attendance of witnesses and the production of documents is found in the enabling legislation under which the inquiry is established, a grant of these powers should be specifically included in the order in council.

11. If specific authorization for the funding of participants in the inquiry is required, the order in council should include this authority, or a related order in council should be prepared and submitted simultaneously. Often this is best handled by authorizing the commissioner to pay for consultants, advisors, participants in the inquiry process, and representatives of the public interest as the commissioner deems advisable. Alternatively, the whole question of participant funding can be left out of the authorizing order in council so long as there is a clear understanding that such funding will be available if the commissioner deems it advisable. The matter can then be dealt with at a later date (see Chapter IV, The Inquiry Structure, "Participants and Participant Funding").

12. The commissioner should avoid, if possible, the inclusion of a specified reporting date in the authorizing order in council. While the commissioner could clearly agree to proceed as

expeditiously as possible, a report date imposed before all of the issues are known may place the integrity of the inquiry in jeopardy. An inquiry will be under constant pressure and is subject to manipulation by all participants if it is known that its life is limited by a defined period. For example, proponents of a project under review may avoid completing unfavourable studies until the inquiry's mandate expires. Similarly, opponents may delay the proceedings in the hope the inquiry will have to conclude that it lacked sufficient information to approve the project. Whatever informal arrangements are made, no final report date should be included in the order in council.

If the commissioner is made aware in advance of particular time constraints (and not artificial time limits imposed by a government for its own convenience), the commissioner can structure the inquiry's investigation and consultation processes to ensure that the inquiry is in a position to advise the government on at least the key issues within the established time frame. Interim reports, reports at the end of phases of the inquiry, or other similar techniques may be used to ensure that the government has some timely advice. These procedures are better suited to meeting a predetermined time limit than an inflexible final reporting date.

13. If final disposition of the inquiry documents is to be provided for, the order in council should state only that the formal inquiry documents are to be left with the public archivist. This gives the commissioner discretion as to the disposition of the various other reports and studies obtained by the inquiry (see Chapter VII, Terminating of the Inquiry).

The order in council establishing the Mackenzie Valley Pipeline Inquiry is found in Appendix A-3; the West Coast Oil Ports Inquiry is Appendix A-4; the McDonald Commission into the RCMP is Appendix A-5; and the British Columbia Royal Commission on Uranium Mining is Appendix A-6. These illustrate the variety of forms orders in council may take.

After the final form of the order in council is approved by Cabinet, the new commissioner should ensure that any communications from the inquiry defining its mandate or describing its activities at this early stage use the words of the order in council. This will avoid redefining the terms of reference of the inquiry inadvertently, either narrowing or expanding its authority.

Once the order in council has been approved, three certified copies should be obtained by the commissioner. One should be available in the Inquiry's office for reproduction, as copies will be required throughout the course of inquiry. The second copy should be tabled at the opening of the inquiry so that a copy of the enabling order in council forms part of the inquiry's formal record. The third is often retained by the commissioner as a personal memento.

II. REPORTING DATE

One of the most important issues to be settled at the time the terms of the authorizing order in council are finalized is the question of whether there will be a reporting date.

Governments often face time constraints, either formal (for example, where decisions must be made in conjunction with decisions of other countries or of agencies over which they have no control) or informal (for example, where legislative timetables should be adhered to). In either case governments may wish to impose a final date by which the inquiry must submit a report for consideration (see, for example, the order in council establishing the West Coast Oil Ports Inquiry, Appendix A-4).

III. PRELIMINARY QUESTIONS

With the inquiry formally launched, it is appropriate for the commissioner to consider a number of general questions about the inquiry and his role as a commissioner before he is required to make any public announcements or decisions. While it may be premature to make decisions about any of these issues, their consideration will greatly enhance the commissioner's ability to respond to the various pressures that will be placed upon him almost immediately after the formation of the inquiry is announced. It will also ensure that decisions are not made early in the inquiry process that foreclose options that the commissioner may later wish to pursue. Too often, proceeding on assumptions or making what appear to be harmless decisions early in the inquiry process may bind the inquiry or give it an appearance to the public and participants which later may be difficult to dislodge.

Before conducting the first press interview or approaching parties with an interest in the inquiry, the commissioner should consider several general questions, including:

1. *Why was the inquiry created and what is my reaction to this?*

This may seem irrelevant, but it does, in fact, have important consequences. Public inquiries are not established in isolation, and they do not operate independently of other events. Participants will probably already have had a history of involvement in the issues before the inquiry and will bring this history with them as they approach and begin participation in the inquiry process.

It is proper for the commissioner to consider, for example, whether he was appointed because there is a hot political issue and the government wished to externalize the problem and thereby avoid direct responsibility for resolution of the issue. If it is a contentious political issue, the commissioner can expect to be stepping into the middle of a high profile, ongoing dispute. It is likely to lead to a very partisan inquiry as participants attempt to use the inquiry process to further their political objectives. The press will lavish attention on the inquiry, and politicians will watch with a wary eye. The commissioner must ask how these pressures relate to his ideas, and what type of inquiry structure and process is suitable to meet the various demands likely to be placed on the inquiry.

On the other hand, it must be asked whether the commission was created merely as a convenient means for the government to shelve an issue. If the government, and often the parties involved, are prepared to have the resolution of the issue delayed, then this too will affect the timing and the willingness of the parties to respond to the inquiry.

A further alternative might be that the issue is so broad and has so many interrelated aspects that no single government department could deal with the whole issue. The inquiry is, therefore, established as a governmental task force to resolve inter-departmental, or even inter-governmental rivalries or disputes. Again, this will shape the type of co-operation that might be expected, and the attitude of non-government agencies toward the inquiry.

Finally, the inquiry may have been set up because of the need to resolve difficult technical questions or to improve general knowledge of the issue, particularly among members of the public. In this case the inquiry is faced with two challenges: First, it must ensure that it is structured so that persons with technical expertise can assist the inquiry in understanding and resolving difficult technical questions. This may best be done through a series of papers or seminars rather than by means of formal evidence and cross-examination. On the other hand, if the purpose is to promote a public awareness of the issue, the inquiry must be able to present the technical information in a way that is comprehensible and relevant to public concerns. It probably will also have to structure its proceedings so that representatives of various public interests will be prepared to participate and, through their participation, relay the necessary information to their constituencies. These are the segments of the public that must be reached, both to provide accurate information and to ensure that, after the inquiry, those representatives of the public most involved cannot attack the inquiry because it failed to involve members of the public with particular interest and expertise.

A brief recital of the various reasons why an inquiry may have been established gives the commissioner an opportunity to reflect upon the implications these considerations may have for the form and structure of the inquiry, the attitude of the participants involved in the inquiry, the pressures from the media and the government, and the expectations created in members of the general public. It is then up to the commissioner to assess these factors and consider what effect they should have on the conduct of the inquiry.

Consideration of the reasons for establishment of the inquiry leads to a second general question:

2. What purposes are to be served in the conduct of the inquiry?

Regardless of the intentions of those who establish and participate in the inquiry, the purposes that the commissioner wishes the inquiry to serve usually govern. While invariably the inquiry will serve a number of purposes, often an overriding function will be perceived.

The purpose to be served will determine the general shape the inquiry will take. An inquiry investigating alleged wrongdoing may wish to establish a formal "judicial" appearance. On the other hand, the hearing officer may conclude that his function is to arbitrate between relatively well-defined positions and attempt to develop a consensus. Even if there is a question of wrongdoing, he may wish to operate in an investigative manner in which the inquiry, through its staff, researches and identifies the issues rather than requiring parties adverse in interest to do so. Alternatively, the commissioner may wish to ensure that no one appears to be "on trial" in the proceedings and, therefore, will structure the inquiry in a way that is non-adversarial.

There are limits in some situations on the ability of the commissioner to shape the inquiry process. For example, often it is not the inquiry that creates an adversarial process; rather, the fact that the parties are clearly adverse in interest ensures that their conduct will produce an adversarial situation. The question for the commissioner, then, is merely to decide on the process that will either accommodate or modify this pre-existing situation. Should the inquiry adopt a judicial format to ensure that the adverse parties feel they have a fair opportunity to present their positions, or should it attempt to prevent the adverse interests from dominating the inquiry proceedings?

Is the purpose of the inquiry to improve public knowledge of the issues? If the inquiry perceives it has a role in public education, then the form of its proceedings will have to reflect this purpose. Certain information before the inquiry that might more efficiently be tabled or filed may have to be presented orally and in detail so that members of the public can follow. Very technical evidence may have to be presented in less technical language so that representatives of the public have the opportunity to participate in its evaluation. Public interest groups may have to be funded or otherwise encouraged to participate in the proceedings. Structures may have to be established that will encourage or even ensure media coverage so that the information generated by the inquiry is transmitted to the public in a regular and comprehensible way.

The need for the public to be involved in the proceedings will also determine where, when, and in what format the inquiry will conduct its proceedings. The segment of the public that the inquiry is intended to reach may determine the location of the proceedings and the type of information program it will undertake.

Finally, and this is often the most difficult issue for commissioners to face, the commissioner must decide how "political" he will allow the inquiry to become. The first response is, inevitably, that the inquiry will not be political at all, and every effort will be made to ensure that it does not become part of a larger political debate. Unfortunately, this is often more easily said than done. Depending on the nature of the subject matter referred to the inquiry and the participants involved, the issue probably is already political. Given the inquiry's terms of reference, what effect will this political dimension have on the parties likely to appear, the atmosphere in which the inquiry will operate, and the public expectations and support for the inquiry? The answers to these questions affect such things as estimates of the length of time the inquiry will take, the localities where the inquiry may be required to conduct its affairs, co-operation amongst participants, and even the name that should be given to the inquiry.

IV. NAMING THE INQUIRY

Rarely do orders in council establishing an inquiry actually name the inquiry. They normally state only that an inquiry will be made into a particular subject matter (see Appendices A-3 to A-6 for illustrations). It is often left to the media to give the inquiry a shorthand title. Thus, an inquiry to investigate and report on the construction of a nuclear facility at a rural town soon becomes the Rural Town Nuclear Inquiry. It is useful, therefore, for the commissioner to give the inquiry its name at a very early date.

There is no real distinction between a royal commission and a public inquiry. Both are established by the Cabinet under an authorizing order in council. The term royal commission can be applied to both provincial and federal inquiries established under general inquiry legislation. It should not be used for hearings under specific legislation. However, the question whether an inquiry should describe itself as a royal commission should be considered (see Chapter I, History and Legal Nature of Commissions of Inquiry, "History").

Inquiries that examine specific projects or questions that are less than national issues have generally not adopted the term royal commission, while general inquiries into national issues have tended to do so. Thus, there was the Royal Commission on Bilingualism and Biculturalism; however, nationally significant inquiries into specific projects, such as the Mackenzie Valley Pipeline Inquiry, have not used the royal commission terminology. There is a certain formality and detachment associated with the term royal commission, and many commissioners have designated their inquiry a royal commission to emphasize that the inquiry is independent of government.

While the order in council will define the subject matter of the inquiry and, thus, suggest the basis for a formal name, there are a number of considerations to be borne in mind when choosing a name. The name should, of course, be descriptive of inquiry and short enough to be used correctly and fully in media reports. A long name will invariably be shortened by the media to the name of the commissioner. This focuses attention on the commissioner rather than the subject matter of the inquiry. The name should be sufficiently different from any government agency or private organization to ensure there are no mistakes in identification or assumptions of affiliation.

The name of an inquiry can significantly affect the public's perception of the approach the inquiry is taking. Sometimes a hearing officer may wish to focus the nature of the investigation and will select a name accordingly (for example, the Mackenzie Valley Pipeline Inquiry, rather than the Royal Commission into Northern Gas Pipeline Construction). Of course, with a name which narrowly defines the scope of the inquiry, there is always the risk that events may change sufficiently to require a broader examination of issues than originally conceived.

For example, the inquiry into construction of an oil port at Kitimat was named the Kitimat Oil Port Inquiry. Shortly after the inquiry was established, the Kitimat oil port proposal was suspended by the proponents and an alternative project at another location was promoted. The commissioner, therefore, renamed the inquiry the West Coast Oil Port Inquiry. This was sufficiently broad to ensure that the inquiry could examine the impact of an oil port at whatever location on the West Coast proponents were prepared to support at the particular time. Not only does a more general name make it clear that alternatives not specifically in mind when the inquiry was created will be considered; it also ensures that too narrow an interpretation of the terms of reference is not confirmed by a name that focuses on a specific issue or location. When in doubt, a general name, consistent with the terms of reference of the inquiry, should be used.

V. AUTHORITY OF THE COMMISSIONER

It is not clear whether it is necessary for the commissioner to take an oath of office after his appointment. In most cases it does not appear to be essential. However, certain authorizing statutes such as the British Columbia Inquiry Act, section 5, require an oath to be administered. In each case the governing legislation should be consulted. Attached as Appendix B-1 is the form of oath required by the B.C. legislation which, with appropriate change, could be used if no form of oath is provided. The oath would, in normal circumstances, be given by the chief justice of the superior court in the province, or, in the case of a federal appointment, by a judge of the federal court or the Supreme Court of Canada.

The legal authority of the commissioner to enter into agreements and incur expenses for purposes of the inquiry comes from the authorizing order in council. Therefore, the commissioner should have a certified copy of the order in council available in the event that further copies are required by persons dealing with the inquiry.

At an early stage, the commissioner will be asked to incur expenses or other obligations on behalf of the inquiry. Leases for premises, equipment rental, bank accounts, and personal service contracts will all have to be entered into, often before the inquiry staff is in place. An inquiry and its commissioner are in a unique position in that the inquiry is not a distinct incorporated identity, nor is the commissioner necessarily a representative of the government. It is clear from the order in council, however, that he has the right to make necessary expenditures on behalf of the inquiry and, by extension, on behalf of the government.

Generally, all contracts should be made in the official name of the inquiry and signed by the commissioner on behalf of the inquiry. It is important that the commissioner not execute agreements in his personal capacity. The form these agreements should take is discussed in Section X, of this chapter, "Relations with Government."

VI. INQUIRY STAFF

A. Secretary to the Inquiry

One of the first jobs of the commissioner is to select a core staff. Since the inquiry will be of undetermined duration, the staff is generally seconded or hired on contract. One of the first staff members to be hired will be the inquiry secretary. This is the person with overall administrative responsibility for the inquiry. Depending on the size and scope of the inquiry, this person may also be the personal secretary to the commissioner, the clerk who attends hearings to receive and record documents and administer oaths to persons giving evidence, and the regular inquiry contact with the government on financial and other administrative matters.

For small inquiries, the functions of personal secretary and secretary to the inquiry could be carried out by one person, with government liaison handled by the commissioner himself. In such a case, what is required is a secretary with the necessary technical skills, the ability to delegate responsibility and organize others and, finally, someone who would be free to travel with the commissioner should it be necessary to hold inquiry sessions in various localities. This should be a full-time position, especially if the commissioner is not full time and a staff member is required to maintain a permanent inquiry presence.

For larger inquiries, it may be preferable to have an executive secretary who can deal with the more complex administrative matters, deal with the government on questions of finance and administration, attend all hearings, travel with the commissioner, and generally be the chief administrative officer. This is clearly a full-time position. A person with government experience is invaluable in advising the commissioner on how to deal with the government bureaucracy. The commissioner will then also require a personal secretary who should have the necessary technical skills and be able to co-ordinate the work of others, particularly when the commissioner and executive secretary are absent from the inquiry office holding hearings or travelling.

Because *ad hoc* commissions of inquiry are usually new processes for those involved, an experienced executive secretary has major responsibilities in ensuring the efficient operation of the inquiry. Often the criticism is made that it is the executive secretary, rather than the commissioner, that makes many of the key decisions that shape that structure of the inquiry, and indeed this may be so. For that reason, it is important that the commissioner and executive secretary are able to work with each other efficiently and co-operatively, and that the executive secretary is the type of person who can work well with others while effectively carrying out the duties of a chief administrative officer. His prime role in the inquiry will be to steer it through the maze of government red tape and to deal diplomatically with government auditors and other officials. He will also be responsible for hiring support staff, determining wages, and generally ensuring that the office's financial and administrative functions operate smoothly.

As official secretary to the inquiry during any hearings, the executive secretary will be responsible for making the necessary arrangements for physical premises and whatever other support facilities are necessary for the hearings, handling accommodation and travel for the inquiry, and co-ordinating demands on the commissioner's time. He will also be responsible for accepting, recording and retaining evidence presented before the inquiry. He must accept and mark exhibits, maintain an exhibit book, and control access to and disposition of all exhibits. The executive secretary should be made a commissioner for oaths so that he can administer oaths to witnesses appearing before the inquiry.

Notwithstanding the executive secretary's important administrative role, it must be clear from the outset that the ultimate authority on administrative matters rests with the commissioner, and that the decisions of the chief technical advisors and counsel to the inquiry must prevail on all important questions of policy with the commissioner acting as referee only where necessary. Most inquiry conflicts result from disputes between the executive secretary with his concern for administrative efficiency and the investigative staff with its concern for a full and complete inquiry.

B. Counsel

Though most commissioners are reluctant to move too quickly on initial staffing, it is of great value to the commissioner to appoint an inquiry counsel and a chief technical advisor at an early date. This will ensure that initial steps taken by the inquiry, which may ultimately shape the inquiry and the public's perception of it, are made within the context of professional advice. The counsel and technical advisor are important advisors in preparing the commissioner for his initial interaction with the public and the press. They will assist in making contacts with major participants in the inquiry and in the difficult task of finding a competent technical staff.

Counsel to an inquiry is an important position, whether or not the inquiry develops into a major judicial-type investigation. If the inquiry does not develop to the point of holding formal hearings, the counsel will still play a valuable role as advisor to the commissioner. He will advise on technical legal issues and on more general questions, such as whether or not particular issues might properly be considered within the formal terms of reference of the inquiry. Whether for technical advice on the signing of agreements or the scope of the inquiry's power to obtain information from other parties, the counsel will regularly be called upon to advise the commissioner.

If the inquiry is one where formal hearings are to be held, an inquiry counsel is essential. First, if there are vital interests at stake or important matters of principle to be decided, one can expect that participants, or at least some of them, will be represented by counsel. An inquiry is at a serious disadvantage if the commissioner is required to consider and rule on legal or technical objections in the absence of independent legal advice. Second, and most important, general guidelines that govern the way commissions of inquiry are required to proceed have now been established in Canada (see Chapter VIII, Judicial Review of Inquiries). Because rules of procedural fairness apply to inquiry decisions, both inside and outside of hearings, legal advice on procedure is essential.

An inquiry counsel with experience in inquiries and administrative law and practice is particularly helpful. A lawyer with only court experience is likely to have some difficulty in coping with the less structured process of most public inquiries. Secondarily, knowledge of the subject area of the inquiry (environmental planning, nuclear industry, transportation, fisheries) is of great assistance, though of less significance than relevant legal experience, owing to the availability of technical support staff.

In most large hearings, counsel will require the assistance of other lawyers, either to deal with areas requiring special expertise or to act as junior counsel to alleviate the work load. The latter role is particularly important when lengthy hearings are required and where the inquiry counsel plays an active role in examining the evidence of others or presenting evidence on behalf of the inquiry. In any case there should be only one chief inquiry counsel, though other counsel may take the lead for particular phases of the inquiry.

It is useful for the commissioner to consider the role that he wishes the inquiry counsel to play. Depending on the structure of the inquiry, the counsel may play a very active or a relatively passive role. Should the commissioner develop a passive style, where responsibility for presenting evidence to the inquiry is left entirely to interested parties, counsel's role is merely that of advising the commissioner on issues in the conduct of the inquiry and advising during the report-writing stage. However, even in this case, if the parties have counsel, matters may arise during the course of the inquiry on which some legal advice would be useful.

Should the inquiry take on a more substantial structure, the role of counsel increases correspondingly. Generally, the counsel can be said to have the responsibility to ensure the credibility and integrity of the inquiry, of the inquiry process, and of the commissioner himself. To do this, the counsel must ensure that the role played by the commissioner is appropriate, that the process adopted by the inquiry is fair and legally correct and, with the assistance of the technical staff, that all of the necessary evidence is before the inquiry.

Later in the inquiry process, the counsel will be involved in the report-writing stage by providing advice on such questions as what evidence the commissioner can rely on and what weight should be given to such evidence. He will also review the final report to ensure there are no statements which are defamatory or which might present other legal difficulties for the inquiry. In the case of a more substantial inquiry, the counsel will facilitate formal presentations of investigations conducted by inquiry staff and will present evidence to the inquiry, either directly through expert witnesses or by cross-examination.

Inquiry counsel will also play an important administrative role in dealing with other participants and governments with respect to the presentation of evidence. This includes helping to organize an orderly sequence of witnesses before the inquiry. He also has a duty to assist participants and to ensure they are advised of inquiry procedures. Like the executive secretary, counsel will be required to travel with the inquiry and to represent the inquiry in various meetings with the participants, the public, and sometimes the media. Consequently, the commissioner should select a person who is capable of performing these various functions and who is compatible with the commissioner in approach and temperament.

C. Technical Advisor

Whatever the number or variety of experts retained, the inquiry should have one chief technical advisor with sufficient technical knowledge to understand and advise on the evidence. However, the technical advisor does not normally perform the role of expert witness and, therefore, need not have credentials necessary to establish formal recognition as an expert. In fact, it is often better to have someone with less than widely recognized qualifications so that he can critically evaluate the various views presented without being identified with any particular position. Since this is a person who must be involved in the inquiry on a full-time basis, chief technical advisors tend to be associated with consulting firms, universities (where they can take leave), or with government departments.

Some of the most successful technical advisors have been individuals associated with government who have had day-to-day responsibilities in the subject matter of the inquiry. A person in this position has the advantage of being knowledgeable about the issues and familiar with the experts. The individual is usually well known to both industry and government; other officials are, therefore, likely to trust him with information they might not be prepared to forward to an independent consultant retained by the inquiry. If he has been involved with government review of the project under inquiry consideration, the commissioner should be satisfied that his involvement has not been so extensive that he could be regarded as biased. This person must be prepared to be critical of government as well as other actors in the area, and this may produce conflict with his peers. A technical advisor drawn from government may tend to be somewhat conservative in an investigative inquiry, but this can be overcome by an active commission counsel and inquiry staff.

If the technical advisor is appointed from the private sector, the commissioner should review his record of appearances as a consultant or expert witness and should particularly ensure that he has not advised any of the inquiry participants just before his appointment.

The role of chief technical advisor is a demanding one. In addition to advising on definition of the issues the inquiry is to examine, the chief technical advisor will be responsible for: organizing and contracting for research, evaluating technical data, identifying expert witnesses and working with them to prepare technical evidence, reviewing technical evidence for the commissioner and advising him, preparing cross-examination of witnesses for commission counsel, reviewing the technical work of the inquiry staff, and assisting the commissioner in writing the final report. He plays a major role in establishing the credibility of the inquiry by ensuring that an adequate technical assessment of the subject matter is available.

As discussed later (see Chapter IV, The Inquiry Structure, "The Inquiry Phases"), inquiries often operate in phases (*e.g.*, environmental, socio-economic, engineering). Most major phased inquiries have found it valuable to hire a number of consultants, each expert in one or more of the different areas the inquiry will examine. However, it will still be necessary to have a chief advisor who can orchestrate the activities of the various advisors. While the chief advisor should not exercise so much control that other advisors cannot speak directly to the commissioner or commission counsel, it is helpful to have one advisor who becomes knowledgeable over the whole range of issues and can be the technical focus and spokesperson.

In order to carry out the responsibilities of the inquiry, the commissioner should also consider hiring any or all of the following staff. Depending on the scope, duration, and complexity of the inquiry and based on the advice of commission counsel, the chief technical advisor, and executive secretary, the following additional staff may be required:

1. *Personal Secretary to the Commissioner.* Often it is important that certain communications from the commissioner, as well as

report drafts, be treated in strict confidence. A private secretary, rather than the secretary to the inquiry, may be a valuable person to have available to separate personal and inquiry business.

2. *Financial Officer.* As described in Section XI of this chapter, "Financing the Inquiry," it may be important to have an officer within the inquiry with full knowledge of the government accounting and auditing system to ensure the procedure used complies with government requirements. Alternatively, it may be possible to have someone within the government set up an accounting and recording system and then merely retain the executive secretary or some other assistant to maintain the inquiry records.

3. *Librarian.* In any major inquiry a librarian is almost essential. One of the most useful things an inquiry can do is to develop a source of information and documentation on the subject under investigation. The librarian would have responsibility for not only obtaining the necessary documentation (sometimes at the request of the technical staff and sometimes on his own initiative) but also for cataloguing and retrieving information. Since the public should have access to the library's facilities, the librarian must be able to set up the library in a way that is appropriate both for technical research and public use.

4. *Community Relations Officer.* As discussed in Chapter VI, in the section entitled "Community Hearings," it may be advisable to have members of the staff whose sole or primary responsibility is regular liaison with the communities most affected by the subject matter of the inquiry. These staff members will travel into affected areas, to carry out community-relations activities, including arrangements for inquiry community meetings.

5. *Public Relations.* As discussed in Section XIII of this chapter, "Public and Media Relations," it is sometimes advisable to have, either as part of the staff or on contract, individuals with expertise in media relations and skills in communicating the information before the inquiry to members of the public.

6. *Word Processing.* In the course of an inquiry, there is regular need for rapid preparation of inquiry material. This includes public announcements by the commissioner, drafts of briefs, statements of evidence, rulings by the commissioner, and an array of other public statements. Since these invariably go through a series of drafts, inquiries soon find that word-processing facilities are an essential requirement. Since much of the documentation is of a very confidential nature, and the facilities will be extensively used during the report-writing stage, it is often advisable to have the equipment and personnel available in-house rather than on contract.

It is highly desirable that the commission counsel, the chief technical advisor, and the executive secretary be full-time employees of the inquiry. Depending on the nature and scope of the inquiry, other advisors can be retained on a periodic basis. These advisors would either have specific functions (*e.g.*, community hearings, public information, press relations), or they would work on particular phases of the inquiry. If possible, a core staff should be retained on a full-time basis to ensure there is continuity and cross-fertilization of ideas. All other staff positions would then be more or less part-time.

Most environmental impact assessment requires an interrelated approach so that the engineering concerns are cross-referenced with the environmental concerns and these with socio-economic concerns, and so on. This can best be accomplished by a staff that works together throughout the various phases of the inquiry. Similarly, when the time comes for writing a staff report or an inquiry report, it is of value to have staff members who have worked together so they can harmonize and rationalize their ideas.

VII. PROCEDURE FOR RETAINING STAFF

A. Disclosure

Whenever a person is interviewed for a staff position, it is incumbent upon the inquiry to determine that the person has no conflicts of interest concerning the matters being examined. Staff members should not have shares in any companies that could be affected by the recommendation of the inquiry, should not have family or close professional ties with any of the major participants, and should not otherwise be in positions in which their actions, and hence the actions of the inquiry, can be viewed as biased. While it may not be necessary in each instance to have the staff member surrender potentially compromising interests, it is important that the inquiry know in advance of such involvement to avoid embarrassing disclosures later.

When hiring commission counsel, in addition to disclosure of financial interests, it is valuable to receive a letter from him indicating which of his or his firm's clients may be affected by the inquiry. In most cases, because the counsel will be an expert in the field, he and his firm will have clients with an interest in the subject matter of the inquiry. A letter outlining the clients and containing an undertaking by the counsel that his firm will not act for them before the inquiry or on matters being investigated by the inquiry should be sufficient. The objective is to ensure there is full disclosure on the record.

A sample letter of disclosure and statement with respect to confidentiality of information is included as Appendix B-2.

B. Contract

The inquiry should enter into a personal service contract with each staff member. This contract, which must be in writing and retained with the inquiry records, should indicate the nature and terms of employment, including remuneration. In the case of independent part-time consultants, there should be a guaranteed minimum time commitment per month for services. There is a form of personal service contract used by most governments which is cumbersome and difficult to use, but which can form a basis for drafting a contract that will be acceptable to the government auditors.

If staff is to be seconded from government departments, the agreement with the department should clearly set out the conditions of the secondment. Generally, it is best to have the person seconded full-time to the inquiry during all or, at least, a particular phase of its operations. This will avoid any apparent conflict should the individual have to operate in this government role while serving the inquiry and avoid close identification between government action and the inquiry. In major inquiries, secondment should mean total release from government responsibilities but, for smaller inquiries, periodic secondments are likely to be adequate.

There is no established procedure that requires staff members to take oaths either to give them authority to act or to ensure secrecy. It is probably inappropriate for staff involved in a public inquiry to take an oath of secrecy. Staff should operate, however, under personal service contracts which specify how they may make use of information obtained through their activities as staff members.

Generally, the contract should indicate that staff members cannot use information obtained through the inquiry for personal gain (*e.g.*, use it in their consulting practice before publication of the final inquiry report). Since this is a public inquiry, all the information obtained by the inquiry staff will ultimately become public information (unlike information provided to private consultants); limitation on the use of information need not extend beyond the inquiry report date, when the documentation is transmitted to the government and made public anyway. While the commissioner may wish to authorize staff to attend conferences or otherwise discuss inquiry events outside the inquiry itself, members of the staff should be bound not to reveal tentative conclusions or information confidentially received by the inquiry. Government officials seconded to the inquiry should be made aware at the outset that their oaths of secrecy as government officials do not apply to their activities within the inquiry.

From the time the commissioner and staff are brought together, it is important they take a very judicial approach toward their activities. For example, a person who joins the inquiry staff should not thereafter take part as a partisan in conferences dealing with the issues before the inquiry or undertake outside activities which would indicate a bias. Obviously, the staff should not accept retainers from any party before the inquiry. In fact, if the inquiry involves a particular industry, it is advisable that staff members not be involved with anyone in the entire industry. If there are certain consultants who must retain contact with their other clients in the industry, these individuals should be clearly identified as consultants for a particular study or in a particular area, so they do not fall under the same general prohibition suggested for regular members of the staff.

There will undoubtedly be requests from the media and others for biographical information on the commissioner and his key staff persons. Each staff member should, upon joining the staff, provide the inquiry with a detailed biographical note. The commissioner should regularly advise of the engagement of staff so that persons with an interest in the inquiry know who to contact and become aware that there is activity within the inquiry.

A sample personal service contract, which can be altered to suit particular circumstances, is found in Appendix B-3.

VIII. PHYSICAL PREMISES

The inquiry should obtain physical premises as soon as practicable and make this location widely known to ensure that the interest generated by the creation of the inquiry has a focus. As soon as the creation of the inquiry is known, consultants with expertise in the area to be investigated seek out the commissioner to offer their services, members of the public have information they want to communicate to the inquiry, and the press will seek contacts.

Having assembled the first staff members, the inquiry should immediately obtain a telephone and ensure that all inquiries are noted. This means the inquiry staff will be instructed to maintain a series of contact lists consisting of: persons who wish to participate in or receive information about the inquiry, possible consultants or advisors, and press contacts. Government departments responsible for the subjects to be investigated should be advised that future communication in the nature of submissions (either opinion or data) should be directed to the inquiry office.

The physical premises should reflect the various functions of the inquiry. Basically, the inquiry has to operate at three different levels. First, there is the commissioner and his private staff operating as the hearing officers. Second, there is a need for public facilities which would include a library, photocopy facilities, and a place where participants, press, and others can come to review the documents and other materials. Third, there is the commission counsel and technical staff. The staff should be located apart from the commissioner's office to show it, in fact, plays a different role in the inquiry. One suggested approach is to have the commissioner at one end, the library area in the centre (since it is common to both and can be made into a public reception area), and the technical staff at the opposite end.

The inquiry office should be centrally located and easily accessible to the public. A building is required where access to the premises is guaranteed on weekends and after hours, so that the public and staff can review transcripts, and other materials at appropriate times during the days when hearings are held. Flexibility in the lease arrangements is necessary since the length of an inquiry cannot be guaranteed and it may be necessary to reduce or expand the space available. A considerable amount of space may be required until the last few months, when public access ceases and only the commissioner and a small group of advisors remain to write the report. It is also desirable that the offices not be physically located in close proximity to the premises of proponents, major intervenors, or government departments.

Generally, government officials are available as consultants to determine what space is available and what rental rates are within the range approved by the government. In addition, an independent person can be hired to advise on the rental market, to assist commission counsel and the commissioner in negotiation of the lease, and to arrange for design of the office space to accommodate the inquiry's needs.

In designing the office, it is important to remember that a great deal of time will be spent there. A small room where a coffee machine and refrigerator can be located may prove useful. Private offices where confidential work can be carried on must be combined with research space, interview areas, and rooms where large staff meetings can be held. Estimates of space required should be generous. The often intense work of an inquiry, conducted in cramped quarters, can lead to major problems at crucial times.

It is also desirable to have relatively inexpensive quarters so that the inquiry cannot be criticized for reckless expenditure of public funds. This point may not seem serious until one realizes that many government officials or participants are housed in less than adequate premises with inadequate equipment. If the inquiry suddenly appears with fancy offices and the very finest equipment, resentment may develop. Expensive premises also may alienate members of the public.

In designing and locating the commissioner's office, one should ensure the office is large enough, and soundproof enough, that he can hold private conversations without fear of his discussions being overheard. It should also be possible for visitors to report at the reception area and attend on the commissioner without going through the staff's working area. The commissioner's office area should also have an office for the executive secretary and whatever support staff the commissioner and executive secretary require. One should recall that the commissioner and executive secretary will be absent during public hearings, yet the commissioner may require a secretary to remain at this office to handle personal correspondence and make other arrangements.

The inquiry staff area need not be elaborate, but it requires a series of offices that are private so that the research staff can communicate with witnesses and participants in confidence. The area should have one large room sufficient to accommodate the entire staff for regular staff meetings. If this is not possible, staff meetings can be held in the library, but it means that the library has to be closed to the public on those occasions. One should also determine whether the commission counsel will be working out of his own office or at the inquiry. Even if working out of his own office, he will require an office at the inquiry from time to time, where he can work with staff or interview prospective witnesses.

The library is often the hub of a public inquiry, as it is the source of information for both participants and the inquiry itself. An experienced librarian is invaluable. The library must attempt to bring together as much of the information as is available on the subject matter before the inquiry in a very short time. The inquiry should also have access to the local, public, or university library so that these holdings are available to inquiry personnel as required. The library may also be used by the executive secretary as the official despository for exhibits, reports, and other materials tabled with the inquiry. Since often only one copy of these materials is available, they are left in the library for review under supervision before being filed away as part of the inquiry records.

Because the library should only be available for public use with a knowledgeable person in attendance, a library assistant may be required. Finally, it is preferable if there are small rooms or other areas nearby where participants can examine inquiry documents and discuss them without disturbing others. There should also be photocopying facilities. Because photocopying can get out of hand, it is recommended that the library assistant be responsible for all photocopying and that a record be maintained to indicate how much photocopying is done by the various parties. It is a matter to be decided by the inquiry whether participants should be charged for photocopying.

IX. RELATIONS WITH REGULATORY AGENCIES

Creation of special public inquiries raises interesting questions as to their relationship with the existing regulatory framework and with government departments that have statutory responsibility in the areas that are the subject of the inquiry. While there is no set policy that should govern special inquiries, in each case the commissioner should understand fully the regulatory context within which he must operate.

Often special inquiries are created to investigate development projects of particular public concern. In this case, there are usually in-house government review processes that have either been carried out or are underway, or there are processes that have been replaced by a public inquiry because of special circumstances. On the other hand, the existing regulatory authorities may merely stand aside, reserving their statutory authority to later review the project and grant whatever approvals are required.

The commissioner must become familiar with the various regulatory and government agencies involved, and must determine the nature of their respective mandates. He must know whether they intend to pursue their statutory responsibilities at the same time as, or following, the inquiry, what information or sources they have that could be used by the inquiry, and generally what sequence of events will take place outside the inquiry process. The inquiry may be as technically perfect as it can be but, if its decision is out of sequence with other decisions that are being made, it may have little impact. So, for example, if a regulatory board intends to conduct hearings and potentially grant permit approval for a project that is also the subject matter of the public inquiry, the best assessment of impacts in the world made after the permit is issued is of very little value.

In these circumstances, the commissioner must develop a satisfactory working relationship with the other statutory bodies involved. For example, it may be prudent to have the regulatory board and the inquiry continue more or less simultaneously so that the ultimate decision maker, usually the Cabinet, will have the benefit of both the statutory agency's and the public inquiry's advice at about the same time. The commissioner should also ensure that his operations are not merely duplications of work carried out by

others. At the same time, he must not give up part of his jurisdiction as granted in the order in council to another body.

In this context, it may also be important to determine what
foreign or international agencies are relevant and what these
agencies are doing. For example, approval of energy projects whose
markets are in the United States, or consideration of fishing interests
with international consequences may require consultations with
agencies outside Canada to ensure that any Canadian decision is,
so far as possible, appropriately timed when viewed in the international context.

Finally, a project such as a major transportation facility may
have major consequences for other transportation projects or other
operations. Therefore, the inquiry must look beyond the specific
project referred to it. For example, an inquiry into a gas pipeline
in remote areas and route selection for that pipeline may effectively
determine the routing for an oil pipeline or a highway. Having
established the infra-structure for one project, other projects are
likely to follow the same route. Similarly, a proposal to construct
an oil port in a particular area may foreclose use of that area for
other facilities or prevent the area from being used for extensive
fishing. Consequently, it is incumbent upon the commissioner to
communicate with a wide range of interests in the subject area to
ensure that the inquiries' decisions are made within the full political, regulatory, economic, and social context.

Traditionally, there is a fear of *ad hoc* public inquiries in the
ranks of existing public administrative and governmental agencies.
Often these officials feel they could handle the situation and resent
the creation of a special inquiry. On the other hand, the existing
regulatory tribunals may recognize that the issue is one they could
not adequately deal with and are, therefore, encouraged by the
establishment of the inquiry. Depending on the situation, their
attitude to the inquiry may be quite different.

It is helpful, therefore, if the commissioner can make himself
known to the other regulatory agencies and establish personal
relationships in addition to whatever formal relationship might
exist. By establishing an informal and regular exchange of information, the inquiry will ensure that it is informed in advance of any
major decisions which might affect its mandate or the progress of
its hearings. Since the commissioner is not responsible for making
a final determination, it is important the inquiry be aware of the
likely time frame to be adopted by government departments and
other regulatory agencies so that inquiry recommendations arrive
in timely fashion to have a real impact on the ultimate executive
decision. Often these initial contacts allay fears, remove suspicion,
and establish a sound working relationship so that the inquiry

and related processes will proceed smoothly and provide mutual support.

X. RELATIONS WITH GOVERNMENT

Soon after being appointed, the commissioner, with or without the executive secretary and commission counsel, should arrange to meet with the government officials responsible for creation of the inquiry and those other government departments with jurisdiction over questions referred to the inquiry for investigation. In some cases, this may mean making contact with provincial as well as federal government departments, since a federal inquiry investigating matters within federal responsibility may also wish to obtain information from provincial officials with responsibilities in related areas.

These meetings allow the commissioner to know personally the key government officials who will have responsibility for dealing with the inquiry and implementing its recommendations. This will include the Minister to whom the inquiry reports, the deputy ministers for the key government departments, along with senior departmental officials.

Within the departments responsible for the inquiry, the commissioner may also wish to make contact with the department press officer and key technical staff who can indicate sources of expertise within or without the government that the inquiry may wish to draw on for staffing. In particular, they may be able to identify financial officers who may assist in the establishment of the inquiry and development of an accounting system that will meet government requirements. Ultimately, the inquiry will deal with these various officials in their respective functions, and it is helpful to have an early meeting, so that future dealings are on a personal basis.

Often, orders in council establishing inquiries will provide that government departments are to co-operate in assisting the inquiry. Whether specifically provided or not, the commissioner has the right to expect such co-operation, particularly from the sponsoring departments. This assistance comes in many forms. The initial contact is to establish a personal relationship, to ensure that government financial and other guidelines are satisfied, and to obtain the assistance of government officials familiar with matters such as office space rental and equipment procurement. These contacts should be made whether the inquiry intends to hire its own staff in these areas or not.

In the case of the government that created the inquiry, early communication can be informal by telephone, usually followed by meetings. For other levels of government or independent agencies, this is best done by formal letters. Most governments and some government agencies require evidence that they have been formally approached to participate in an inquiry. Such approaches should be at the ministerial or the most senior regulatory level. Even though the commissioner or his staff may know more junior officials who will undoubtedly be responsible for ongoing dealings with the inquiry, initial contact would still be at the highest level. A sample letter of formal introduction is found in Appendix B-4.

The purpose of the initial communication is formally to advise the department or agency of the inquiry's existence, to state the mandate of the inquiry in brief and general terms (often attaching a photocopy of the order in council), and to advise that, under the inquiry mandate, that department will be approached for information and assistance. In some cases it may be sufficient merely to say that such demands will be made as the need arises, to request co-operation, and to ask for an initial contact person, if it is not to be the deputy minister or board chairman. If the commissioner wishes to have an early meeting, it is advisable to indicate that an initial meeting will be requested shortly to discuss the work of the inquiry.

Commission counsel should make a point of informing the government officials, particularly those that may be seconding officials to the inquiry that he is not counsel to the government but rather is counsel to the inquiry. The government will undoubtedly have to work with commission counsel to a great extent in the establishment of the inquiry and to that extent the commission counsel does offer his services to the government staff assisting the inquiry. It must be clear from the outset, however, that commission counsel's responsibility is to the inquiry and not to the government, just as the responsibility of seconded government staff is now to the inquiry. Often a brief discussion about the independence of the inquiry will avoid difficulties later.

In dealing with foreign governments, it is important that the inquiry first communicate with the Canadian Department of External Affairs in Ottawa (even if it is a provincial inquiry) to advise of the intended communications. Of course, foreign governments can only be requested to assist an inquiry, and this may affect the form and timing of any request for co-operation. Since the question of direct contact between a Canadian inquiry and a foreign government is one fraught with international diplomatic considerations, it is valuable to have initial meetings with foreign government or foreign agencies set up through External Affairs and the Canadian embassy or consular officer in the area. The representative of the inquiry should meet directly with his foreign counterpart. This often means a round of meetings with External Affairs and consular officers to review the inquiry's mandate and intended mode of procedure and to allow them to arrange the initial meetings. Once this formal contact has been made, it is possible for the inquiry staff to make direct arrangements with foreign officials, either to have them appear or to benefit from any study or work they have done in the area. Thereafter, it is only necessary that External Affairs be kept informed of these discussions or arrangements made with foreign officials.

Meetings with the appointing government should include discussions on the government's role and responsibility in relation to the inquiry. Initial discussions should cover accessibility of government documents and witnesses; the likely timing of the inquiry to determine how it fits in with existing government activity; public participation, and the related question of intervenor funding; relationship with other governments, both provincial and foreign; the issues the inquiry is likely to consider; and the general structure of the inquiry. All of these issues should be discussed in sufficient detail to enable the government officials to relate the proposed inquiry budget to the scope of the inquiry as the commissioner sees it.

It is very difficult for the commissioner to deal with all these issues before holding preliminary inquiry sessions, but generally preliminary sessions cannot be held until there is a certain public awareness of the issues and understanding of the nature and consequences of involvement in the inquiry process. On the other hand, the commission will require funds before it can enter into this process and, hence, the need for an interim budget. Experience indicates that it will probably be necessary to prepare a budget before preliminary hearings can be held. If this must be done, it is imperative that the preliminary nature of the budget be made very clear to the government officials at these early meetings.

These early meetings with government ministers and their senior officials are extremely important. Ministers often create an inquiry in order to externalize a problem by referring the matter to an independent commission rather than accepting direct responsibility. To that extent they are anxious to remain apart from the inquiry. But most ministers are also anxious to ensure there is no question of the inquiry's being a captive of government and no suggestion of ministerial attempt to influence the structure or outcome. For these reasons ministers will often be reluctant to engage in detailed discussions or, sometimes, even to call the commissioner in for consultation.

On the other hand, it is essential that the commissioner bring the ministers along as he develops an awareness of the problem and ideas on how the inquiry may proceed. Ministers establish inquiries for particular purposes, and it is valuable for the commissioner to know the purpose, whether he agrees with it or not. Also, before the commissioner is caught up in the public debate over such matters as terms of reference and scope of the inquiry, and public participation, it is helpful for him to gain an understanding of the ministers' current position. He will then know whether his understanding of the inquiry and the way he intends to proceed is in accord with the ministers' preconceived ideas. If it is not, the commissioner then knows that he must persuade the government to a certain extent so that the inquiry will not be regarded by government as an unmanageable, and even hostile, operation.

The inquiry must work to maintain a good working relationship with the political ministers. This is best done by communicating with them early and keeping them regularly and fully informed of the inquiry's activities and intentions, so that they are not surprised by any public act taken by the inquiry. An inquiry requires the support of the ministers to ensure that government officials and agencies, in the exercise of their statutory responsibilities, do not foreclose inquiry recommendations by taking decisive government action while the inquiry is in progress, and to ensure that any recommendations the inquiry makes will be openly and fully received.

Inquiries should play a role in determining government policy. To ensure this happens, the inquiry must earn the respect of the politicians, not only by demonstrating technical skill but also by satisfying the relevant governments that the inquiry is being conducted with full knowledge of the impacts of their work. Since the commissioner was appointed by the government, there is initial recognition of the commissioner's integrity. It is necessary to build on that by an early demonstration of the seriousness of the inquiry's work to satisfy government officials, so far as possible, that the inquiry is an aid to the government rather than a threat to it.

It is difficult to draw a line between advising the ministers so they do not regard the inquiry as a threat and shaping the inquiry to conform to preconceived ministerial ideas. In most cases the commissioner was selected because of expertise in the subject area or impartiality and integrity, and the ministers are content to allow the commissioner the freedom to exercise his authority as he sees fit. At least initially, the commissioner will be regarded as the authority on how to proceed and, therefore, should take the initiative. Contact should be on the basis of advising the government as to the direction of inquiry investigations in order to avoid misunderstanding. It should not involve the commissioner's seeking approval for any particular course of action.

An established avenue of communication at the senior official level in the Minister's office is essential to the running of the inquiry. The Minister is usually unavailable for immediate contact and is spread so thinly over a number of issues that it will be impossible for him to keep on top of a fast-moving inquiry. It is essential, however, that there be feedback to the inquiry on the current political thinking as well as someone within the Minister's office who can direct the departmental staff to respond to the inquiry's needs. The Minister's executive assistant, senior policy advisor, or some other person in close and regular communication with the Minister should be designated as principal contact for the inquiry. This is especially important if there are a number of ministers with responsibility for creating the inquiry.

The ministerial contact will also ensure that official communication with the Minister can be carried out quickly. It may be important from time to time for the inquiry to have on record the fact that it has officially communicated with the government on a particular matter. This is facilitated by having someone in the Minister's office who can confirm that the communication has been received and, if a reply is necessary, co-ordinate a response. If official correspondence is to go to a number of sponsoring ministers, there is value in having one executive assistant who is the prime contact and who has responsibility for communicating with the other offices.

This person plays a dual role. First, he advises the inquiry as to the current political and bureaucratic situation, the attitudes of officials and participants as expressed to government, and other information which will assist the inquiry to understand the context within which it is proceeding. Communication should, in most cases, be directed to inquiry counsel or some other staff member and not directly to the commissioner. Second, the staff and the commissioner must have someone within the Minister's office as a well-informed liaison who can keep the Minister informed as to what is going on in the inquiry, who can serve as contact person if the inquiry is having difficulty getting action through the civil service, and who can build the personal rappport necessary to maintain feelings of mutual confidence between the government and the inquiry. There is no escaping the fact that a public inquiry has a public or "political" dimension to it. The role of this individual as a contact with the inquiry, therefore, becomes a crucial one.

It is also essential to have a contact person at the official or bureaucratic level in each of the sponsoring departments since it will be necessary to deal with the department on such matters as budget, discovery of documents, and government staff witnesses. If the inquiry is located in an administrative region of the government, it makes sense to have two contacts, one in the local area and a second in the capital. This will mean that communication with the public service may be duplicated, but it ensures that the government officials feel they are fully informed. While always ensuring the government does not unduly influence the inquiry, it is important that these officials do not feel isolated from the inquiry. Otherwise, they may become suspicious and eventually hostile to the inquiry process. Experience indicates that as long as the government officials are kept informed and the reasons behind inquiry actions are explained, they will be co-operative without interfering. Since government officials are often reluctant to establish formal contact with an independent inquiry, this is something that must be initiated by the inquiry staff.

In addition to these forms of communication, the inquiry should consider whether it wishes to hold a briefing for key government officials. Such a briefing would have two general objectives: (1) to inform the officials of what the inquiry has in place and the general direction of its activities, and (2) to obtain the advice and suggestions of officials on sources of expertise and modes of procedure.

The decision to hold such a briefing must be taken very carefully. It ensures that more than just the Minister and deputy minister have knowledge of the inquiry's activities; it taps other sources of information. But it does have the appearance of treating government in a different way than that of other participants. Also, if the inquiry should disregard the advice of the officials, this may have a detrimental effect on working relationships that would not have occurred otherwise. Generally, an introductory series of informal meetings with the Minister, deputy minister, and a few key officials, followed by meetings between inquiry staff and government officials at a more technical level, is preferable to formal briefing or in-house sessions with government officials.

Finally, there are the early contacts with government that can best be described as reviewing the red tape necessary for the orderly operation of the inquiry. Personal service contracts, leases, and so on have to be approved by the government or, at least, fall within the government guidelines; it is generally regarded as sensible, therefore, to have the agreements in a form that is familiar to the government officials and, hence, is likely to be routinely approved. It is suggested that in each case an official government form be obtained and modified to suit the inquiry's needs. Official government forms (with government identification) should not be used, but forms incorporating the same general content usually mean requests will be more easily passed.

It is also useful at this time to get official guidance from the government as to how the contracts are to be processed. In particular, an official letter from the government should be placed on file that indicates instructions for audit purposes. Since the inquiry records ultimately have to form part of government records, or be subject to government audit, detailed instructions should be available from the beginning to ensure that accounting records are established in a manner acceptable to government audit, that hiring contracts are entered into where required, and that leases are in a form that can be accommodated by government policy. In some cases the inquiry may not be required to satisfy these government financial controls. If so, this fact should also be confirmed in writing.

XI. FINANCING THE INQUIRY

Some inquiries are funded out of general revenue of the government. Others are funded out of the budgets of the departments whose ministers are sponsoring the inquiry. This latter method causes numerous difficulties.

Government departments are invariably pressed for funds. They are continually concerned that the amount of money allocated to their department is not sufficient for the responsibilities they have. When an *ad hoc* inquiry is funded out of departmental budgets, it is a threat because it takes funds away from the department and gives them to a process over which department officials have no control. Bureaucrats dislike the idea of departmental money going to a group of "outsiders."

When funds come from a particular department, there is a further problem since the inquiry is not under the same budgetary controls as that department. Government departments have budgets that are supervised by departmental officials and regularly revised. An inquiry does not have an ongoing budgetary position and does not participate in the battle for departmental budget dollars. In most cases it is required to advise the government at an early date what funds are required for the current fiscal year. A sum is then allotted to the inquiry. If further funds are legitimately required to fulfil the inquiry's mandate, further funds are somehow found.

The funding of public intervenors is usually treated as a special budgetary allotment. As a result, money granted the inquiry can be moved from function to function, but no funds can be moved in or out of the allotment for participant funding (see Chapter IV, The Inquiry Structure, "Participant Funding").

If the commissioner has any influence in the matter, he should urge that the funds for the inquiry come out of general revenues or a special fund so that it cannot be said that funds for the inquiry are at the expense of other departmental projects. To ensure that the impartiality of the inquiry is not put in question, the commissioner should also not receive all of his funding from a government department that will be the subject of the inquiry's investigation. For example, an inquiry into the environmental impacts of a major energy project should perhaps report to and receive its funds from both the Ministry of Environment and the Ministry of Energy, rather than solely from the energy department whose projects are under review.

Government officials are, at least initially, somewhat nervous about appearing to influence the inquiry or restrict its independence through budgetary restraints. Consequently, they often merely request an initial budget from the inquiry, which they will then review and process. Generally, they will not interfere with a decision by the commissioner that certain functions, facilities, or staff are required.

The commissioner must also ensure that he is not bound by rates of remuneration, requirements for tenders, or any other such procedures that often form a part of ordinary government procurement policy. It must be recognized that an inquiry, unlike an ongoing government department, does not have the lead time to adopt procedures which can be justified in other circumstances. Also, because it often requires work to be undertaken and completed in a short time frame and cannot offer employees even a guaranteed term of employment, it is often necessary for an inquiry to pay higher remuneration or compensation in order to attract people of high technical competence.

At all times the financing of the inquiry must be solely within the authority and discretion of the commissioner. The government's obligation is to appoint a trustworthy person as commissioner and, having done so, they must rely on the commissioner's good sense and judgment in determing what funds are required to carry out the inquiry's mandate. While the commissioner will agree to follow government guidelines as to audit requirements and record keeping, the decision as to whether any expense is justified or warranted, both initially and on an ongoing basis, must be left solely to the commissioner. To do otherwise would be to permit budgetary controls to fetter the inquiry's independence and affect its ability to fulfil its mandate.

Since most governments will recognize that it is up to the commissioner himself to decide what information is required by the inquiry and in what form, they should be prepared to recognize that the commissioner should not be required to return again and again to have funds allocated for specific information to be collected. A system whereby every decision of the commissioner must be confirmed by a government act authorizing the expenditure of funds is intolerable not only from an administrative point of view but also on the basis of policy, since it will appear that all decisions to obtain information have been vetted by the government. Whether this is the case or not, a commissioner's position is weakened in they eyes of the public and the participants if he cannot agree to have particular evidence heard or particular studies undertaken unless he first goes back to the government to ensure it will allocate the funds necessary to commission that work. For this reason, from the outset, the commissioner should establish a process whereby he will be responsible for preparing an inquiry budget that will be approved by the government in timely fashion. Thereafter, it will be the obligation of the commissioner to ensure the funds are properly allocated and, following government guidelines, properly spent.

The inquiry must receive funds early in order to initiate its operations. But the government will demand a statement of the total requirements of the inquiry at least to the end of the fiscal year before it seeks a grant of funds. Sometimes the sponsoring departments have funds within their budgets which can be used by the inquiry on an interim basis until a separate allotment to the inquiry is granted. This means they will use funds designed for their own use and, hence, will put pressure on the inquiry to obtain independent funding quickly.

The inquiry, is, therefore, put in a very difficult position. Before it defines its terms of reference and identifies all of the issues with which it must deal, it will be asked to determine a budget. Since the budget depends on how long the inquiry will take, the number of hearing days, whether expensive research will have to be undertaken, whether there will be a recommendation for participant funding and, if so, how much, this is almost impossible. It may be necessary, therefore, for the inquiry to produce a preliminary budget soon after senior staff has been appointed, with the clear understanding that the first real budget will come later.

It may be appropriate for the commissioner to request an interim allotment of funds without labelling this even a preliminary budget. The commissioner could then draw on this interim allotment to establish the inquiry and retain staff, giving some breathing space before it is necessary to present a budget.

If a budget is demanded at an early date, often this "tentative budget" submitted to the government for approval, becomes the official budget. Therefore, if it is necessary to complete an interim budget, the commissioner must be very generous in his assessment of the length of time and the amount of funds required. This will ensure that, when a more realistic budget is prepared, the inquiry has more money than required and is not in the difficult position of having to go back to the government for further funding.

In the preparation of a budget, whether an interim budget or a more complete one, the inquiry must adopt general categories so that it can reallocate funds as it proceeds. It should also be stipulated for a stated period, for example, to the end of the current fiscal year. This means that, if the inquiry continues beyond the stated period, it can go back to the government for additional funds. A form of inquiry budget is included as Appendix B-5. Discussion of budgets for funded participants is found in Chapter IV, The Inquiry Structure, "Participants and Participant Funding."

XII. INQUIRY PARTICIPANTS

It is important for the commissioner and his senior staff, particularly the chief technical advisor and inquiry counsel, to make initial contact with the major groups and individuals that are likely to participate in the inquiry. Obviously, if the inquiry has been established to review a particular development or project, there will be a project proponent and perhaps a series of proponents for alternate projects. In addition, there will be local or regional citizens groups with an interest in the project as supporters or opponents, local municipal councils, chambers of commerce, native groups, and others. Government departments and agencies with statutory responsibility in the area may also wish to participate.

An effort should be made to communicate with these various groups and interests to become known to them and to understand, informally, their positions. The commissioner should make himself well known to the participants, so they all understand the rules of the game and so that confidence and trust can be established. There is often fundamental distrust of any government process, and elements of the public may have to be reassured that the process will be a fair one which will allow them to effectively participate. The proponents too, must be reassured that they will be fairly treated. An inquiry is likely to be a new experience not only for the participants but also for many members of the press and government officials at all levels, including local. Each of these groups is likely to be exposed to the commissioner and the inquiry process.

An initial evaluation of the abilities of these various interests to participate in the inquiry should also be made; methods of communication should be developed so they can be kept informed and, where necessary, consulted. It is important that organizations with an interest in the subject matter of the inquiry be kept routinely informed of the inquiry's activity.

The commissioner may wish to hold a series of informal meetings with these potential participants in the inquiry process. The commissioner should travel to the area directly affected by the activity or project referred to the inquiry. Informal meetings may be held with public interest groups in the area, local elected officials, and organizations. Generally, it must be demonstrated to the citizens most directly affected that the inquiry is prepared to receive the benefit of their opinions. Such trips would also help the commissioner understand the physical area to be examined and would demonstrate that he is prepared to search out information, rather than merely sit back and wait for individuals or organizations to come before him.

Such meetings would not be a substitute for public hearings, nor should they be captive meetings sponsored by any particular group within the community. Often it will be most appropriate to arrange these meetings through the local mayor, chief, or band council; but they should be informal, designed merely to have the commissioner appear in the community and to meet people so that communities feel they have personal contact with the inquiry. The commissioner should also make it clear that he wishes to meet a broad range of community members in these sessions so that he is not used by segments of the community, who may attempt to make their views known to him apart from the public hearing process.

Developing a personal contact with the citizens, particularly local officials who are often overlooked in the major government decisions, and gaining a personal appreciation for the physical characteristics of the area is very important. For local citizens, to hear that an inquiry has been established and then to know that the commissioner is in their midst soon afterward is likely to enhance the credibility of the inquiry.

All that the commissioner can expect to do at this early stage is to make personal contact with the range of interests likely to be represented in the inquiry and to assess their relative sophistication. These preliminary sessions should be very low-key affairs, with the commissioner making direct contact with the groups rather than using formal public notices and other procedures which may suggest that hearings are underway. It should be made clear that the commissioner is not at this time hearing evidence on the substance of the issues before the inquiry but, rather, wishes to make contacts with the various communities to understand the issues and peoples' feelings.

At these sessions, the commissioner will also explain, in a preliminary way, his role and his terms of reference. He should indicate the intention to keep the local citizens and groups involved. At this stage the commissioner should also attempt to identify the range of interests likely to be affected and not merely to note those interests that are clearly identifiable by their organization. To some extent, therefore, he may wish to encourage affected parties to organize themselves to participate in the inquiry.

The commissioner can also begin the process of gathering information. He should ensure that he has pencil and pad with him at all times because individuals will communicate with him, and it will be important that he retain their names and addresses in the event further contact is required. He should note the names of individuals who are reputed to have information and keep a separate list of people who want to be kept informed of the inquiry's activities so they can be added to the mailing list. His early impressions should also be documented.

In the case of hearings involving major development projects, the approach to proponents will be somewhat different than the approach to local citizens. While citizens will generally welcome an inquiry, either as an opportunity for them to be heard or as an opportunity for the various points of view to be presented before any decision is made, proponents often regard the inquiry process as just another administrative hurdle they must overcome before their project can commence. They often, therefore, approach the inquiry in a hostile, or at least a reserved, manner. There is a history in the Canadian regulatory process, part fact and part fiction, which has produced these attitudes.

The Mackenzie Valley Pipeline Inquiry was one of the first major inquiries of a formal nature that industry was required to undergo outside the established regulatory processes. In that case the proponent consortium spent a considerable amount of money, time, and effort in presenting and defending its project, only to have a competing project, which was not as well researched or studied by the inquiry, gain ultimate regulatory approval. As a result, industry is reluctant to go through an *ad hoc* inquiry process (as distinct from a formal regulatory process) without some indication from the government that there is a commitment to the project in principle.

In the West Coast Oil Ports Inquiry, industry requested that the government declare that a west coast oil port is in Canada's national interest and, as a matter of policy, should be constructed. This would then allow industry to examine the various options and determine which proposal to present to the inquiry and to relevant regulatory authorities. This project, or alternative projects, would then be researched, and the industry would spend the considerable sums of money and time needed to examine these proposals in an inquiry, in a regulatory approval process, or both. Industry said it was not prepared to spend these vast sums of money without some agreement in principle that the government is prepared to entertain an application for that project.

This concept of an approval in principle has very important consequences for the inquiry process. Should industry take the position that it demands agreement in principle before it will conduct the research and prepare the necessary documentation for a thorough inquiry, the ability of the government, whether through its institutionalized processes or an independent inquiry, to obtain all the information it requires will be severely curtailed. It will mean that whatever is required will have to be dragged out of the proponents who, while complying because they want the project to proceed, will not be completely open. Either the necessary information will have to be obtained through government activity, or there will simply be less information upon which to base a decision.

On the government's side, there will then be tremendous pressure to provide such a commitment, whether formal or informal. Should such a commitment be given, it raises serious questions for the inquiry. How can there be an independent inquiry into the question of construction of a major project if the ultimate decision makers, the government, have already made up their minds that, as a matter of policy, the project is one that should proceed? An inquiry would be severely limited if its only function were to determine the impact and assess how adverse impacts could be reduced or mitigated. Most major inquiries have the authority to conclude that the impact is likely to be so severe that the project should not proceed at all. To many people the real question is whether the project should proceed, and not the lesser issue of how it should proceed, and any commitment by the government before the inquiry begins will dramatically change the dynamics of the process.

From the inquiry's point of view, it is a much less significant inquiry if its only objective is to determine how to mitigate impacts. For one thing, many interested parties will not wish to participate in an inquiry which assumes that the project will be constructed no matter what the impacts. From the proponents' point of view, there is little incentive to do more than the minimum research.

The second approach of a proponent may be to avoid involvement with the inquiry — to "hide in the weeds" — so that the public inquiry process carefully examines and reveals the problems associated with a competing project and leaves the critical assessment of the proponent's project incomplete. The strategy is to participate to the extent necessary to allow one to say that the project was before the inquiry, but not to be the major proponent whose project is the centre of the public review.

It is important, therefore, that the inquiry not appear to be so narrowly structured that it will closely examine only one project and allow another one to circumvent the inquiry process and, owing to lack of investigation, be considered a preferable project. The commissioner must make it clear to proponents and potential proponents that he intends to examine all possible alternatives, though the "main" project will obviously receive the bulk of his attention.

It is important for the commissioner to remember that at the outset all of the participants, proponents or otherwise, will be unclear as to his intentions. As expressed earlier, the scope and structure of an inquiry is often very personal to the hearing officer, and a wide range of inquiry structures may be used. The participants should not feel that the inquiry is establishing a "life of its own" by developing its own concept of timing, procedure, and issues to be considered without consultation with affected persons.

Also, many of the participants will require funding and, therefore, at an early stage there must be some mutual understanding between the inquiry and participants concerning the important questions of funding, duration of the inquiry, cost of operation, intended participation, and the role expected of the various participants. It is important to establish at least some basic appreciation of the inquiry's intentions so that everyone involved can make plans based on a mutual understanding of what is likely to take place.

XIII. PUBLIC AND MEDIA RELATIONS

Generally an inquiry is launched by the government's issuing a formal press release advising of the inquiry's creation and the appointment of the commissioner. Soon thereafter it is appropriate for the commissioner to hold a brief press conference of his own to state his initial plans in fulfilling his mandate and to indicate where he can be reached during the initial organizational period. This will serve notice that the commissioner is getting on with the job assigned to him and will establish a contact point where potential staff, consultants, and members of the public can communicate with him.

Generally, an inquiry is created in response to public pressure or public concern over major issues. It is important, therefore, that representatives of the public be kept informed of the inquiry's activities and how they can participate in the process.

This need for communication can be met by regular press briefings or press releases by the commissioner even before the inquiry starts. Information could include the activities of the inquiry and the inquiry staff, the nature and type of evidence that is being developed and when it will be presented, any research undertaken, identification of the inquiry staff and their expertise, and the travel, inspections, or other research being undertaken by the commissioner himself. All this information not only demonstrates to the public that the inquiry is active but also helps to explain its activities to the often skeptical public and participants. This is likely to ensure that there is broad knowledge of the inquiry's activities, that any actions taken by the commissioner are clear and public, and that any delay in start up of the formal hearings of the inquiry is understandable given the preliminary activity undertaken.

Before any public hearings can be held, even hearings of a preliminary nature, there must be some public education undertaken to ensure that people are aware of reasons why they should participate in the inquiry process, what information they should bring, and how it should be presented.

This public information program can often be generated, initially, by using personnel and materials available through government departments with responsibility for the area or the issues before the inquiry. Circulars and other promotional information is also often available from project proponents or local organizations. This material should be used by the commissioner for his informal sessions to encourage general public awareness of the issues and facilitate preparation for active participation. Usually one of the first tasks, once the inquiry staff is in place, is to put together information circulars so the inquiry has some documentation that it can take to the public.

In undertaking this initial public education, it is important that the inquiry not be perceived as attempting to stir up public controversy and create issues where none exist. For that reason the information presented must be relatively technical and generally descriptive, though it must be in a readable format. While public relations consultants may be useful to assist in the packaging and distribution of the information, many are not suitable to the somewhat formal, even judicial, nature of a public inquiry. Care must be taken to ensure that inquiry documentation does not appear too slick or designed to produce unnecessary controversy.

IV

The Inquiry Structure

I. PRELIMINARY HEARINGS

Terms of reference for public inquiries are usually cast in general terms, and it is usually necessary for the commissioner to define the scope of his inquiry further. The commissioner must also determine the timing for the hearings, the procedure to be followed in those hearings, and the form of public participation.

Traditionally, these questions have been dealt with by the commissioner in consultation with his staff. While this is certainly the prerogative of the commissioner, there are benefits to be achieved if the commissioner's decisions on these matters are made after a round of preliminary sessions in which persons outside the inquiry staff have an opportunity to present their views. Very often these participants have a history of involvement in the issues before the inquiry that places them in a better position than the commissioner or his staff to evaluate the range of issues, the amount of information available, the time required for preparation of additional information, and the ability of participants to mobilize for a hearing and otherwise contribute to the process.

These preliminary sessions can be as formal or informal as the commissioner desires. Parties can be called into the commissioner's office, individually or as a group for informal discussions; or the commissioner, with inquiry counsel but as few other staff as possible, could travel to meet the participants (see Chapter III, Establishing the Inquiry, "Inquiry Participants").

An inquiry may wish, in addition to these sessions, to hold public sessions that are more like formal public hearings, though they will deal only with preliminary procedural and terms of reference issues. These preliminary hearings, too, can be as formal or informal as the commissioner desires.

Preliminary hearings should be called as early as possible after certain groundwork has been laid. It is important there be a general understanding of the inquiry and its mandate and that all potential participants be aware of the hearings and of their right to participate. If certain procedural developments are taking place — for example, if there is a filing date for project applications or major government decisions are pending — it is best to have these matters resolved so that participants and the inquiry have a common base of understanding before discussing the structure and timing of the inquiry.

Generally, it is best if preliminary hearings are held at the locality most directly affected by the events that are to be the subject matter of the inquiry or the locality most accessible to potential participants. It may be necessary to hold a number of preliminary meetings at various localities over a period of time.

Public announcements for preliminary hearings must be carefully drafted and reviewed, since initial public reaction is to assume that representations may be made on the substantive issues before the inquiry. The notice must, therefore, indicate it is a preliminary hearing, that questions of the inquiry's terms of reference, timing, and the role participants wish to play in the proceedings are to be discussed with the commissioner, but that is not yet the time for submissions or witnesses to deal with the substantive issues before the inquiry. The idea to be communicated is that the hearing is a matter of process rather than a discussion of the issues. The notice should specifically state that the inquiry will hear from the public on the issues at a later date (see form of preliminary hearing notice, Appendix B-6).

Because the preliminary hearing is primarily concerned with process, it is the organized groups that attend, often represented by counsel. It is the opportunity for citizen groups to make themselves known and often to request consideration for participant funding. Project proponents (if it is that type of inquiry), their supporters or competitors, and even governments may appear. It is, in fact, the first formal occasion for participants to make themselves known to one another and to indicate publicly the role they see for themselves in the process.

Once it is determined that there will be public participation, it is valuable to consult the various public groups to determine the nature, extent, and form of that participation. It is difficult for an inquiry to impose terms of participation. There are no standard rules for public participation, and each inquiry must determine how it will structure public participation, who will be the participants, and what the timing for participation will be. In all of these questions it is important to get the views of the groups expected to participate so that they understand from the beginning what the inquiry expects of them. A successful public participation program can only be accomplished if there is broad public acceptance. Thus, the consultation process must be a real one and not appear to be an exercise to convince participants that the rules of the game as established by the inquiry are to prevail.

The procedure to be followed at a preliminary hearing will vary depending on the formality the commissioner wants to convey. The hearing should begin with the commissioner briefly outlining the mandate of the inquiry, some of the events that have already taken place, and the reason for the preliminary hearing. He should then indicate the procedure to be followed, whether there will be a question-and-answer format or presentations by participants. He should again emphasize that the inquiry will return at a later date to hear submissions on the substantive issues.

The commissioner should also introduce himself and his staff and indicate briefly the nature of staff responsibilities. He should also advise how participants can communicate with the inquiry both by telephone and in writing and outline where and how the public can get necessary information.

To assist the participants who wish to address the hearing, the commissioner may also suggest an agenda for the meeting, indicating that he would like to hear from them on such questions as participant funding, the timing and organization of the hearing, the role that various parties feel they can or would like to play in the proceedings, and the location of hearings.

It often assists the process if inquiry counsel has prepared and distributed a submission on the issues to be considered at a preliminary hearing. This submission may be prepared following a series of informal meetings with the various participants and direction from the commissioner as to how the hearings should be structured. With that information, plus technical advice, the counsel can put together a suggested format and make it public so that participants have something to react to at the preliminary hearings, giving a focus to the procedural debate. This process has another important advantage. Because these recommendations are seen to emanate from inquiry counsel rather than the commissioner himself, participants can criticize the submission and appeal to the commissioner without feeling they are criticizing the commissioner himself. This establishes the commissioner as an impartial arbiter from the beginning.

Counsel's submission may include recommendations on the location of hearings, the order and phasing of the hearings, the identification of participants, production of documents, discovery of witnesses, order of examination and cross-examination, form of public participation, and the starting date for the inquiry hearings. It should be distributed to interested participants about two weeks in advance to enable them to decide whether they wish to intervene or comment on the procedure at the preliminary hearing (see sample form of inquiry counsel submission on procedure, Appendix B-7).

II. PARTICIPANTS AND PARTICIPANT FUNDING

By the time preliminary hearings are held, the various participants will have had an opportunity to consider the role they wish to play. Participation in an inquiry is generally an expensive and time-consuming effort and rarely does any public interest group have the resources to participate fully throughout. Also, it is almost impossible for one particular group to represent the various public interests that are likely to come before the inquiry. As a result, in most cases there will be some form of coalition of interests for purposes of participation and also for purposes of obtaining funding. Sometimes this will occur naturally; other times it may be necessary for the inquiry to encourage the formation of coalitions.

At the same time an effort will be made by the various individual groups to maintain the flexibility to have a separate and independent intervention. If the concept of formal and community hearings is followed (see Section V of this chapter, "Form of Hearings") there exists the possibility of the coalition's being representative of the groups at the formal hearings while, at the same time, allowing each individual group to participate separately in the community hearing in its locality.

The inquiry must maintain an updated list of all the groups and individuals who have indicated an intention to participate. Initial communications should go to all of these groups individually. By the time of the preliminary hearing, some of these groups may have come together in a coalition, especially if inquiry counsel has recommended that funding be limited to major interests representing a number of participants.

The question of public participation and the funding of public intervenors is a crucial element in the inquiry process, and it is usually not completely under the control of the commissioner. The practice in Canada has been for government to fund intervenors directly but to use the inquiry as the vehicle for delivery of the funds. Funding for intervenors is a separate allocation from the government according to criteria agreed upon, and these allocations cannot be used for other purposes within the inquiry. While the inquiry plays an important role in advising government on the amount of funding, the ultimate decision is made by government.

This process of participant funding, however, is not universally adopted. In some cases the question of participant funding is left entirely to the commissioner and merely forms one element of the inquiry budget. The government may also fund community preparation costs (including counsel) but not advocacy, so that participant funding is a hybrid of inquiry and government funding. In other cases, both the inquiry and the government may agree to establishment of an independent funding panel with responsibility for determining the level of funding and the allocation of funds to particular groups.

The structure developed ultimately depends on the government, since the funds are government funds no matter how they are administered. As grantor, the government makes the final decision on conditions to be attached to these funds and on their allocation. The commissioner's views on funding are likely to be given considerable weight and in some cases are considered the definitive judgment. However intervenor funding is structured, it is important the issue be resolved early, well before discussions with participants. The government commitment to intervenor funding should be clear, and agreement should be reached on the criteria for funding.

The commissioner should, at the preliminary hearing, review the criteria for funding public participation if the government has agreed that funding will be provided. The guidelines issued for the funding of intervenors at the Mackenzie Valley Pipeline Inquiry have been subsequently adopted by a number of federal and provincial inquiries and provide a useful guideline (see public participation funding criteria, Appendix B-8).

A common criterion for government funding is the formation of coalitions. This ensures that funds are not spread over a large number of groups so that only overhead and operating expenses are covered, with little left for effective research. It also ensures that work is not duplicated by a number of groups. An integrated approach toward research and participation is essential for effective participation, and the funding mechanism is one way to ensure that this happens.

The guidelines usually also provide that applicants for funds must have a record of interest and involvement in the issues before the inquiry, so that "instant organizations" are not created without a recognized constituency solely to cash in on available government funds. An applicant must also represent a distinct public interest that, without participant funding, would not be able to participate before the inquiry and must be sufficiently well organized to be able to account for funds granted. This prevents narrow allocation of funds to a few established interests, and ensures that there is a clear account of how the funds are spent. This government accounting should be done after the fact to verify that the funds were spent on inquiry business, rather than in advance as a tool for controlling participants.

The commissioner must consider how forcefully he will apply the funding criterion that groups represent coalitions of interests. To the extent that this is enforced, the funded coalitions will become less homogeneous and fewer in number.

For example, a number of groups that have traditionally opposed one another, but that are united in opposition to a particular project, perhaps should not be regarded as members of a single coalition. Similarly, groups with a tradition of independent action, especially if they have an independent source of funds, are unlikely to wish to be part of the same coalition. Often these groups resent the fact that the name of a coalition developed for the inquiry will become known while their group, with a history of involvement in the issue, will have to take a back seat during the inquiry. Many of these groups require publicity both to demonstrate to their constituents that they are active and to facilitate fund raising, and they may not be content to be part of a coalition unless other groups are subordinate to them and the coalition operates under their name.

Consequently, it will be necessary for the commissioner to determine what groups of interests must be represented and then to ensure that there is adequate funding for each group, keeping in mind these imperatives, the personalities involved, and the roles the inquiry sees for each group. Skilful creation of viable coalitions will pay dividends later.

Funding is a difficult matter to organize since each participant may have very different ideas about the issues involved, the time the inquiry will take, and the amount of money required to do the various things they wish to do. All that can be demanded is that participants prepare a detailed budget which outlines their requirements and the expected budgetary consequences.

The commissioner then receives these budgets and reviews them to ensure a consistent pattern. For example, the commissioner may conclude that the likely number of hearing days is substantially different from that estimated by particular participants and, if there is a *per diem* item for hearings in the budget, he will make the appropriate adjustment. Similarly, counsel should all receive approximately the same rate or allocation of funds. It is then up to each participant to decide whether it wants a very expensive lawyer for a short time or a less expensive lawyer for a longer period. Office overhead expense should be rationalized to ensure particular participants do not budget for overhead that is substantially greater than for others involved in the process. All the budgets should cover the same time period. If, for some reason, the inquiry is to carry on beyond that date, additional funding may be required for those participants still active.

While the responsibility of deciding whether or not participants should be funded rests with the government, it is usually the commissioner's responsibility to review the budgets to ensure that they make sense in the inquiry context. Upon receipt of the various budgets from the participants and a rationalization of the items, a detailed budgetary review should be carried out by the inquiry.

Once the commissioner is satisfied that the budgets are supportable, they are then forwarded to the government or *ad hoc* funding panel for direct funding of the participants. In other cases the government may issue the funds to the inquiry, which then dispenses them to the participants.

Dispensing funds is best done on an intermittent basis so that, while there is a commitment for funding over a long period of time, the participants must come back at regular intervals for funds. This ensures that the inquiry panel or government can demand receipts and other accounting records for the funds on a regular basis and can verify that the participant is, in fact, still actively participating in the inquiry. Difficulty could develop if all the funds were spent by a participant at an early stage of the inquiry so it could not be active at a critical later phase.

Although there is a risk that participants will misuse funds, funding to participants should meet stated criteria, but otherwise there should be no strings attached. Participants must use the funds for proper inquiry activities. There should be an approved budget and an accounting process appropriate for government audit purposes. Beyond that, it should be the responsibility of each participant to ensure that funds are properly spent within the established guidelines, and there is no need for day-to-day supervision of funds. It is the participant who must take responsibility for expending the funds, not the inquiry.

From the commissioner's point of view, the issue of participant funding raises a number of questions. First, it may be necessary for the commissioner to estimate the inquiry budget, including allocation of funds to participants, before the participants have sufficient time to determine their actual needs and prepare a preliminary budget. This "preliminary estimate" by the commissioner becomes the ultimate allocation of funds. Any early estimate of funds likely to be required for participants must be presented to government in a tentative way to ensure that the commissioner has not prejudged the extent and cost of intervention.

In addition to the major funding to coalitions of interests or representation groups, it may also be advisable to provide lesser funding to other interests. These are groups or individuals whose interests are covered by one of the major intervening groups but who require some financial assistance, either to participate in selected segments of the inquiry or in recognition of particular circumstances that cannot be dealt with by the other major intervenors. This category would also include intervenors who, though expected to play major roles in the inquiry, have their own independent source of financing, so that merely token financing is required to demonstrate the inquiry's desire for their active and continued participation.

Another funding approach is one that involves a matching formula. In those circumstances funding is given up to a certain maximum, provided the participant itself contributes a certain amount of funds. Because the government does not bear the total cost of the intervention, this technique forces the participant to be more mindful of its expenditure and, because public fund raising is often involved, to demonstrate it has a broad constituency.

Groups may come forward demanding public funds on the basis that they represent a broad range of interests; however, it is almost impossible to demonstrate that they do, in fact, represent that constituency. One way of demonstrating that there is wide support for the group is to demand that they go to the public for funds, to supplement funds available through the inquiry. It must be remembered, however, that many broad-based groups may not be able to raise funds because their constituents are not financially able to support them or the organization legitimately requires these funds for its other activities. Historically, public interest groups in Canada have not been well funded.

When the inquiry has identified potential public intervenors and determined how those interests are best represented, it must then determine the role the inquiry wants these participants to play. If the commissioner wishes to take a "judicial" approach, responsibility for collecting and presenting evidence and challenging the evidence of others will rest primarily on the participants. In that case they must be well funded to carry out technical research and to acquire able legal representation at the hearings. If the commissioner sees the inquiry as one in which inquiry counsel presents the evidence and public groups merely monitor the proceedings, then much less funding is required. Similarly, if the public interest groups are to be used to fulfil a public information function, a different formula for funding will be required than if the inquiry performs that function itself. Generally, to determine an appropriate level of participant funding, the commissioner must decide the role to be played by the participants, make sure they are willing and able to perform that role, and fund accordingly.

III. INQUIRY PHASES

Once the scope of the inquiry is defined, the commissioner, perhaps after preliminary hearings, may conclude the inquiry should be structured into a number of phases. The purpose of phasing is to have all of the evidence on a particular issue before the inquiry heard at the same time. This gives the inquiry some focus; it also ensures that research and the attendance of consultants and witnesses on a particular issue is required at one stage of the inquiry and is not repeated throughout.

In most environmental impact assessments of major resource projects, phasing falls into such general categories as construction, environmental impact, and socio-economic impact. The first phase is some form of a technical phase in which the project and its engineering and construction characteristics are described. This phase is very much a data-gathering period that allows the inquiry to understand the nature of the project.

Subsequent phases will examine the various impacts of the proposal under appropriate headings. Generally, the environmental and the socio-economic impacts can be distinguished by focussing first on the physical environment and then, in a socio-economic phase, by considering the impact on people as a result of these impacts on the environment. This may mean, for example, that the environmental phase deals with the impacts on fish, while the socio-economic phase considers the impact on fishing and the fishing industry. While the distinction is artificial, it has a logical basis and proves more appropriate than an examination of all impacts at once.

The significance of phasing is that all of the various participants will call their evidence on a particular subject within that phase before moving on to another phase, when all of the participants will be called on again. Without phasing, the proponent of a development would likely call the evidence first, including all of its engineering, construction, environmental, and socio-economic evidence.

This would mean that at the critical opening sessions of the inquiry, the proponent alone would have the floor and, hence, all of the media attention. By the time all the other participants called their evidence, media attention would be reduced, and the impact of their evidence would be lost. There is also a danger that, having called all of its evidence, a party may become largely inactive for the balance of the hearings. Phasing ensures that all participants have an opportunity to be active throughout those sessions of the inquiry of interest to them. Phasing also helps the public understand the interrelationship of evidence presented by different interests because the evidence is presented from different points of view at about the same time.

Finally, phasing enables the inquiry, if necessary, to write an interim report after a particular phase. For example, if an early phase should demonstrate that it is impossible to construct the project as proposed or that the actual construction schedule will be much different than originally assumed, these conclusions should be made known before the subsequent analysis of the impact begins. One could visualize the situation where it becomes clear that the construction schedule originally proposed is unrealistic, and a new different construction scheme is required. It would then be appropriate to consider the environmental implications of the new construction scheme rather than the one originally proposed. Without phases the proponent would have presented all of its evidence on environmental and other impacts based on a faulty premise, and the inquiry would either have to recall those witnesses or proceed without the proponent's evidence on the true construction schedule.

Similarly, if the government wishes to use the inquiry technique as part of its institutionalized decision-making process, it is possible to phase an inquiry so that it can report to the government on various issues as it goes along. This would allow the government to take action, if desirable, before all of the matters referred to the inquiry have been examined.

A commissioner concerned about time constraints could use phasing as an effective tool to ensure that he is in a position to report to the government at the time particular information is needed without limiting the total scope of his inquiry.

Phases may also aid in determining the timing of the inquiry. Often participants are able to estimate the time for particular phases so that the commissioner can schedule breaks between the phases. This not only assists in planning but also allows the inquiry to take breaks in hearing sessions at logical points. The hearing process is a tiring one, and breaks are essential. It also gives the commissioner the flexibility to schedule phases at convenient times. For example, an inquiry into fishing rights cannot proceed when fishermen are away fishing; a technical session involving academic witnesses may be difficult to organize during the summer months, when those academics normally conduct field research.

A two-stage decision-making process is another possibility. The first phase would be a general review of the project to determine whether, in principle, the project should proceed. Once that is done, a more detailed assessment of particular impacts could be made. This two-phased approach would mean that the general policy questions would come early and an interim report could, if appropriate, be filed by the commissioner. The inquiry would then proceed to deal with the specific issues. This procedure would allow the government to have some information available to it outlining the general issues before the more specific (and more time-consuming and more expensive) examination takes place. A two-phase inquiry with interim reports is a way of co-ordinating inquiries and established government decision-making processes.

IV.   INQUIRY TIMING

Timing considerations include the question of when the inquiry will start, how long each phase will be, how much time will elapse between phases, and how long the full inquiry will take. These issues must be dealt with because such matters as length of staff contracts, leases, and budget, all depend on them and will arise early in the proceedings.

In determining when an inquiry should start its hearings, the commissioner should recall that affected persons must be given reasonable notice so there is an opportunity to prepare (see Chapter VIII, Judicial Review of Inquiries, "Notice"). The timing and pace of hearings is shaped, however, not only by legal considerations.

Those who are in favour of a particular project will wish to proceed with the inquiry as quickly as possible, since they have a great deal of money riding on the project and delay is costly. Also, often the project is urgently needed and undue delay can be contrary to the public interest.

It is always easier for inquiry counsel and project proponents to proceed with an inquiry than it is for the intervenors. The proponent, who has largely completed his research and planning, has made the application or proposal that brought about the hearings. Inquiry counsel relies on government officials and other professional consultants who similarly are knowledgeable in the area or have the time to become expert quickly. Other participants, however, are often only in the process of organizing and, hence, need much more time to prepare. In addition, these participants have a separate role in informing the public about the project and obtaining public comment and support. Often they can determine their position only after a certain amount of public consultation. For this reason the participants will invariably require more time before the hearings than will the inquiry staff or the proponents.

Another issue of major concern relates to the overall length of the inquiry. Most participants, including the inquiry staff, need to know how long they are expected to be away from their other duties. Because of the *ad hoc* nature of the process, the inquiry must hire staff that can be freed from other duties. The duration of the inquiry, therefore, becomes a critical factor in determining who is available to join the staff of the inquiry or of the participants.

Many of the staff for the various participants will be engaged on a part-time basis. For example, there may be consultants who will be required only for a certain phase. This means that participants must have some indication of when that phase will take place so they can engage the particular consultant for the time that phase is underway. The same thing is true for counsel and others who are scheduled to take active parts only in certain phases of the inquiry.

If there is a time limit for reporting to government, this will cause further problems. The participants will object to any established time frame because of their fear that it will be insufficient to complete a thorough analysis of the problem. Participants often feel that the government that establishes the inquiry, and even the commissioner, are not fully aware of all of the issues. A limited time frame may seriously underestimate the complexity of the issues and create a false expectation by the government and public that the inquiry will be in the position to report at an early date. Participants, concerned about their ability to be ready and to "keep up," will reject any time frame that appears to restrict the amount of evidence or the number of issues that can be considered; they will likewise reject one that creates a pace too hurried for their limited resources.

The inquiry should be cautious of being too specific about timing. Continuous revision of the official time frame will cause confusion and damage the credibility of the inquiry. As mentioned earlier, hunting or fishing seasons, harvest times, community events, or meetings of participant organizations might require rescheduling because of unavailability of premises or people.

It should be kept in mind that it is difficult to hold hearings over the summer months because advisors, consultants, and potential expert witnesses are often unavailable. Similarly, one cannot schedule hearings around the Christmas vacation period. Depending on the location of the hearings, one must also be cognizant of potential travel problems. For example, hearings in isolated communities must rely on airline schedules that will accommodate large numbers of participants and witnesses. Weather and availability of accommodation vary and must also be taken into account in scheduling.

Another consideration in timing is to ensure that there is adequate time between phases to allow participants to review documentation and prepare for upcoming hearings. Having breaks at convenient points will allow participants to re-examine the evidence on a completed issue, write tentative recommendations, and use that material in preparation for subsequent phases. Also, it is unfair to expect a commissioner and members of his staff, not to mention the participants, to sit in hearings weeks after week. For any hearing, three weeks on and one week off may be the maximum schedule. Participants and staff must not only prepare witnesses currently attending but must locate experts and prepare the evidence they intend to call later. They cannot operate for long periods of time when they have to be both in the hearing room and preparing witnesses. There is a great deal of effort required outside the hearing room to ensure that the hearings operate effectively and efficiently. It is false economy to have long series of uninterrupted hearing days. It is more efficient to allow participants time for adequate preparation outside the hearing, rather than have them grope about in the hearings because of lack of preparation.

A hectic hearing schedule affects participants unequally. Those with substantial funds can hire the additional staff required for speedier hearings, while participants without funds, usually citizens' interest groups who rely on a few people to do their work, are left behind. Public interest groups generally require an extra amount of time for information to be considered by the larger groups they represent and to obtain instructions.

Finally, a schedule of hearings should be considered a flexible document that is reviewed from time to time as the hearings progress. Often the evidence of certain witnesses takes longer than anticipated, or evidence suggests that certain phases must be expanded and others contracted. Hearing schedules should, therefore, be considered as informal guidelines and should be regularly reviewed and revised as circumstances warrant.

V. FORM OF HEARINGS

One of the most important preliminary decisions to be made is the form that will be used by the inquiry to allow participants to present information. In most statutory tribunals the form of hearing is well established. The hearings usually are modelled on court proceedings, with counsel, cross-examination, and other accoutrements associated with judicial proceedings. A commission of inquiry, because of its power to determine its own rules of procedure, has the opportunity to adopt very different forms of hearing, depending on its needs, provided it complies with the statute under which it was created and meets certain minimum requirements established by law. These controls may be no more than common sense or they may be quite sophisticated, depending on the nature of the inquiry.

In determining what type of hearings to conduct, the commissioner should first consider whether there will be affected parties who must be given a fair opportunity to be heard (see Chapter VIII, Judicial Review of Inquiries, "Fair Opportunity To Be Heard). If there are, then legal advice should be sought to determine the applicability of the "rules of natural justice" and the shaping effect those rules will have on the type of inquiry the commissioner wishes to conduct.

But there are also non-legal considerations. These include, (1) the number and nature of participants from whom the commissioner would like to hear, (2) the amount of time and money available for the conduct of the hearings, and (3) the nature of the evidence likely to be presented. If the participants are organized, have funds available, are likely able to retain counsel, are generally located in one area, and are similar enough that they can all participate in the hearing, then one form of hearing suitable to meet those participants' needs will be satisfactory. If, on the other hand, the participants range from relatively unsophisticated (in terms of inquiry procedure) groups to large well-financed organizations, if some participants are in scattered localities with no easy or central place to meet, or if the commissioner is satisfied that a particular form of proceeding would result in undue hardship or would treat one type of participant more favourably than another, he should be prepared to vary the hearing structure.

The form of hearing may also be varied if the commissioner believes a particular procedure will entail an expense greater than is warranted by the issues before the inquiry or if it will take undue time. For example, a formal hearing requiring counsel is not only a more expensive way to participate but also requires sufficient lead time to allow participants to prepare. On the other hand, a hearing that merely involves participants coming together to file submissions can, generally, be conducted in a much shorter time frame.

The nature of the evidence to be presented has a great impact on the form the inquiry should take. If the evidence is very technical, it may require a different form of hearing than less technical presentations. Similarly, if the evidence is very controversial, it may have to be presented in public where it can be challenged, rather than merely added to the data generally agreed upon. If credibility is an issue, cross-examination may be essential. If vast amounts of money are involved or property rights are at stake, the proponent may demand, and should receive, a structured form of hearing where he can be sure his technical and legal advice may be properly used. In the same way, if a certain locality is particularly affected, the form of hearing should be structured to ensure that local residents have an opportunity to make their views known in a form suitable to them.

Faced with these conflicting demands, the commissioner may wish to use more than one form of hearing. While there are certain problems inherent in such a procedure, there is no reason it cannot be adopted. In fact, it has been successfully employed in a number of major hearings. By proceeding in this way, the inquiry must be sure that evidence received in one form of hearing can, if necessary, be challenged in another form. However, having established this right, experience has shown that rarely do participants require evidence to be re-presented or challenged in another hearing.

While variations and combinations of hearings are possible, the following types of hearings are the most commonly used.

A. Formal Hearings

A formal hearing is the traditional form of hearing. It is largely modelled on judicial proceedings and invariably involves the hearing officer's considering evidence that is presented through examination of witnesses and cross-examination by the various participants and by the inquiry staff. It usually involves lawyers and includes expert witnesses presenting technical data. There is the opportunity for argument by counsel on both substantive and procedural matters. It is the form of hearing most often required when rights of individuals are directly affected and brings with it a range of minimum requirements imposed by the courts or by inquiry statutes (see Chapter VIII, Judicial Review of Inquiries, particularly "Natural Justice" and "Evidence"). It has the great advantage of being structured so that participants know what is expected of them and how their information is to be presented. Participants are given the opportunity to hear the evidence and to challenge that evidence in a public forum. The primary disadvantages are the cost of conducting hearings of this type (both to the inquiry and to the participants), the time such hearings require, the relatively formal and technical procedure that results, and the adversarial tone it encourages.

B. Community Hearings

This type of hearing usually involves the hearing officer's attending a meeting where local representatives are able to come forward and present their views. Such proceedings may or may not be under oath and usually do not include the opportunity for cross-examination. Few rules of procedure are followed, and the hearing officer receives opinion evidence along with the technical information that comes from experience in the local community.

The advantage of this form of hearing is that it provides a local and comfortable setting which encourages participants to appear because they are not intimidated or hampered by the cost of more formal participation. The information provided may be of variable quality and veracity, and it is disadvantageous that there is no opportunity for challenging it except through submissions in response. Also, if contrary evidence is to be presented by persons who are not from that locality, it can only be done at another community hearing or at a later date in another context.

One further comment on community hearings is required. Very often they are discounted as having less probative value than other hearing forms and as being merely an opportunity for citizens to let off steam. They are more than this. Information presented at these hearings is often the only, or the best, source of information available to the inquiry. Advice on local conditions, attitudes, and potential impacts are often best received first hand rather than from others studying the area or the people. Community hearings are useful because they not only allow participation by groups or individuals who might not otherwise attend but they can also be the best source of valuable technical information.

C. Seminar Hearings

This form of hearing has been successfully used where there is a recognized pool of experts with differing opinions on a particular subject and the commissioner wishes to hear these views and give the experts an opportunity to comment on and question the views of others. The inquiry organizes a panel composed of experts, either representing participants or not directly affiliated. Each expert is given an opportunity to present his views and to question other members of the panel. Following this exchange, other participants may be given an opportunity to question the panelists.

The advantage of the system is that it allows technical information to be presented by technical experts in their own way and permits others familiar with the subject matter to question this information. It can be relatively informal and unstructured and does not rely on legal counsel.

This type of hearing has a number of disadvantages, however, including the fact that the evidence may be presented by experts in a way that is understood only by the members of the panel (and perhaps the commissioner), but not by the participants or members of the public involved in the issue. The result may be a verbal free-for-all where personality and forcefulness of presentation play a larger role than the soundness of the opinions presented. Also, if one of the experts, in fact, represents a viewpoint held by a participant, that participant will wish to protect the credibility of that point of view by protecting that witness from unfair comment or harassment, something that is difficult to do in this type of hearing.

D. Submissions

Hearings may be conducted by the commissioner's merely attending at a place to hear the submission of whoever wishes to appear before him. The only questions put would be those that the inquiry staff or the commissioner himself wishes to direct. If written submissions only are accepted, the structure is usually considered to be a supplement to one of the other forms of hearing rather than a form of hearing itself. The advantage of this form of hearing is that it can be quickly and inexpensively put together, and it is less intimidating to participants who wish to have their views known. Its major disadvantage is that there is no pulling together in a public forum of the various points of view and no public testing of the evidence. As a result, most of the real work of the inquiry is done by the inquiry staff after the submissions have been presented.

As suggested, each form of hearing has various advantages and disadvantages and there may be combinations that best suit the needs of the particular circumstances of each inquiry. For example, hearings involving major technical projects often combine formal hearings (where the rights of the proponent may be adequately protected by counsel), community hearings (where local people may present evidence of impact), and written submissions (where those who are intimidated by public forums may participate). A form of hearing may be used which would allow a community-type hearing but would include presentation of technical data and data from various localities at one sitting. Or, the inquiry may call in experts to explain the various sides of an issue in a locality, then proceed to a community-type hearing.

Each type of hearing can be complemented by a variety of techniques to bring the evidence before the commissioner most efficiently. For example, issue papers, containing information and divergent views on a particular issue, can be prepared. These papers may exclude the need for hearings on the subject (if there is no controversy) or act as a focus for further proceedings. The inquiry can also conduct seminars or conferences. Papers can be presented and informed comment solicited in a general exchange of information and views. Debates, academic dialogue, and written and verbal exchanges of all sorts can be used to support the hearing format. The form of hearing, or combination of hearings or the use of complementary techniques, is up to the commissioner based on his assessment of the issues, the participants, and the resources available to the inquiry and the participants to provide the best possible information.

V

The Inquiry Process: Procedural Rules

Much of the work of the commissioner and his staff to this point has been directed toward preparing the inquiry and the participants for the public hearings. We now turn to the difficult task of establishing the "rules of the game" to be used by the inquiry at the hearing to obtain and evaluate the information that participants wish to put before it.

Once the inquiry has become familiar with the general state of the information to be represented and the participants, it should consider issuing procedural rulings to indicate to the public and participants how the inquiry proposes to go about its task of collecting information in a public hearing format. Because these procedural rules should be known well in advance so participants can structure their participation according to the inquiry rules, they are often issued in the form of preliminary rulings in advance of public hearings.

As discussed earlier, the inquiry may wish to issue draft procedural rules, usually through inquiry counsel, and then hold preliminary hearings to hear the views of the participants on the procedures suggested. A form of inquiry counsel submission on procedure is found as Appendix B-7.

The commissioner, after reviewing the submissions of various parties, can prepare and issue his rulings which will then constitute the procedure for the hearings. Whether preliminary hearings are held or not, the commissioner should still issue rulings or advice to the public which will explain the procedures to be followed. Normally this is done by an inquiry document issued over the signature of the commissioner. These rules should then be communicated to the participants and to interested members of the public.

The rules adopted should cover a broad range of procedural issues. These rules may be amended and varied by the commissioner in the course of his activities. They should not, however, be changed to such an extent that participants may be prejudiced because certain evidence was presented under one set of rules and other evidence was presented under other rules. While it is possible to have different forms of hearings (see Chapter IV, The Inquiry Structure, "Form of Hearings"), it is important that, within each type of hearing, the rules remain relatively constant throughout the inquiry. For that reason the commissioner, having considered the nature and structure of the hearing he wishes to conduct, should make the procedural rules well enough known in advance that participants will be prepared to present their evidence in the form and at the time required by the inquiry.

I. PROCEDURAL RULINGS

By this time the commissioner and inquiry staff will have reviewed the terms of reference closely and done sufficient background research to have an understanding of the issues to be considered in the course of the public hearings. The commissioner and inquiry counsel will also have considered what procedural requirements are imposed by the courts or by statute. In reaching these conclusions, the commissioner may also have the benefit of a series of preliminary hearings on procedure in which the terms of reference, phasing, and timing of the hearings will have been discussed. He will have met informally with participants, government officials, and others who can assist the inquiry in understanding the nature of the issues before it. He will also have an understanding of the evidence that is likely to be presented in various phases of the inquiry, a rough idea of the number of witnesses likely to be called, and some idea of how long the inquiry process will take at each particular phase. The inquiry is now ready to respond to the information provided by making determinations as to the structure and the specific rules that will govern the public hearings. A sample form of procedural ruling is found in Appendix B-9.

II. SCOPE OF INQUIRY AND TIMING

Armed with the information that has been assembled through preliminary rulings or otherwise, the commissioner should share with the participants any determinations concerning these issues. For example, he may wish to clarify particular issues that were the subject of controversy in defining the scope of the inquiry's terms of reference. Before the public hearings, the commissioner may wish to rule that particular matters are or are not considered by the inquiry to be within its terms of reference. Such decisions must be made carefully so that the inquiry does not prejudge issues by ruling important information to be beyond its terms of reference. But it is necessary to ensure that participants do not prepare evidence on issues which the inquiry has already determined are beyond its terms of reference.

The inquiry should also take the opportunity to set out the phases or general subject areas that will be covered and the order in which they will be presented. For example, in an inquiry examining the impacts of a major development project, the commissioner may wish to indicate that the public hearings will first deal with a description of the engineering and construction of the project, to be followed by examination of the environmental impact and the mitigating measures to be used, and to be completed by a review of the social impact on communities affected. This allows the participants to determine whether or not they will be active at all phases and allows all parties to make some general determinations as to the extent and timing of their participation.

The question of the timing of the various phases should also be addressed, but only in a general way. It is much too early for the inquiry to know with any certainty when the various phases are likely to occur. As a result, it is often better to announce only the phasing and the starting date for the first phase. If it is considered necessary to give some guidelines as to the timing for subsequent phases, this should be done in a general way with ample time left between the phases in the event that the public hearings take longer than expected. Guidelines as to likely starting date for subsequent phases are useful so that tentative assurances can be given to expert witnesses who often must be approached many months in advance.

Setting out likely hearing dates for subsequent phases, however, presents serious problems. The inquiry may be faced with the situation where expert witnesses have been arranged for a particular month and evidence has been prepared for presentation and yet, owing to circumstances beyond anyone's control, the proceeding phase has taken longer than anticipated. The inquiry must then either terminate the evidence being presented (this may exclude relevant information that should logically be on the record before the next phase is undertaken) or allow the ongoing phase to continue. In the latter event, the inquiry runs the risk of having experts who are prepared to give evidence in the next phase excluded because they are not available when that phase actually comes before the inquiry. Either way, the inquiry will suffer.

Most inquiries approach this timing problem by outlining the sequence of issues to be dealt with, starting with the first issue, then proceeding as long as possible in the order established. To assist the participants, while making it clear that it is not binding, the inquiry will often suggest possible timing. Updated hearing schedules are then published from time to time as the evidence unfolds.

Proceeding in this way is not, however, always possible. For one thing, the inquiry may have a reporting date or may otherwise be restricted in how long it is prepared to hold public hearings on issues at various times of the year. The difficulty in scheduling expert witnesses has already been mentioned. The problem of the order and timing of evidence is one which, therefore, must be handled skilfully and must be regularly reviewed, taking into account the demands of the inquiry and of those likely to attend as participants and witnesses.

III. STATUS OF PARTICIPANTS

The preliminary rulings should define who is to be a participant in the inquiry and what rights and responsibilities this status carries. Generally, any person should be able to become a participant in the inquiry by merely appearing and requesting participant status. This is consistent with the idea of a true public hearing in which any member of the public, whether individual or group, has a right to participate. Any person whose rights are affected, particularly if they are affected in a manner or to a degree different than the general public, should automatically be considered a participant (see Chapter VIII, Judicial Review of Inquiries, "Standing").

A participant should have the right to participate in the appropriate manner in inquiry proceedings. Each participant should also have the right to receive all notices of hearing and whatever other information the inquiry may send out to keep interested people informed (such as newsletters) and should be given an opportunity to present a submission to the inquiry at the appropriate time and in the appropriate way. The inquiry should maintain an up-to-date list of participants.

There may be a substantial number of people who want to be recognized as participants because they wish to be kept advised of developments and have the opportunity to make submissions. In addition, they may also wish to call expert evidence and to participate in the cross-examination of other experts. In most situations, however, there will be relatively few participants who have a special interest in the subject matter of the inquiry and who will, therefore, actively participate on a regular basis.

The inquiry should recognize as major participants those

who will be active more or less continuously throughout the
inquiry or through major segments of the inquiry. These parties
should have special rules and responsibilities, particularly with
respect to the production of documents. This will normally include
the parties that are the subject of the inquiry, the government,
inquiry counsel, and those intervenors (generally the coalitions)
who will regularly represent the interests of segments of the public
at the hearings. Because of these special obligations, the major
participants should be identified well in advance of the hearing
so they can organize themselves to comply with the rulings of the
inquiry.

When the inquiry has determined which parties are to be
regarded as major participants in the proceedings, it should next
determine what are the consequences of such a designation. The
formal rules of participation in the public hearings (discussed in
detail below) should apply to major participants, entitling them to
present evidence, cross-examine witnesses, demand production of
documents, and participate in any meetings to assist in the
planning of the inquiry.

A related consideration is the difficult question of who will
receive copies of the official inquiry transcript. Preparation of a
transcript, particularly on a daily basis, is a very expensive procedure, and inquiries are wise to consider carefully the number
and distribution of such transcripts, since it is likely that a large
number of participants will request copies.

In many cases people who do not attend the inquiry on a day-
to-day basis will not have occasion to use the transcripts. This is
especially true if there are copies of transcripts available to them
at local public libraries. On the other hand, participants present
on a day-to-day basis require transcripts, as do certain participants
who rely on the transcripts to inform themselves as part of the
preparation for their appearance later in the inquiry. The issue is
often resolved by the inquiry's declaring that major participants
have a right to receive copies of the transcripts, while those not so
recognized may use copies made available to members of the public
through libraries.

The question of distribution of the transcript should be left
to the commissioner. Generally, the procedure followed is to require
that the government and well-funded participants arrange and pay
for their own transcripts. Transcripts are provided without charge
to the major participants representing public groups or other non-
profit organizations. If funding for major intervenors comes from
the government through the inquiry, it does not make much sense
to require them to pay for a transcript and then provide them with
the funds, unless for accounting purposes. This technique is also

a useful way to give more money to the public participants by having the transcript costs absorbed as a cost of the inquiry. The provision of transcripts is regarded as one of the benefits of being recognized as a major participant.

In public hearings where submissions only are made and questions asked only by the inquiry (the commissioner and his staff, including inquiry counsel), it is normally not necessary to indicate a distinction between classes of participants. The various participants will merely appear before the inquiry to make their submission and answer questions.

It may be desirable, however, for the inquiry to identify those participants likely to have substantial relevant information and require them to participate in a different way than the general public (for example by filing a list of documents in their possession relevant to the inquiry's terms of reference). The inquiry may wish to indicate the issues these participants are to cover in their submissions and even to identify particular persons it would like to hear. While this may not require a special designation as a different class of participant, it is useful for the inquiry to identify and place different requirements on those participants who have information of particular significance.

IV. FORM OF PRESENTATION

As discussed earlier (see Chapter IV, The Inquiry Structure, "Form of Hearings"), the inquiry should indicate at an early date the various forms of evidence that will be received. Generally, it should provide for receipt of written submissions, oral presentations, and expert witnesses. The inquiry may also decide to hold different types of hearings depending on the form the evidence is to take. An ancillary procedural matter to be determined is whether or not all or any of the evidence will be presented under oath.

There appears to be no requirement that evidence before an inquiry be sworn. However, the order in council establishing an inquiry will often give the inquiry authority to receive sworn evidence. Many commissioners do not like the idea of having sworn evidence. There may be a concern that having evidence under oath gives the proceedings a court-like formality that detracts from the type of hearing they would like to hold. It must also be recognized that witnesses appearing before the inquiry may be giving expert opinion evidence, hearsay, and general rumour on a range of issues and that, therefore, requiring an oath may in practice be meaningless. It is also difficult to conceive a situation where evidence given in an information-gathering inquiry hearing could ever be the subject of perjury proceedings.

Other commissioners, however, may feel that the act of giving an oath re-enforces in the minds of all participants the fact that the proceedings are serious and that they are required to provide information with the same care and sincerity as in any judicial proceeding. While the recognizing the looseness with which information may be presented, they still value the idea of preserving the ability to take judicial proceedings should it be proved that a witness deliberately lied. This concern is particularly relevant in inquiries that directly affect rights and property of individuals. In inquiries into wrongdoing or where credibility is an important issue, the witnesses are routinely sworn.

As a result, most inquiries require the witnesses appearing before them to be sworn. To indicate that everyone's evidence is considered equally significant, there is usually the requirement that the evidence be sworn whether it be expert testimony or oral submissions by individuals at public hearings. Only written submissions filed with the inquiry but not spoken to are received as unsworn testimony. There is no distinction between evidence received under sworn oath and that received by affirmation.

Before adopting detailed rules for the presentation of evidence, the commissioner should consider the more general question of the form and order to be followed in the presentation of information in the public hearings. In general inquiries, there are no real problems. The presentation of information is a matter of considering in what order, logically, the information should be presented so as to provide a sequence of events that can effectively and efficiently be used by the inquiry.

When an inquiry deals with a review of a development project, it will invariably have a range of intervenors, from those supporting the proponent to those who are relatively neutral but have issues they want addressed, to those who are clearly opposed to the project and are likely to remain so throughout the course of proceedings. The inquiry does not create this situation; it inherits it from the fact that it is examining an issue in which there are proponents, opponents, and a range of other interests. In these circumstances there will be at least the following categories of evidence:

1. Evidence of the proponents and supporters, which will support the project being examined.
2. Evidence of the opponents, which will oppose the evidence called by the proponents.
3. Evidence of a range of third parties who have interests they wish to see represented or protected which may support the evidence of opponents or proponents depending on the issue.

This group may also include government and other regulatory officials who may have supporting or critical evidence for the inquiry. However, third parties will not usually take a position for or against the project.

4. Evidence called by the inquiry counsel in the interest of the inquiry's general investigative function. This will be neither for nor against the project but, rather, will provide a critical assessment for all sides and will ensure that the interests and objectives of the inquiry are promoted by taking steps to see that all of the relevant information is available.

A preliminary procedural issue to be considered, therefore, is the order in which the various parties will call their evidence and cross-examine (see Chapter VIII, Judicial Review of Inquiries "Order of Presentation"). Part of this question, is the role to be played by the inquiry counsel.

Generally, the procedure followed is that a proponent will lead in the presentation of evidence in all of the phases of the inquiry. The rationale is that the inquiry has been called because of the proponent's application to undertake the project and, presumably, he has conducted the most research and is best suited to present information before the inquiry on the range of issues raised by the proposal. Public interest groups in opposition to the project are particularly adamant that the proponent go first. They regard themselves as forced to react to the proponent's initiative and, therefore, want to hear the full description of the project before calling contrary evidence. While it is sensible that the proponent lead evidence describing the project, the inquiry should be prepared to re-examine the order of presentation in other phases to determine whether other parties may be better prepared to begin the presentation of evidence.

In determining the order of presentation, the inquiry may decide more than what is the logical way of proceeding. It is often suggested that there is an onus on a proponent. In other words, the order of presentation urged by the participants reflects the judicial concept that one of the parties to the proceedings carries an onus that, if it is to be successful, must be discharged in the course of the inquiry's proceeding. It is usually said that the proponent has the onus to describe the project and its likely impacts, to establish that the public interest requires the project to proceed, and to demonstrate how impacts might be mitigated. If it successfully discharges this onus, the inquiry is entitled to report favourably on the project, and the decision makers may grant the proponent the approvals it seeks. The objective of the opponents is merely to ensure that the onus is not discharged.

There is nothing that they must prove; they merely have to demonstrate that the proponent has not proven its case.

While the incidence of both the evidentiary burden (burden of adducing evidence) and the burden of proof (ultimate burden of persuasion) is an important factor in judicial proceedings, its appropriateness in general public inquiries is not at all clear. First, most proponents involved in public inquiry processes will not accept the concept that there is any burden on them. Invariably, they take the position that they are merely one of the participants in the inquiry. They are prepared to accept a role consistent with the fact that they have the bulk of information, but they do not accept the proposition that they have an onus to discharge. Therefore, they do not accept the proposition that they must present evidence first in all of the phases.

A decision must be made by the inquiry as to whether there is an onus to be discharged and, if so, who has it and whether the onus shifts to other parties. Leaving the order of presentation flexible, depending on who has the best information, suggests that the inquiry does not place the entire burden of proof on any one participant throughout. The inquiry should consider whether an onus rests on more than one party and, if so, it should set the order of presentation accordingly.

In reviewing the burden of proof, the commissioner should review the issue with inquiry counsel to distinguish it from the standard of proof, which basically deals with the question of what degree of doubt a commissioner can have about an issue and still come to a conclusion. These related, but distinct, concepts should be understood before scheduling decisions are made.

The inquiry may wish to indicate at an early stage the order in which evidence is to be called and the order of cross-examination. It should be made clear, however, that the order may be varied by the commissioner at his discretion. This will ensure that the commissioner can hear evidence and cross-examination in the order that will best assist the inquiry, rather than according to a rigid formula. For example, particular parties may have regarded certain issues as priority items. Since they are well prepared, their evidence or cross-examination may be scheduled early. At other times, these same parties may be less interested and should be allowed to defer their participation.

While this flexible order of presentation is preferable, it does hold the potential for abuse, and the commissioner must be careful that it is not manipulated for ulterior motives. For example, where a public inquiry is covered by the media, there may be attempts by parties to have their evidence presented or their cross-examination undertaken before newspaper deadlines or at a time when the proceedings are filmed or recorded. These extraneous reasons for requesting priority in cross-examination must not become reasons for ordering the timing of evidence or cross-examination.

V. ROLE OF INQUIRY COUNSEL

Through meetings with participants and advice from staff, inquiry counsel will soon develop an understanding of the issues to be addressed by the various parties. The inquiry must then determine the role of the inquiry counsel in presenting evidence. In some cases, for efficiency of effort, control over the proceedings, or because none of the participants is capable of assembling the evidence, inquiry counsel may be assigned the principal task of presenting witnesses. In such circumstances inquiry counsel will act very much like any other counsel except that he should regard his "client" to be the inquiry, not the commissioner. It would be a disservice to the inquiry if the commissioner alone decided what he was to hear.

On the other hand, the commissioner may wish the participants themselves to carry the major responsibility for calling evidence. In that case, it may be in order for inquiry counsel to advise the participants of some of the issues that, in his opinion, should be addressed in evidence and confirm that this evidence will be called by one or more of the participants. This would be the exercise of inquiry counsel's responsibility for ensuring that evidence is called on all issues relevant to the inquiry while, at the same time, ensuring that those participants with the greater interest in particular evidence call that evidence.

There is a danger that, if inquiry counsel appears too willing in the first instance to call evidence, public participation may collapse. Many of the participants, particularly the public intervenors, may leave all or substantially all of the evidence to be called by inquiry counsel because it is much easier for participants to limit themselves to cross-examining rather than undertaking the time-consuming task of preparing witnesses and arranging for their attendance. If inquiry counsel is not diligent, the result may be that participants will sit back, content to make their case through cross-examination or by calling only a few witnesses in rebuttal.

Inquiry counsel should take the position that he will not guarantee calling any particular evidence and will not indicate to the participants the evidence he intends to call until after the major participants have presented their witnesses. It is the responsibility of the participants to be satisfied that, after they sit down, all necessary evidence to support their position is before the inquiry.

Inquiry counsel will then call whatever additional evidence is required to complete a comprehensive review of the issues.

If there are a substantial number of issues outside the experience and information of participants, or if participants are unable to bring certain evidence before the inquiry (for example, if participants have a history of being in an adversary position with the government so that government officials are not inclined to co-operate with them), inquiry counsel may still play a major role. It may also be necessary to have inquiry counsel call certain evidence because it is expensive or because it is evidence of an international nature involving foreign government officials, who cannot co-operate with specific interests but will assist the inquiry itself. These factors mean that inquiry counsel may still spend a great deal of time calling evidence.

The problem with extensive evidence presentation by inquiry counsel is that much of this evidence, while important, may be of a rather routine nature. Ideally this background information should be presented to the commissioner before the more refined evidence is presented. If calling this basic data is to be the responsibility of inquiry counsel, and he is to call additional evidence at the end to ensure that all gaps have been covered, he could be obliged to call evidence twice within each inquiry phase. While this may not necessarily be inappropriate, it does detract from the proposition that the responsibility for calling evidence before the inquiry rests primarily with participants.

In inquiries that involve project developments, both proponents and inquiry staff have advice and research capabilities, while many of the other participants lack resources. These other participants may be able to ask questions, but they cannot be expected to participate actively in the full range of the inquiry. The purpose of intervenor funding is to correct this imbalance. Participants then are in a position to call the evidence they feel must come before the inquiry. The tendency is to request inquiry counsel to undertake to call certain evidence so that they can spend their limited funds in calling more witnesses relevant to their special interest. While this may be acceptable to the inquiry, it is important that the amount of participant funding reflect the role participants actually wish to play.

The best approach is a form of co-operation whereby inquiry counsel agrees to call difficult-to-obtain evidence or evidence that requires a more formal approach by a non-partisan counsel. He will often agree to call this evidence early in the phase, while retaining his right to call clean-up evidence at the end. The funded participants, on the other hand, will undertake to call stipulated evidence as part of their responsibility to the inquiry.

Generally, the commissioner must ensure that the participants seek the attendance of witnesses if they feel that their attendance is important and have inquiry counsel call them only as a last resort. Forcing inquiry counsel to call witnesses on behalf of participants weakens the participants' responsibility for determining what evidence they feel should be called, and turns the matter into one of obtaining directions from the commissioner. More important, it sets the precedent whereby participants need merely advise the inquiry of the witnesses they want to appear and then leave it to inquiry counsel to arrange their attendance. Such a procedure could be accommodated, but it means the participants themselves will play a minor role in calling evidence.

If the commissioner feels that the responsibility for calling this evidence should be borne by inquiry counsel, then arrangements must be made beforehand whereby participants merely advise counsel of the evidence that should be presented and counsel then arranges for the attendance of those witnesses. This procedure does, however, effectively prevent inquiry counsel from cross-examining those witnesses. It also has the serious drawback of again returning the responsibility for calling evidence to the inquiry staff, something participant funding was designed to avoid. Also, inquiry counsel becomes the servant of the participants, calling their witnesses at their request. This may conflict with his duty to the commissioner and to the inquiry as a whole.

If inquiry counsel is able to maintain his independent position and leave prime responsibility for calling evidence to the participants, he should advise participants of issues he would like them to address if there is doubt whether such evidence will be presented. It is also often important for inquiry counsel to contact people who may not be planning to participate (*e.g.*, proponents of competing projects), outline what information the inquiry wants, and request their appearance. It is usual for participants to indicate to other participants the nature of evidence they expect to present or the nature of the evidence they wish to elicit in cross-examination. This ensures that the person presenting a witness or panel of witnesses has notice of the issues to be raised and can, therefore, have the people with expertise in appropriate areas available.

Inquiry counsel may also wish to write participants indicating the nature of evidence he wishes them to call at various stages and obtain from them an undertaking that such evidence will be presented. Usually this can be done on an informal basis but, if there is a reluctant participant, it may be necessary for counsel to indicate the nature of the evidence that the participant should present and obtain a formal undertaking. If that undertaking is not forthcoming, it may then be appropriate for inquiry counsel to arrange for subpoenas to be certain that that evidence does come before the inquiry.

Often witnesses will not be totally within the control of inquiry counsel. For example, counsel may wish to call government witnesses to give evidence. These witnesses may feel that government policy prevents them from speaking to particular issues or may be unwilling to be as forthright in explaining particular issues as the inquiry may wish. Since inquiry counsel is responsible for assisting these witnesses in the preparation of their evidence, it is not possible for him to cross-examine if he finds that the witness is reluctant to present a comprehensive statement. In these cases, it may be necessary for the commissioner to permit greater freedom than usual in re-examination or to allow inquiry counsel to ask supplementary questions as a matter of direct evidence rather than cross-examination in order to obtain the elaboration required. Since no participant should be allowed to cross-examine its own witness, this is a delicate matter and requires planning before it can be properly carried out. Inquiry counsel is in the unique position of having to call evidence that is necessary to round out information before the inquiry through witnesses who are not fully within his control.

The question has been raised whether there is a need for witnesses to appear clearly as representatives of particular interests or whether it is sufficient that information come before the inquiry without attribution to a particular view or interest. For example, if a proponent calls a panel of witnesses, is it important that one of the witnesses be able to give undertakings on behalf of the proponent company? A problem exists when a witness is prepared to give evidence in his personal capacity but not as a representative of the government or party he served as consultant.

In every case it will be necessary to review the particular situation. It may be important that a participant be formally represented before the inquiry if the inquiry is seeking undertakings from a particular branch of government or a particular company. On the other hand, if it is merely factual information that is required, and no one is seeking undertakings or otherwise attempting to get information on behalf of the named company or government, then formal identification loses its significance.

VI. DISCOVERY OF DOCUMENTS

Inquiries are created at a particular time with instructions to examine an issue and to report. While the commissioner himself may be familiar with the subject area (though this is not always the case), and while knowledgeable staff can be retained, rarely does the inquiry have the documentation necessary to ensure a comprehensive data base.

One way to ensure that it quickly develops this data base is to require that all parties with information relevant to the work of the inquiry, including governments, make that information known to the inquiry. This is usually done by the inquiry's ordering named parties to file a list of all the reports, studies, or other documents relevant to its terms of reference in their possession or power. Upon a review of these lists, the inquiry can decide which documents to review or to obtain.

Unlike courts, inquiries do not have a pre-existing formal procedure whereby parties can discover and compel disclosure of relevant written material and other evidence held or controlled by other parties. It is necessary for the inquiry to design its own discovery procedure, usually following preliminary hearings, and to prescribe the procedure in its rulings or orders.

This power to compel the production of document lists and the documents themselves flows from specific statutory powers under the public inquiry acts or other special acts that authorize establishment of inquiries. It also flows from aspects of the rules of natural justice (see Chapter VIII, Judicial Review of Inquiries, "Disclosure" and "Discovery"). An example of a procedure requiring production of a list of documents is found in Appendix B-7, and a sample list of documents is found as Appendix B-10.

Commissioners often forget that, unlike judicial proceedings, inquiries do not have the range of preliminary proceedings that assist participants in gathering information and in focussing and clarifying the issues. Judicial proceedings have pleadings in which the parties outline the nature of the dispute and the specific issues in dispute. There are also discoveries, in which opposing parties examine each other under oath and review the documents likely to be relevant; interrogatories (formal written questions and responses); and pre-trial conferences, in which matters of organization and procedure can be discussed and clarified. Without these supporting procedures, an inquiry is at a considerable disadvantage unless it adopts similar or analogous techniques.

To ensure that participants are not surprised by the revelation of major reports or studies during the course of the hearing, with the likely consequence of an adjournment so that the report can be studied, the exchange of lists of documents by the major participants is required. There is then an opportunity for the parties to receive and review these documents in preparing for the hearings.

A list of documents is not, however, the only discovery technique that should be considered. After an exchange of documents, a commissioner may convene preliminary conferences at which the parties would be asked to disclose information with a view to defining which issues are controversial and should be dealt with in the context of the hearing and which are necessary to have on record but should be dealt with by filing relevant documents without calling witnesses. For example, the commissioner may wish to adopt a procedure whereby evidence is merely filed with the inquiry and only cross-examination on that evidence takes place during the hearing. Alternatively, detailed statements of evidence could be filed, with the witness giving only a brief summary before cross-examination.

Another alternative is to have a pre-hearing conference at which the parties may agree on the areas that require cross-examination. Written questions on relevant matters addressed to other parties and their corresponding replies (interrogatories) may be filed with the inquiry, making it unnecessary to cover those issues in the hearing itself. These interrogatories, accompanied with demands for relevant material in their possession, can often dramatically reduce the number of witnesses. All these procedures are designed to ensure that hearing time is devoted only to the controversial issues or to matters of credibility.

The success of various discovery procedures will vary, depending on the sophistication of the parties and their willingness to co-operate, and on the commissioner's view of how much of the inquiry's work is to be conducted outside of the public eye. If the commissioner is satisfied that all major interests are sufficiently well represented, if he is desirous of saving hearing time, and if he does not regard the public hearing process as a public information exercise (which means that all information must be publicly presented and discussed, not for the benefit of the commissioner, but for the benefit of the public), then the inquiry can consider these various techniques. If, on the other hand, interests are not well defined, and the commissioner wishes all of the issues discussed in public, then only a limited pre-hearing process may be appropriate.

Generally, the demand for a list of documents is directed only to those parties who can be regarded as major participants or who, while not directly participating in the inquiry, are known to have relevant information, such as governments. This list of documents to be prepared by the various participants should, in all cases, be prepared by the participants themselves. For example, inquiry counsel should not be placed in the position of undertaking to provide a complete list of documents in the possession of the appointing government. It must be made clear that the obligation to provide a list rests with the government and not with the inquiry. Therefore, inquiry counsel can only state he is advised by the government that the list is complete and accurate.

An order requiring participants to prepare a list of documents should also require each of the participants to file his list with the inquiry and serve it on the other named participants. This ensures that each party has a full list of the documents relevant to the inquiry.

Each list of documents should identify a contact person and, where possible, an accessible location where the documents can be inspected. Since certain documents may be of general interest, it is a wise practice to allow participants and governments to file with the inquiry library a copy or copies of documents that will be in regular use. Participants can review these documents at the inquiry library instead of attending and reattending at the participant's office to review the materials.

Where necessary, the inquiry may be required to obtain a particular document and make copies available. Otherwise, each participant should provide a photocopy facility, where portions of documents can be photocopied by the participants should it be necessary for the adequate preparation of their case.

The list of documents should include all of those documents in the possession or power of the participant, even those that it may wish to claim are privileged communications and, hence, are not required to be produced. Documents which would ordinarily be relevant to the work of the inquiry, but which can be withheld by participants under established grounds of privilege, should, in any event, be made known. (See discussion of whether privilege is available in inquiries, various forms of privilege, and grounds for non-production, in Chapter VIII, Judicial Review of Inquiries, "Privilege"). Procedures may then be devised whereby the inquiry agrees that it will exclude the document from production or receive and review this information on a confidential basis.

Receipt of information on a confidential basis by a public inquiry is, on its face, a contradiction. It may, however, ensure an opportunity for review by the inquiry of documents whose public disclosure would unduly and unfairly prejudice a particular party. Some inquiries take the view that, unless a document is made public, they will not review it. If absolutely necessary, others will receive the information on a confidential basis, rather than proceeding without that information. The question of whether or not the inquiry is prepared to receive information on a confidential basis should be dealt with in the preliminary rulings.

One further issue is whether or not parties who have not been required to prepare statements of evidence, such as members of the public, are entitled to receive documents or a list of documents. Inquiries will often permit members of the public who have not filed a list of documents to receive copies of documents if they require them for preparing their submission to the inquiry, provided they use the inquiry office to review the lists and obtain documents for this purpose. Usually these parties will work with the inquiry librarian, who will ensure that requested documents are made available at the inquiry library for review.

Government departments should also be required to provide a list of documents. The list will either be filed by inquiry counsel or by lawyers representing the government. Documents themselves should be available in the area where the inquiry is located or holds hearings. This is particularly important when documents may, as in the case of federal government material, be located only in Ottawa, and far from the centre where the hearing is taking place. Normally government document lists are prepared by a co-ordinator within the department of government responsible for sponsoring the inquiry. This officer ensures that other government departments prepare lists, and a comprehensive government list is then submitted.

It is useful to have the various document lists deposited in central locations where they can be reviewed by members of the public. These lists should also be available in the hearing room in the event reference is made to a report or study that a participant wants to verify has been disclosed in the list.

Inquiry counsel will be required to file a list of documents in the possession of the inquiry itself. This is because the inquiry staff will generate its own documents or, in the course of its research, identify documents that may not be in the possession of any of the participants or governments involved.

Participants must file supplementary lists of documents from time to time as additional documents are prepared or brought to their attention. The inquiry may have to issue reminders requesting supplementary lists. Similarly, if witnesses or participants refer to studies which are not part of that participant's list, the inquiry may require that a supplemental list be filed.

The safest policy in deciding what should be included in a list of documents is to be as comprehensive as possible. Generally, one should consider all of the witnesses or evidence that may be presented to the inquiry, and have all of the documents to be referred to or relied on in the preparation and presentation of this evidence listed. When the witness appears on the stand or a submission is prepared, there should be no reports referred to or relied on that are not part of the list of documents.

While the list is to be comprehensive, there are a number of policy decisions to be made in deciding what is to be included and what is not. One question is whether independent consultants' reports have to be listed. Generally, the soundest position to take is that, if the participant has the right to demand possession of any documents, they should be listed.

Another question arises when a preliminary and then a final report is prepared. Usually a participant will only list the final report. Often other participants are more interested in the earlier draft since it may contain more information of interest to them before it is reviewed and redrafted by the listing party. There is no way to compel production of these drafts other than by requesting production if their existence is known. In deciding whether to compel production of earlier drafts, the commissioner should consider whether it advances the work of the inquiry, especially if the draft is inconsistent with the position now being addressed by that participant and whether such an order might encourage "fishing expeditions" that would unduly delay the work of the inquiry. Generally, it is sufficient if only the final report is listed and not the earlier draft of that report unless it is specifically requested and there is a good reason for its production as, for example, when the author of the draft is called to give evidence (see Chapter VIII, Judicial Review of Inquiries, "Privilege").

Some participants will take a narrow view of what a "report" is. While it is not necessary, obviously, to list all of the correspondence, memoranda, and other minor communications related to issues before the inquiry, anything that represents a bringing together of information should be listed as material relevant to the inquiry. This will include some correspondence, though most letters and similar written communications would be excluded.

It must be recognized that the success of this procedure depends on the good will of the parties. The inquiry's terms of reference are likely to be so broad and the number of relevant documents so large that it is impossible for any party, in most circumstances, to state categorically that these are the only relevant documents. For example, in any technical area one must consider which of the standard texts or basic engineering documents are relevant and should be listed. It is for this reason that most inquiries do not require that affidavits be sworn attesting to the completeness of document lists, as would be the case in judicial proceedings.

There is really no substitute for a voluntary production of documents. For example, the subpoena does nothing more than compel a party to appear before the inquiry and bring the relevant documents. It does nothing to ensure complete production of documents beyond evidence the witness will present but still within the inquiry's terms of reference. Nor does it give disclosure far enough in advance that these documents can be studied before the witness attends. The procedure is useful only if a party refuses to provide a document list at all.

The list should be made available to the major participants in sufficient time to permit them to review it and decide what documents they require. It is also important that the contact person is known and the procedure for receiving and reviewing the documents is in place. Once the inquiry starts, production will be demanded on short notice and the commissioner should be satisfied that major sources of information have been "pre-tested" so that the mechanism and procedure is adequate when proceedings begin.

Experience has shown that discovery of documents, while important as a matter of form, has only limited practical application. In most inquiries actual production of documents from the list has been minimal. More often, documents that form part of a witnesses' statement of evidence are demanded once the evidence is presented. Though these reports may be on the general list of documents, in most instances production of the report will not be demanded until the witness relying on the report has participated in the hearings.

Generally, one can assume that, if a document is included on the list of documents, it will be produced. Most participants in a public inquiry process will produce all of the relevant documents and will not claim privilege. Documents of a sensitive nature will generally not be listed on the grounds that they are irrelevant to the terms of reference or that they are preliminary to listed documents. While the general list of documents is a valuable way of bringing together research, it is often not totally comprehensive.

VII. STATEMENT OF EVIDENCE

Many inquiries have adopted a procedure, now well established in regulatory proceedings, whereby witnesses appearing are required to file a complete statement of their evidence at a specified time before the witness is scheduled to appear. Often the statement of evidence also includes sufficient information on the witness to qualify him as a person capable of giving expert opinions on the subject matter covered in the statement. A list of all reports, studies, and other documents that the witness will refer to or rely on in the course of his evidence is often included as well. (See sample rule requiring statements of evidence as part of preliminary procedural rulings, Appendix B-9 and sample of statement of evidence, Appendix B-11).

Like the discovery of documents procedure, the filing of statements in advance is particularly useful in proceedings where there is no other procedure available to assist participants in knowing the nature of information to be presented. Filing a statement of evidence allows other participants to review the evidence and determine what expertise they require for purposes of cross-examination. It also gives participants an opportunity to review the statement in detail and, hence, more efficiently prepare cross-examination. The theory here is that better prepared cross-examination will take much less hearing time.

Statements of evidence filed with the inquiry should also be transmitted to the other major participants. Because of timing and a desire to ensure that the inquiry, through an error on its part, is not criticized for inadequately informing the parties, the responsibility for preparing and distributing the statement of evidence is often given to the participant calling the witness.

The use to which a statement of evidence is put once the witness actually appears varies. In some cases the practice has been merely to table the statement as the evidence of the witness and immediately make him available for cross-examination. This has the advantage of shortening the time required to process each witness and avoids the often laborious task of reading a detailed statement already in the possession of interested participants. It does have its disadvantages, however. For one thing, the public appearance of the witness and the impression he creates arises only in the context of responding to questions in a defensive position. Often a more favourable view of the witness is created if he also has an opportunity to express, in his own words, what he has stated in his written testimony.

Appearing for cross-examination only encourages some witnesses to answer questions by repeating sections of their statement to get it in the hearing transcript. Cross-examiners may feel it necessary to repeat the evidence before putting questions. In either case the process of questioning is lengthened and may fill any time saved by filing the statement. Finally, it can be very confusing for the media and public, because questions are being asked that are based on written materials that only the participants will have read. Not only is it confusing, it is counter-productive, if one of the inquiry's functions is to educate the public on the issues.

An alternate way of proceeding is to require the witnesses to read their entire statements of evidence into the record before being questioned. This ensures that the transcript is complete and accurate. It also makes it possible for those who have not received a statement of evidence and those reporting the proceedings to know all of the evidence without having to read a background statement of evidence. On the other hand, it is a long and often tedious process since witnesses are reading evidence already in front of all those directly involved and, because they read from prepared material, their presentation is often flat.

A compromise is to have the full statement of evidence filed with the inquiry and the witness asked to adopt the written statement. Then he is asked to summarize or "highlight" the statement of evidence within an agreed time limit. In some cases the summary is also provided in written form, much like an "executive summary" of a report. The witness then takes the inquiry through his filed statement of evidence, reading sections of particular significance. Alternatively, the witness may outline his major conclusions without repeating much of the material in the written statement.

The advantage of this approach is that it allows the witness an opportunity to present his statement in his own terms and to verbalize the key aspects so the public and the media can become acquainted with what he has to say without searching out the filed material. While some witnesses often run beyond their allotted time, so that the summary is not much shorter than the full statement, this can usually be controlled. Of some concern is the problem of witnesses' presenting their summary in a way that is an extension of their statement as filed and is, in fact, "new evidence."

Whatever approach is adopted, the procedure should be outlined and all parties informed well before the first witness is called since, depending on the format adopted, different preparation is required.

If witnesses are not required to read their full statement of evidence, the complete statement of evidence must be sent, along with the verbal transcript, to those who are to receive a full inquiry record. Otherwise, the transcript merely records cross-examination, and the evidence itself is not available for review.

VIII. OPINION EVIDENCE AND HEARSAY

The commissioner may also advise in his preliminary rulings how he intends to deal with opinion evidence and hearsay. Under strict rules of evidence, individuals are entitled only to give evidence of what they know on the basis of their own observation. They are not entitled to give opinions on the ultimate issues before the court. The right to give an opinion is reserved for those individuals who are recognized as expert in the field. The procedure is to have an expert present his qualifications, be "accepted" or "qualified" by the tribunal as an expert in a particular field, and then present his expert opinion on matters in that field and that field only.

Courts of law also want to receive the best evidence on facts before them. They, therefore, require witnesses to state only what they know on the basis of their own observations. They normally reject as hearsay the evidence of one person about what another said, if the intention is to ask the tribunal to accept the truth of that evidence. (For a more detailed discussion of opinion evidence and what constitutes hearsay, see Chapter VIII, Judicial Review of Inquiries, "Evidence".)

It is left to the discretion of the commissioner to decide whether he wishes to be bound by the legal rules of evidence or to vary them. He is not bound as a matter of law. The practice adopted by most commissioners is to allow hearsay evidence and to hear opinion evidence from a broad range of witnesses, some of whom would be considered experts and others not. The reasons are not hard to find. From the public's point of view, it indicates a willingness to listen to a range of experience. From the inquiry's perspective, these opinions may still be the best, or the only, sources of information available.

There are often circumstances in which individuals may be regarded as experts even though they possess no formal technical qualifications. For example, an experienced fisherman may be able to give very good and specialized evidence on current and weather conditions in a particular marine area even though he has no formal training that would qualify him as an expert. In any event, testimony by lay "experts" of this kind has even been recognized in judicial proceedings as sufficient to support convictions for environmental offences. With this judicial precedent, most inquiries allow lay evidence to be received.

If this "opinion" evidence is allowed, it should still be necessary for the person calling the witness to qualify him and to allow others to cross-examine him on his qualifications. This may be done first so that a determination can be made initially as to his expertise before the evidence is admitted. An alternative practice is to present the witness's qualifications, hear his evidence, and then allow cross-examination to determine the extent of his expertise and the basis for the opinions expressed. While allowing parties to examine and cross-examine on expertise before hearing evidence has the advantage of placing that evidence in its proper context, in public inquiries this procedure seems overly legalistic. If it is decided that such information will be allowed to be presented in any event, there is little advantage to be gained by arguing over qualifications before hearing the evidence. Since credibility of witnesses is rarely an issue in public inquiries, and since most good witnesses will set out their areas of expertise and qualify themselves adequately before giving their opinion, there is little reason to investigate witnesses' technical qualifications formally.

The matter is one, however, that is within the discretion of the commissioner, who can refuse to hear opinions of witnesses he determines to be non-experts. Whatever the practice, the matter should be resolved and a procedure established before witnesses are called to give evidence. A consistent procedure should be maintained throughout the hearings.

IX. CROSS-EXAMINATION

The right of participants to cross-examine the witnesses called by other participants is considered by hearing participants to be fundamental. It is not, however, an unqualified right, and variations in the use and scope of cross-examination may be appropriate (see Chapter VIII, Judical Review of Inquiries, "Questioning or Cross-Examination").

In some circumstances cross-examination may properly be excluded. For example, in community hearings where the commissioner is interested in getting the feelings and personal reactions of individuals, cross-examination would add little in the way of evidence and might discourage people from coming forward to speak. Similarly, if the structure of the hearing is such that the commissioner wishes to receive the oral submissions of individuals, even though the submissions may contain mixed factual information and opinion evidence, cross-examination may be neither appropriate nor useful to the inquiry.

The purpose of cross-examination is to allow parties adverse in interest to challenge and "test" the information presented and to elicit further information, which might work against the interest of the party calling that witness.

In a public inquiry the concept of a party "adverse in interest" is difficult to apply. Generally, commissioners will allow any of the participants to cross-examine evidence that is called. As a result, cross-examination is often abused in the sense that it is not used for the purpose of challenging and testing but, rather, it is used by participants who support the evidence presented. This can lead to an abuse of the inquiry process, especially if the rules provide for advance notice of evidence to be called. By allowing parties similar in interest to cross-examine each other, evidence in support of a particular position may be presented unexpectedly through "friendly cross-examination" rather than under the ordinary rules for the presentation of evidence.

Given the fact, however, that many participants would say they are neutral or are cross-examining for purposes of providing more information for the inquiry, it is difficult to restrict cross-examination. Normally all the commissioner can do is structure the order of cross-examination so that parties clearly opposed to the interest of the party calling the witness are given an early opportunity to cross-examine. This will ensure that at least the initial cross-examination functions as it was intended.

Finally, the commissioner must decide whether to allow all participants, or merely those identified as major participants, to cross-examine. Consistent with the concept of a full and complete public inquiry, many commissioners provide that all the participants in the proceedings (*i.e.,* anyone present), can cross-examine evidence called by others. To ensure that the matter does not get out of hand, however, commissioners may also provide that they will call on major participants to cross-examine first. Experience has shown that, by the time these participants finish their cross-examination, there are relatively few questions left, so that other parties rarely participate in cross-examination. Alternatively, it may be appropriate to require that, except for major participants who cross-examine directly, all parties must submit their questions to the commissioner or, preferably, to inquiry counsel who will address the questions on their behalf.

There is one further aspect to consider when determining the order in which evidence is to be presented or cross-examination conducted, and that is the role of the inquiry counsel. This will vary, depending on the size, scope, and subject matter of the inquiry. Often, if there are well-organized parties on both sides of an issue and the general public interest is also well represented, inquiry counsel will play a relatively modest role. This means that he would call evidence and cross-examine last, playing a "clean-up" role to ensure that gaps are filled and evidence is clarified for the benefit of the commissioner.

On the other hand, inquiry counsel may be required to be the dominant, and sometimes the sole, cross-examiner. He will thus be the first person to cross-examine all of the parties, on whatever side of an issue they appear. As discussed earlier, the commissioner should carefully consider the role of inquiry counsel and allow him to cross-examine or call evidence in whatever order is consistent with this role.

In all cases, however, parties must be given some opportunity to respond to prejudicial information. If no cross-examination is allowed, alternate forms must be available. Usually this means participants are given the right to present their views in opposition to those presented, either at the time or at a latter point in the proceedings.

Where witnesses are called before the inquiry by participants and asked to provide evidence in the same manner as witnesses in a court proceeding, the denial of cross-examination would be singularly inappropriate. In these circumstances, parties, at least those that regard themselves to be adverse in interest to the party calling the witness, should have an opportunity to cross-examine.

The main purposes of cross-examination are to get admissions of fact from parties which may be against their interest and to get further information which may help the party cross-examining to build its case. Cross-examination can also be used to explore the areas of expertise of a witness, to limit the subjects upon which he should be regarded as an expert, or merely to clarify the meaning of evidence the witness has presented. Cross-examination as to credibility — designed to demonstrate that the person is untrustworthy or has misled the inquiry and, therefore, should not be believed — is rarely used in public inquiries.

When cross-examination is allowed, it may, in certain circumstances, be limited to varying extents. The commissioner, in deciding on any limitation of cross-examination, should be aware of the legal requirements of the rules of natural justice and procedural fairness. He should also, however, consider whether these limitations might lead participants to conclude that they are being unfairly treated and, hence, damage the credibility and public acceptance of the inquiry.

Restricting cross-examination is always a very troublesome matter. In most cases it should be possible to obtain estimates of cross-examination time from various participants in order to assist in the scheduling of witnesses. There is nothing more disruptive than having witnesses, especially experts who have travelled great distances, sit around because cross-examination of the preceding witnesses has taken much longer than anticipated. Because statements of evidence are available in advance, it should be possible for inquiry counsel to get estimates of the cross-examination time from counsel for the various participants. This works better in theory than in practice since cross-examination is invariably much more lengthy than expected. Every effort should be made, however, to make realistic determinations of cross-examination time.

Because of the interrelated nature of most issues before an inquiry, there is often a temptation for participants to ask all of their questions of a particular witness the first time he attends. This ignores the phasing of the inquiry and the fact that the witness will re-attend at a later phase. The commissioner must ensure that the cross-examination does not go beyond the issues before the inquiry in each phase. At the same time a witness should not be forced to return where there is only a small amount of additional evidence of a minor nature to be presented. In those cases the commissioner may wish to have questions related to another phase asked of the witness at the time he first attends.

Any limitation on cross-examination must be carefully considered from both the legal and public perspectives. Time limitations can be perceived as arbitrary and may be counter-productive. One party may be conducting a very useful and instructive cross-examination when his time runs out and he is forced to cease and turn over the cross-examination to a party who is less prepared and who may, in fact, waste the inquiry's time. The procedure might also lead to the situation where certain participants assign their cross-examination time to others. Time limitations may appear beneficial from an overall efficiency standpoint; however, the procedure may prove to be less than successful because the limitations are necessarily aribtrary without recognition of either the significance of the information presented or the fact that lengthy cross-examination may genuinely assist the inquiry in carrying out its responsibilities.

Limiting cross-examination to certain parties involves similar difficulties. While cross-examination may theoretically be limited to parties adverse in interest, it is often difficult to identify those parties. Many participants who may appear to be opposed to other participants may, in fact, see their role as merely gaining information or educating the public without advancing any particular interest.

Procedures have been devised in which only the commissioner or inquiry counsel are entitled to cross-examine. This is often appropriate where parties are asked to make submissions on particular topics and the purpose of cross-examination is merely to clarify submissions. In hearings of this type, it is important that inquiry counsel or the commissioner appear neutral in questioning and that alternative ways of correcting unchallenged information be provided for participants. This procedure would probably work in circumstances where a long series of requested submissions are presented with little or no public involvement in the proceedings. It would not work well where expert witnesses make submissions in the presence of parties adverse in interest and in the presence of the media.

One of the most successful techniques for restricting time spent on cross-examination, while being fair to all the participants, is to allow cross-examination but encourage or require like-minded participants to work through one counsel. This forces generally similar interests to co-operate before cross-examination to bring together their information. Duplication is avoided, and individual participants are permitted to develop expertise in particular areas delegated to them rather than attempting to address a wide range of witnesses and issues without having adequate time to prepare.

Unless there is a statutory right to cross-examination, restriction of cross-examination is dependent upon the wishes of the commissioner. A commissioner who requires cross-examiners to make their points quickly and succinctly, who is prepared to question the relevancy of a line of cross-examination that appears to go beyond the interest of the inquiry, and who will rule certain lines of questioning as irrelevant or of only peripheral interest will soon alert the participants that, unless they are rigorous in their cross-examination, the impact will be lost. Ultimately, the participants must ensure the efficient use of cross-examination. If they feel their efforts are gaining them little, and in fact may be alienating the commissioner, they will soon restructure their cross-examination to make more efficient use of inquiry time. Ruling matters irrelevant or cautioning parties must be done carefully and in recognition that the proceedings cannot be restricted to lawyers; however, these are the best techniques available to commissioners to ensure relevant and efficient cross-examination.

If there are particular problems, such as reporting dates or severe scheduling difficulties, the commissioner may have no choice but to limit or even exclude cross-examination. In addition to limiting who can cross-examine and for how long, the inquiry may obtain undertakings that witnesses will return at later dates or that further questions will be answered in written form and filed as part of the inquiry record. Whatever procedure is used, there must always be a sense that the limitation is sensible and fair. It is very difficult to control evidence-in-chief; it is, therefore, unfair to allow great freedom in chief and then to severely restrict cross-examination.

The role of the inquiry counsel in cross-examination will have a great impact on shaping the inquiry. For example, should inquiry counsel cross-examine first or last? Inquiry counsel has the responsibility of examining all of the issues before the inquiry to ensure all evidence necessary for a proper investigation is presented to the commissioner. He may, therefore, want to hear the evidence-in-chief and the cross-examination of all other participants before undertaking his cross-examination. This will enable him to pursue lines of cross-examination that may not have been fully developed by a participant because the participant's particular concern did not demand such development. It will also ensure that issues not touched on by other participants, but important to the inquiry, are examined and will give him the ability to "mop-up" or finalize the evidence on any issue on behalf of the inquiry.

On the other hand, inquiry counsel may be assisted by the most knowledgeable and experienced advisors on the issues before the inquiry. As a result, his cross-examination may be more efficient and precise than the cross-examination of other participants. It gives the proceedings a more professional tone and allows evidence to be processed more quickly if inquiry counsel cross-examines first. Because of this experience and expertise, inquiry counsel's evidence can cover a wide-range of issues of interest to a number of participants and include all the basic data that must come before the inquiry. Thus, participants can merely pick and choose particular points of interest to them without taking the time required to canvass a range of issues. Any issues of interest to the inquiry but not canvassed can then be dealt with by the commissioner himself.

Having cross-examined first, it is difficult for inquiry counsel to then follow up lines of cross-examination by other participants that may be necessary for a full understanding of an issue. If issues are raised and not pursued to the full extent of their relevance, inquiry counsel would fail in his responsibility to ensure that all of the evidence, including that which goes beyond the interests of participants, comes before the inquiry. For this reason, inquiry counsel is generally asked to cross-examine last.

A further alternative is to allow inquiry counsel to examine witnesses first, to make use of the expertise, and then again last, to fulfil his special responsibilities to the inquiry. Such a procedure seems unfair since no other participant is given the same right, and it may lead to an over-emphasis of the role of inquiry counsel.

If the commissioner has funded participant groups to participate in the evidence-gathering process, then they should be given the opportunity to do that, including presentation of evidence required on the record but not relating directly to their concern. Though this may take longer than a co-ordinated and systematic cross-examination by inquiry counsel, the difference would not be so great as to be outweighed by the advantage of having inquiry counsel close out cross-examination, satisfied everything the commissioner needs is before him.

The commissioner also has an opportunity to question the witnesses. Questions designed to clarify the commissioner's understanding of evidence should be addressed to the witness in the course of the evidence, unless such a procedure unduly disrupts the flow of information. Any extensive cross-examination by the commissioner should take place after the evidence is in, preferably after everyone else has completed cross-examination. This leaves the primary onus on the participants to elicit the required information.

As in the case of inquiry counsel, a commissioner with extensive experience in the subject area may wish to begin cross-examination. However, this is usually unsatisfactory. Some participants are intimidated, while others may conclude, on the basis of the cross-examination, that the commissioner views matters in a particular way, and may tailor their answers to respond to that perception rather than present their case in their own way. The participants usually expect the commissioner to be completely impartial — something extensive, particularly aggressive, cross-examination is likely to betray.

X. MAINTAINING A RECORD

The concept of an official record is one that has been imported from traditional judicial proceedings and incorporated, in varying degrees, into the public inquiry process with very little thought. In judicial proceedings a court is bound to make a decision only on the basis of the formal evidence presented and admitted before it in public proceedings, that is, on the "record." Except for a limited range of notorious matters of general public knowledge, which the judge is deemed to know without proof at trial (matters of which he is permitted to take "judicial notice"), all other facts must be established on the record. A similar concept of "record" has been applied to formal administrative proceedings in which the tribunal determines the rights of parties before it (see Chapter VIII, Judicial Review of Inquiries, "Record").

This idea of an official record has been adopted to some extent in most public inquiries. Generally, it has meant that the inquiry keeps a public record of all the submissions it receives and, when it holds public hearings, it records the proceedings in a transcript. It also means that all materials presented to the inquiry by witnesses are given exhibit numbers and formally accepted.

These procedures are sound ways of ensuring information filed before the inquiry is consistently dealt with and forms part of the documentation and information the inquiry will use in the course of its deliberation. It is often not clear, however, whether commissioners regard an official record as merely a sound administrative technique or as a legal requirement that limits the manner in which the inquiry receives its information and controls what information it can consider in reaching its conclusions. Inquiries headed by legally trained individuals tend to use the concept as it is applied in judicial proceedings; others tend to use it more as an administrative arrangement.

While a record need not be maintained for purposes of an appeal, a record makes the information that is to form the basis of the inquiry's decisions publicly gathered and publicly available. The credibility of a public inquiry is enhanced if the decision is clearly seen to be based on information publicly presented rather than on information secretly obtained.

A public record can be adopted in recognition of the differing scope of information provided to a public inquiry and to a judicial proceeding. Strictly applied, an official record would greatly increase the cost and the time for conducting an inquiry. It would be necessary for each of the participants to understand the concept of a record and to incur the cost of providing appropriate information. Many commissioners, especially if they have expertise in the subject matter under investigation, resent the waste of time and effort in presenting information that they already know or can find more easily outside of the hearings.

Since there is no onus on parties to provide information to the inquiry, the consequence of failure to provide information in the record to support any position is unclear. Unlike a judge, who is assumed to have no knowledge of the matters in issue so that everything must be proved before him, a commissioner may be expected — in fact required — to make use of his particular expertise. Is it a proper use of inquiry time, in those circumstances, to lead routine information that is well known to the hearing officer and perhaps even to all major participants? Leaving aside the value of such information as a public education tool, can one say that information that is not on the public record should not be available to the inquiry, particularly when the inquiry is requested to investigate and report and is authorized to hold public hearings, but is not required to obtain information only through the public hearing process?

It is advisable to operate as closely as possible to the traditional concept of a public record to encourage participants and inquiry staff to publicly present all of their information so the commissioner can make a fully informed decision. At the same time, one must recognize that the scope of the information of which a commissioner can take notice, particularly if he is appointed commissioner because of his expertise, must be much more broadly interpreted than in judicial proceedings.

What constitutes the official record must also be broadly interpreted. It will include all of the transcript of proceedings, exhibits, and other formal documents of the inquiry. It also includes the written submissions of individuals and the results of any field trips taken by the commissioner in the course of his investigations. This extends to photographs, notes, and even observations made or information orally received in the course of these visits.

Judicial proceedings have the concept of a "view," which permits the judge to examine the scene of an accident or other place of concern. However, he does so only in the presence of the litigants and subject to strict rules as to the information to be obtained and the purpose to be served by the view. Personal trips and examinations routinely conducted by commissioners go well beyond the judicial concept of a view.

The transcript of proceedings is an important part of the official record. It also serves a very useful purpose in the day-to-day operation of the inquiry. Transcripts can be obtained by engaging court reporters or by entering into a contract with an independent reporting service. Any agreement for transcripts should include transcribing, printing, and distributing in the form and the number required by the inquiry.

For public hearings where cross-examination is allowed, it may be important to have a daily transcript. Very often cross-examination of witnesses requires that the transcript of a witness' evidence be available later the same evening or early the next morning at the latest. For community hearings or public hearings where submissions only are received, a daily transcript is not required since the transcript is not intended to assist the day-to-day proceedings but merely to provide a permanent record of the hearings.

The transcript, besides forming part of the official record, is also an important tool in securing an accurate, permanent record of the inquiry proceedings and as a source of documentation for the final report. Witnesses should be requested to review the transcripts to correct any errors, except for matters of style. Most transcripts provide for errata sheets to be prepared and inserted in subsequent transcript volumes.

XI. SUBPOENA

Under its authorizing order in council, an inquiry is invariably given the power to compel the attendance of witnesses. The source of this power is the inquiry acts or other specific statutory provisions. This means that it has the legal authority to issue a document compelling a person to come before it at a specified time and place to give evidence and to bring with him all documents relevant to the issues before the inquiry. A sample form of subpoena for an inquiry is set out as Appendix B–12.

The right to compel the attendance of witnesses is essential, though its use in practice is extremely limited. It does, however, let it be known that the inquiry must be taken seriously and that compliance with its requests for information is not merely a voluntary action by the participants to be performed at their convenience; the order of a judicial officer, when formalized, must be obeyed. Parties recognize that, since their attendance can be compelled by subpoena, they are well advised to comply voluntarily with the request to attend. The result is that rarely does a subpoena have to be issued to compel the attendance of a witness.

When a subpoena is issued by an inquiry and served on a party, failure to comply entitles the inquiry to go before a court to have its order made an order of the court. Further refusals to comply place the party in contempt of court and subject to the penalties, including incarceration, that would be available in judicial proceedings (see Chapter VIII, Judicial Review of Inquiries, "Contempt").

In a judicial proceeding the subpoena is available to officers of the court, including lawyers, as of right and usually requires nothing more than a request and the payment of conduct money to be served along with the subpoena. In an inquiry the use of subpoenas must be circumscribed somewhat and is generally a matter of discretion. While in judicial proceedings the number of parties is usually more limited and parties abusing the subpoena process can be penalized through costs, the same control is not available in inquiries. Nor is the matter of costs a real deterrent since in many inquiries the attendance of witnesses is paid for by the inquiry or by the government through participant funding (see Chapter VIII, Judicial Review of Inquiries, "Subpoena").

There are also a number of procedural implications of the use of subpoenas. Concern is sometimes expressed that it may be used as a technique for harassment or for allowing participants to go on "fishing expeditions" in the hope that they will uncover something relevant to their interests. These concerns can be met by a procedure that gives the commissioner discretion in granting subpoenas.

The inquiry must also be careful that the subpoena is not used by participants as a technique to circumvent other rules of the inquiry. For example, an inquiry that requires statements of evidence to be filed in advance could have this important procedural rule circumvented by a participant calling its evidence by issuing subpoenas. Witnesses appearing under subpoena are merely required to attend and bring information with them. They are not required to prepare a statement of evidence for filing in advance of attendance.

These difficulties can be overcome by a procedure whereby a subpoena is issued only as a last resort when it is clear that voluntary attendance is impossible. It is, therefore, recommended that a subpoena power not be given to all participants as a matter of right but, rather, that it be a power exercised by the commissioner upon application by any party. In those cases where witnesses are genuinely hostile and will refuse to attend unless ordered to do so, it may not be reasonable to expect a statement of evidence. The subpoena could be issued and the requirement for a statement of evidence waived.

A suggested subpoena procedure involves participants' making application to the commissioner who, after hearing the application and any other submission, has the discretion to issue the subpoena. The application to the commissioner should state whether the subpoenaed witness will be able to comply with the advance filing of written evidence requirement. If the witness will file such a statement, the subpoena could be issued as of right. A subpoena of this type would be required in those instances where public service statutes or other employment arrangements state that a witness cannot be paid his salary or expenses for participating in judicial proceedings unless he attends under subpoena. Often employees, even though willing to attend and to comply with all the rules of the inquiry, still must be subpoenaed to allow them to receive their salary.

If, on the other hand, the participant advises that no statement of evidence will be filed, further procedures may be necessary. The applicant should be required to state the reason the witness is being subpoenaed, the nature of the evidence that will be adduced, and the attempts made to have the witness appear voluntarily and in accordance with the inquiry rules. He should state that, in his view, without a subpoena the witness could not attend and why it is important that the witness be heard. Upon receipt of such an application, the commissioner may wish to have inquiry counsel communicate with the witness to see whether he will voluntarily attend as a witness if for some reason he objects to appearing as a witness on behalf of a participant. In extreme circumstances the commissioner himself may wish to intervene in securing the witness's attendance.

In cases where it is only through the exercise of subpoena power that the witness's attendance can be secured, the inquiry should issue the subpoena and require the participant to circulate as much information as possible to the other major participants concerning the evidence likely to be adduced by the witness as a substitute for filing the statement of evidence. (A copy of an application for subpoena is found as Appendix B-13, and a sample statement of evidence of a witness appearing under subpoena is found as Appendix B-14).

XII. GOVERNMENT WITNESSES

Public inquiries often find that the issues referred to them for investigation are already the subject of a certain amount of study by various government officials in exercise of their statutory duties. It is usually essential that this information, and the government witnesses responsible for it, appear before the inquiry.

Governments no less than private individuals, are required to co-operate with public inquiries. Generally, both provincial and federal governments are prepared to co-operate, though there is often disagreement as to which government officials should appear before the inquiry and as to their ability to speak on questions of government policy.

Normally governments, whether participants or not, are

required to file a list of documents and otherwise indicate the information they have relevant to the issues before the inquiry. Inquiry counsel may file the list on behalf of the government that established the inquiry, but it is the responsibility of the government officials to prepare the list. Governments may claim privilege and refuse to produce documents on the usual grounds of privilege, plus "Crown privilege" (see section "Privilege", particularly "Public Interest Privilege" in Chapter VIII, Judicial Review of Inquiries).

It is also possible that the government will have in progress or will initiate further studies of particular interest to the inquiry. These further studies are then prepared, and the government officials who conduct them may be called to appear before the public hearing.

Attendance of government witnesses before inquiries is now a recognized practice in most jurisdictions. However, the tradition of government departments themselves is not to appear as parties before regulatory bodies or other agencies whose responsibility it is to report to government. On the other hand, in most project development proceedings, it is government officials who have the most information because they have been conducting studies in the area or have supervised the activities of others. Some governments take the position that an inquiry they establish is designed to report to them, and it would be inappropriate for the government to appear through its agencies as an active participant in the proceedings. On the other hand, attendance by government witnesses is now commonplace. Provincial governments have appeared before federal inquiries, and federal officials have participated in provincial proceedings without objection.

There is no established procedure for government witnesses appearing before public inquiries. However, most governments have adopted the practice of making their officials available. In those circumstances, the government witnesses are permitted to undertake whatever responsibilities are required, such as preparing a statement of evidence. Whether additional research by a government witness will be permitted depends on the government and the particular situation. While the witness is preparing a statement and attending before the inquiry, his salary is paid by the government since his attendance is the exercise of a public responsibility by a public official. Practices have also developed whereby the federal government will pay the expenses for its witnesses to attend the inquiry. Some governments will also allow their officials to appear as witnesses on behalf of participants who wish to call them. Others will allow employees to attend only if they are represented by government counsel or by inquiry counsel.

In almost all circumstances, the government witnesses are

required to state they are attending in their personal capacity and that none of their evidence necessarily represents government policy. They are also advised that they are prohibited from answering questions involving government policy. All of the arrangements and the terms for the attendance of government witnesses should be established by meetings involving the commissioner, inquiry counsel, and the government departments concerned. These meetings should be held before the hearings so that the rules governing the attendance of government witnesses are known and understood by participants well in advance.

Government witness must be informed that inquiry counsel is counsel to the inquiry and not to the government. He will represent the inquiry's interests during the attendance of witnesses before the inquiry and not necessarily the government's interest. Even those government witnesses who appear at the request of inquiry counsel should be aware that, although counsel will assist them in preparation and presentation of their evidence, they are there at the request of inquiry counsel but not as an inquiry counsel witness. This distinction is often difficult to understand, but it is important for purposes of the inquiry.

Inquiry counsel will often be put in a position of formally requesting the attendance of government witnesses where, for example, the witnesses' evidence, while relevant, does not advance any particular interest or where all the participants want to cross-examine. In those cases inquiry counsel's invitation to government witnesses should make it clear that they are appearing on behalf of the government or by virtue of their government responsibilities, and they will be subject to cross-examination by inquiry counsel as well as by the other participants. Inquiry counsel will work with the witness, if the witness requests, to advise him as to the means of preparing the statement of evidence and the issues that should be addressed, but he will still be permitted to cross-examine.

In all cases where a government official requests assistance, independent counsel should be arranged. One procedure is to advise any government witnesses requesting counsel of the person within the justice department of his government specifically assigned to advise witnesses with respect to their participation in the inquiry. Counselling of the government witness is then left to other government representatives. The federal government has established a procedure whereby a witness requiring counsel from the Department of Justice is obliged to follow certain channels within his own department. The witness's department then makes a formal request to the Department of Justice, which, upon review of the case, decides whether or not to provide counsel.

In those cases where the evidence is called at the request of inquiry counsel but the witness does not appear as an inquiry witness, the particular witness may prepare his statement of evidence in consultation with inquiry counsel. Counsel should merely indicate the form to be followed, the timing for the statement of evidence and, in some cases, ask that the witness in his statement of evidence at a minimum cover certain issues. The final review of that statement of evidence is done by the witness, his department, and the Department of Justice lawyer. The result is that the substance of the evidence is outside the control of inquiry counsel; it is, therefore, appropriate for inquiry counsel to cross-examine the witness.

An inquiry can also make arrangements with the Department of Justice to identify a regional officer in the area where the hearings are being held who could be called upon to appear on behalf of government witnesses on short notice. With a local contact counsel and the name of the Department of Justice counsel in the capital responsible for the inquiry, it should be possible to assure government witnesses that their legal rights as government officials will be protected.

XIII. FOREIGN EVIDENCE

Traditionally governments will not allow their officials to participate in the regulatory process of another country. Most governments take the view that a foreign regulatory process is a matter internal to that country, and they do not wish to appear to be interfering in the internal affairs of another state. They also do not wish to submit themselves to a foreign country's jurisdiction.

There have been exceptions to this rule. Canadian officials appeared before an inquiry into a coal mine disaster in Virginia, and both federal and provincial officials attended various U.S. hearings on acid rain.

For its part, the United States has not appeared before the National Energy Board and does not normally submit itself to a foreign jurisdiction. While it is clear that it is impossible for a Canadian regulatory process to compel attendance extra-territorially, the United States has voluntarily provided documents, studies, and other information in regulatory processes dealing with projects of interest to both countries.

The U.S government is also concerned that an employee of the government or its agencies would have his views taken as the official U.S. position. It is the U.S. State Department that speaks on behalf of the United States, not any of the particular agencies or departments. There is a concern that, even if a witness states that he is appearing on his own behalf and is not representing the government, his views will be taken as the official government position.

At the West Coast Oil Ports Inquiry, steps were taken early to ensure that American evidence was available to the inquiry. Initial contacts were made directly with the agency believed to have the information and expertise useful to the inquiry. Following this initial contact, a formal contact was made through the Canadian Department of External Affairs and the Canadian embassy. As a result of these communications, inquiry counsel met with Canadian embassy officials in the region. Communications were also directed to the U.S. Department of State through the officials responsible for U.S.-Canadian relations.

Following negotiations, an arrangement was made between the inquiry and the U.S. government through the Department of State for the attendance of U.S. government witnesses. This arrangement included agreement that the U.S. could select or approve the official who would appear, that the statement of evidence would be prepared in the United States and sworn before a U.S. official, and that the representative would only answer questions by way of clarification. Any other questions would have to be directed to him in writing for official response later.

This arrangement was considered to be satisfactory by both sides. The success of the arrangement depended on how strict an interpretation was to be placed on the condition that cross-examination would be limited to questions of clarification and would not extend to elaboration of the evidence. This ultimately depended on the approach of the witnesses giving evidence.

Generally, the experience was that the witnesses who appeared were prepared to answer almost all questions as a matter of clarification and, if they ran into difficulties, were prepared to respond in writing at a later date. Witnesses expressed the view that they did not face any questions that could not be answered as part of clarification. The consensus is that the arrangement worked well.

When the American government witnesses attended, inquiry counsel would table the statement of evidence-in-chief that was sworn under seal in the United States. This would then become an exhibit just as would the statement of evidence of other participants. Inquiry counsel would then ask the witness "Do you regard the evidence filed as your sworn evidence as being true and binding on your conscience?" The witness would then answer "yes." It was the view of counsel that a witness who prepared a sworn statement and stated that the evidence was binding on his conscience was in much the same position as other witnesses giving sworn evidence. The benefit of this system was that American evidence was offered within the same general rules as those governing other witnesses and was available on the public record in Canada.

An alternative approach is to take statements of evidence from Americans in the United States. This could be done by having the inquiry counsel attend, much like an examination in a foreign jurisdiction, or by arranging for the commissioner to hear the oral testimony of American officials in the United States. There is a risk that evidence taken in this way may be regarded by parties as prejudicial since the participants would not have an opportunity to cross-examine that evidence. Also, it might be objected that the commissioner's powers do not extend to foreign jurisdictions. Consequently, the suggested method of having U.S. witnesses attend the hearing in Canada appears to be preferable, and at least one precedent exists for such an arrangement.

VI

The Hearings

Rarely will one form of inquiry procedure meet the different needs of the inquiry and all the participants. For that reason various forms of procedure have been reviewed (see Chapter IV, The Inquiry Structure, "Form of Hearings"). To ensure that the benefits of each form of hearing are achieved and the potential difficulties minimized, the inquiry must adopt flexible, yet distinct, procedures.

I. SUBMISSIONS

Hearings conducted through the use of submissions, that is, people coming forward to present their material and answer questions from the commissioner, require substantial support to be successful. Because analysis of the submissions does not take place in the public forum, the inquiry must have a staff qualified to review the various submissions, not only to understand their significance but also to relate them to one another. This is a very difficult task, yet its importance to sound inquiry judgment must not be under-estimated. What is required is a staff that can receive a submission, understand its significance, draw out whatever further information is required, and analyse how that submission affects other submissions. Without the benefit of participants indicating the interrelationship between submissions through questioning, the inquiry must develop an ability to go beyond each written submission to place it in the context of the overall evidence.

So that this task can be effectively carried out, the inquiry procedure should require that the submissions be filed far enough in advance of the proposed hearing date that the staff can analyse each submission. They should also be filed early enough that the secretary to the inquiry can determine how long the hearing is likely to take and when, in the course of that hearing, each submission is likely to be heard.

Through preliminary rulings and advertisements, the inquiry should indicate a final filing date well in advance of the tentative hearing. This lead time is required because, invariably, people are late in filing their statements, and it would be a mistake for the inquiry to proceed without hearing them. It also gives the staff an opportunity to determine the number of presentations and, in consultation with the technical staff reviewing the submissions, to make a preliminary estimate of how long each submission will take.

The submissions can be rather lengthy and often are accompanied by colour photographs or other such audio-visual aids. Requiring too many copies may place an unnecessary financial burden on participants who wish to make a submission. On the other hand, there should be a copy for each commissioner, if there is more than one, and one copy that is tabled as the official exhibit. It is also preferable that there be one additional copy for use by the staff. That copy can then be reproduced, at inquiry expense, to provide whatever number of copies are required for review or distribution. In most cases making additional copies is just a matter of photocopying. However, if the submission includes photographs or other aids that do not easily photocopy, the inquiry should be sure it has sufficient copies from the participant to properly carry out its review.

Submissions should include the name and telephone number of the participant and the name of any organization that he represents. The brief should also include, in addition to the submission itself, a biographical note on the person making the presentation and a list of any reports or studies that the person has relied on in the preparation of the submission.

The commissioner should be sure that sufficient staff review of the submission has been completed so that he can obtain an estimate of how long each submission is likely to take for both presentation and questions. He should also arrange a grouping of submissions so that similar submissions, where possible, are presented at about the same time. Armed with this information, the commissioner, through the executive secretary, can set up a hearing schedule.

The hearing agenda or schedule will set out the order in which submissions will be presented and provide a timetable for presentation. This timetable should be confirmed with the participants by telephone and their attendance at the time specified confirmed. Once this has been done, a list of submissions and the time of their presentation should be made public through posting, a public information program, or sending a copy to every person making a submission. Representatives of the public, the media, and other participants will know when the various submissions are being made so that they can attend as spectators if they wish.

Before the hearing the commissioner should meet with his technical staff to review the nature, extent, and significance of questions that technical staff wish to have answered or issues they wish canvassed. In this way issues are properly understood and major questions are appropriately highlighted. If questions are to be asked only by the commissioner, staff instructions on each submission should be settled in enough time before the hearing that, should further briefing be required or research undertaken, a rescheduling of the presentations can be accomplished and a supplementary timetable issued. If, on the other hand, inquiry staff are also entitled to ask questions, there should be an understanding of the nature of the questions so that the commissioner is satisfied the questioning is relevant and assists the work of the inquiry.

At the opening of each session of the hearing, the commissioner should introduce the members of the inquiry staff who play a role in the proceedings. Staff would include, in addition to the commissioner himself, any technical advisor sitting with him, inquiry counsel, any staff members who may be questioning or advising, the executive secretary, and any other support staff who play a public role. Also, if the proceedings are transcribed, the commissioner should describe the nature and operation of the transcription facility.

The commissioner, following some explanatory comments on the procedure to be followed, should call on presenters according to the schedule. When the individual presenting a brief is called upon, he should be comfortably seated at a central table, located within easy view of the commissioner, that has a microphone, if required for transcription, and a pencil and paper for making notes of questions. He should be sworn (if this is the procedure adopted), and his statement of evidence, as submitted, should be given an exhibit number and formally accepted by the inquiry. The individual should identify himself for the record, indicate if there are any additions, errors, or changes in the submission as filed, and identify any others who may be with him for the presentation. If there is more than one author of the submission, the presenter should indicate which sections of the submission are the responsibility of others so that questions can be directed to the appropriate person. The commissioner may at that point wish to confirm that the submission, as amended, represents the complete statement of that witness. Participants should be reminded that the submission, plus whatever comments they make orally in the course of their presentation or in answering questions, constitute their total evidence before the inquiry.

The commissioner will have advised presenters by this time whether it is his intention to have the submissions read fully into the record, summarized, or accepted as read and proceed directly to the questioning. If the brief is to be summarized, a time limit should be set.

Following presentation of the submission, the commissioner should allow the inquiry staff to ask questions first, if they are to participate actively in the proceedings, so that he, as commissioner, will have an opportunity to tie together all of the information in the brief by questioning last.

After the questioning, the commissioner may wish to give the person making the submission an opportunity to make any concluding comments and then thank him for his attendance and allow him to step down. This procedure can be modified as required. For example, it is not necessary to have the submission under oath. However, since the verbal exchanges are to form part of the inquiry record, an oath may be appropriate, especially if other forms of hearings are to be used where evidence will be taken under oath.

Briefs can be presented without filing in advance. This retains some spontaneity and prevents potential participants from being intimidated by the requirement for a written presentation, but it also makes it difficult to schedule presentations and requires an immediate response by the commissioner and staff without the benefit of considering the information before the questioning is to commence. Whatever procedure is adopted, it should be known by participants in advance and consistently followed throughout.

II. COMMUNITY HEARINGS

In situations where the inquiry wishes to receive the comments and evidence of members of local communities, the use of community hearings has become an established practice. The participation of local residents is often desirable because of the public policy benefit of involving those individuals most affected and because the views of these individuals may provide the best, and sometimes the only, evidence on certain issues of importance to the inquiry. This is particularly true for outlining local conditions or predicting socio-economic impacts.

The structure of community hearings should be set out in the preliminary rulings so that the procedure to be followed is generally known in the community. The rules should also indicate the process to be followed by those who wish to present information and how this information will be integrated into the inquiry work.

Generally, community hearings are informally structured and conducted in a way that will encourage local residents to participate.

By definition, the form of community hearings may change from community to community depending on local preferences or customs.

There is no established way of co-ordinating and structuring the conduct of community hearings. They can either be organized by the inquiry after receiving advice from the community as to their form and timing, or they can be turned over to local community groups outside the inquiry, which then host the inquiry.

If the inquiry is to take responsibility for planning the hearing, it must structure the planning process to allow for input by both the communities involved and the participants. For example, the inquiry might consider establishing a community planning secretariat made up of inquiry staff and representatives of the communities where hearings are to be held. Alternatively, the inquiry could create a secretariat made up of all of the participants in the more technical hearings. The advantage of such a system is that all participants in the inquiry have an opportunity to determine the conduct of community hearings. This is particularly useful if the inquiry wishes, for example, to have the proponent of a particular scheme participate in community hearings.

Allowing community-based organizations to arrange the hearings has the obvious advantage of planning by those who are most sensitive to local needs. The disadvantages are that there may be competing interests within a community, and the inquiry may be seen as captive of one element of the community to the exclusion of anothers. It is also possible that attempts to be responsive to community needs may produce lack of focus in the hearings. Another possibility is that the timing chosen may not serve the needs of the inquiry itself. Generally, community hearings planned by the inquiry, but based on the advice of the community and the participants in the inquiry (or at least those participants who represent community interests), will provide the best balance between community needs and the needs of the inquiry.

Because community hearings must be responsive to community needs if a broad cross-section of participation is to be achieved, it is essential that the inquiry involve communities directly in planning the timing and procedure for community hearings. Often an inquiry will retain a community relations officer, whose prime responsibility is to plan community hearings which meet the inquiry's needs while being responsive to local considerations. The inquiry should develop a general understanding of the evidence available in a community and determine when, given the general structure of the inquiry's work, such information would be most effectively received. The inquiry must then work with the community to ensure that a community hearing at that time is both possible and beneficial from the community's point of view. The inquiry must provide sufficient information to the community and otherwise prepare it for participation in the hearings. The community must be informed well in advance of the date of the hearing since scarce community resources (meeting rooms, hotel space, and transportation into the community) may have to be shared.

The community officer must be sufficiently in touch with the community to be confident that members of the community will appear and will have accurate enough information to provide a considered response. Often the timing and location of a community hearing will affect the likely success of the hearing in eliciting information. Community hearings are major community events. Since they take place within established social patterns and inter-relationships, the inquiry must be careful that it does not alienate any segment of the community or appear to favour any particular group. Often these social signals are not readily apparent to an outside inquiry. For example, the entire inquiry staff staying at the hotel run by a participant, may suggest a bias.

Similarly, the hearing should be held at what can be regarded as neutral ground so that no element of the community feels it cannot participate or that the inquiry is biased. Thus, for example, in a community that has both native and non-native populations with separate social and administrative systems, it may be necessary to hold separate hearings for each group if no mutually acceptable location is available. Native people may be reluctant to attend a hearing held in a part of town or at a facility where they are routinely viewed as outsiders, and non-natives may be reluctant to attend a hearing held in the native social centre.

The timing and duration of the community hearing should be left largely to the community hearing organizers. If the logical time, from the inquiry's point of view, for a community hearing in a fishing village is at the time of the year the residents are away gaining a livelihood, obviously the community hearing will not have the advantage of input from these residents. Similarly, hearings held on days and times when most residents are at work will severely limit the number that can participate. The inquiry community hearing officer should be in a position to advise as to the times best suited for a community hearing (if the inquiry has the luxury of continuing for a number of months) and also to comment on the location, timing, and order of presentation. For example, some inquiries have found the procedure of visiting a community in the morning and holding community hearings in the afternoon and evening to be an effective way of establishing the inquiry's presence in the community.

The most appropriate timing for a community hearing may

be difficult to determine. It must conform not only to the inquiry's needs, but also to the needs of the local community. If community hearings are to be called in conjunction with more formal technical hearings, the interrelationship of the two hearings must be considered. Community hearings tacked on to long formal hearings may suggest that the community hearings are merely perfunctory sessions, and the real evidence before the inquiry is presented in the formal hearings. Participants may also feel that so much evidence has been presented before the community was consulted that the community hearings are too late in the process to affect the commissioner's views.

On the other hand, often information must be presented at the technical hearings before the inquiry can expect meaningful community comment. Hearings concerning the technical impact of a proposal may be prerequisite to an informed expression of opinion on the likely community impact. Community hearings based on lack of information or misinformation lack impact and may even become an information process in which residents spend more time asking questions than giving the commissioner the benefit of their views.

The inquiry has a great influence on the question of whether proponents of a project should be in attendance at community hearings. There is often a desire by the community to ask proponents questions or to have the proponents there to hear what the community has to say. On the other hand, attendance by the proponents may result in the hearing's becoming an information session in which the community is content to ask the proponents questions rather than make their views known. Some persons in communities may feel intimidated by the proponents or may be inhibited in giving their own views which may be contrary to the "expert" opinions of the proponent.

In all cases the commissioner, executive secretary, and a court reporter should be in attendance so the inquiry record at the community hearings is as complete as the record of formal hearings. The secretary will retain exhibits and briefs presented to the inquiry. The inquiry entourage must not be too large. It would be overwhelming for a small community to have a large sophisticated inquiry staff with its elaborate equipment descend upon it. Inquiry staff should consist of the minimum number required to compile a full and accurate record.

The commissioner should indicate that information obtained at community hearings will be evidence before the inquiry in the same way as if it had been presented in formal technical hearings. He must then decide what weight to give to evidence at community hearings in relation to the more technical evidence at the formal hearings. In some cases evidence at the community hearings may be as good, if not better, than evidence at the technical hearings because participants will speak from actual experience rather than merely express theoretical conclusions. This experience is often over a long period of time and, consequently, may have greater credibility than short-term studies conducted by technical experts. If the commissioner is to give the evidence at community hearings the same or similar weight as evidence at formal hearings, he should make this fact known and take the evidence under oath so it cannot be challenged as somehow inferior.

Generally, community hearings are informally structured, and this fact should be communicated well in advance. It should also be reflected in the physical set-up for the hearing. For example, it may not be necessary to have elaborate facilities (*e.g.*, projection equipment, blackboards) that would be required for more technical evidence. The commissioner need not appear on a raised platform. In hearings conducted in facilities such as school gymnasia, it is always an error to put the commissioner on the raised stage. Rather, the commissioner and the people appearing before him should all be on the same level to facilitate communication. While separate tables are required for the commissioner, the executive secretary (to retain exhibits), and the court reporters, the rest of the inquiry staff should sit in the audience unless they are required to play an active role in the hearing. There should be a table facing the commissioner from which people may speak to the inquiry.

In community hearings it may also be necessary to have interpreters to ensure that all segments of the community can participate. In this case there is a standard form of oath for an interpreter in judicial proceeding (a copy is found in Appendix B-15) that should be administered before any witnesses are called.

Since in most community hearings there is no cross-examination of witnesses, it is not necessary for other participants in the inquiry process to have any formal status. Members of staff and other participants should not take over the front of the hall. At some point the commissioner should introduce staff members and explain what role, if any, they are playing in the proceedings.

Other inquiry participants who have evidence that is contrary to evidence presented at community hearings have no opportunity to cross-examine; they will, however, have the opportunity to call contradictory evidence at the technical hearings or to encourage people who disagree with the evidence to speak at other community hearings. The result is that no one can complain about lack of opportunity to meet and contradict evidence presented at the community hearings.

Because most of the people in community hearings will not

be legally trained or expert at hearing procedure, and because many will be emotionally involved with the issues before the inquiry, it is particularly important for the commissioner to demonstrate an unbiased and judicial attitude. The commissioner will have to be very flexible in the way he treats people appearing before him. Some will require special consideration or procedures so that their message can be fully presented. The residents of a community are often familiar with the people appearing and are tolerant of special privileges accorded to those who cannot participate in the usual way. The important thing is that the community feels the hearing was fairly and properly conducted, that everyone had an opportunity to express himself, and that procedural or technical barriers did not prevent some people from participating.

While a community hearing may not be governed by formal rules, it is important that the commissioner retain the proper amount of decorum and courtesy. The community hearing is still part of the evidence-gathering process of the inquiry and, as such, must be under the control of the commissioner at all times. The commissioner will want to be sure the community hearing is not taken over by the more vociferous or better organized and that it is not used by participants as a media event for their own purpose. The commissioner may decide it is inappropriate to allow applause or other expressions of support from spectators. Rather than representing a spontaneous expression of community views, such action may be a deterrent to people who oppose the views of the vocal majority.

The procedure to be followed is similar to that in hearings where submissions are presented. The major difference is that it is usually impossible to require people wishing to participate to attend according to a fixed timetable. As a result, a typical procedure would involve the commissioner's calling the inquiry to order, making some preliminary comments on the purpose of the community hearing and its role in the context of the total inquiry, indicating the procedure to be followed during the hearing, identifying key members of the inquiry staff and perhaps indicating their availability for discussion after the hearing, and then inviting people to come forward. Sometimes it may be necessary for the inquiry to arrange in advance for one or two individuals to appear first and "break the ice." Often community leaders such as the mayor or president of the chamber of commerce will make their presentation early and thereby encourage other citizens to come forward.

The commissioner may also wish to advise the audience, at the start of the proceedings and at intervals throughout, that people wishing to appear should give their names to the executive secretary so he can then provide the commissioner with an updated list of appearances. This allows the commissioner to call people forward by name and gives some indication of how long the hearing is likely to take.

When an individual comes forward to the witness table, he should be required to identify himself, spell his name for purposes of the inquiry record, and then make his presentation in the form he desires. Because it is very difficult to assign time limits in advance, it is up to the commissioner to ensure that no person takes an unduly long time to make a presentation or otherwise abuses the process. While the commissioner should, through careful interjections, limit the far-ranging views of some, he must be careful not to discourage the timid or inarticulate from appearing. Patience is generally the key to a full hearing. After the witness has appeared, he should be thanked and allowed to stand down before the next witness is called.

At the end of the hearing, the commissioner should thank the community, indicate whether transcripts will be available in the community for those who wish to ensure the inquiry record is accurate, and reassure the participants that their contributions were valuable and will be taken into account by the inquiry.

III. FORMAL HEARINGS

When one thinks of hearings in the traditional sense — that is, the formal procedure for the technical review of major issues — one is probably thinking of what are often called formal or technical hearings. It is often these formal hearings that give the inquiry the bulk of its useful information and that normally take the most time, money, and resources to organize and conduct.

A. Physical Arrangements

In determining the location for the formal hearings, a number of considerations should be kept in mind. First, the hearings often require large numbers of very expensive consultants, many of whom have to travel to the hearings. For that reason, the hearings should be held at a location reasonably accessible by airplane and other modes of transportation. It should also be at a place where there is suitable hotel accommodation, preferably near the hearing room, or adequate local transportation.

The hearing room should not be located in a government office or in the same office building as participants in the inquiry. The physical separation of the inquiry from any of the participants and from the government is a symbolic expression of the inquiry's independence. It also avoids the situation where media reporters, after speaking to the commissioner, seek out one of the participants conveniently located nearby for comment to the exclusion of other participants.

Formal hearings can be satisfactorily held in large meeting rooms in hotels or in community halls. If a hotel is used, care should be taken that the hotel is not too ostentatious, and that the hearing room has direct public access, can be closed off, and is not located in the proximity of noisy activities (*e.g.*, a temporary partition away from another regularly used meeting area).

The size of the hearing room will vary depending on the number of people participating and the amount of evidence the process is likely to attract. It should be large enough to accommodate the number of people expected, even on the heavy days. At the same time it should not be so large that the participants feel lost during the less popular days. A room with moveable partitions is ideal. Because the transcription facilities and television equipment cannot be easily moved, it is best to obtain hearing space that will allow this equipment to remain standing throughout the formal hearings or large portions of it. Facilities should be used that can remain set up for, at least, entire phases of the inquiry. It is very disruptive and costly for the inquiry to remove the equipment involved in transcribing and recording the hearings every weekend because the hall is to be used for other purposes. It is also valuable to find a facility that can be locked, as it will be necessary to leave expensive equipment overnight. Many participants may also wish to leave reports and other documents of importance to them in the hearing room rather than move them back and forth each day.

If there is to be a daily transcript there must be space for transcribing the proceedings in the vicinity of the hearing room. These are basic physical requirements for those hired to record the proceedings and make transcripts.

It is useful to have a room for photocopying, telephoning, distributing statements of evidence, obtaining transcripts, and otherwise assisting the inquiry participants, the press, and the public. Access to photocopy facilities nearby is essential. Often a witness will refer to a document which should be photocopied immediately and made available to the commissioner and other counsel.

A separate room for participants to interview witnesses and prepare is also welcome. Participants' offices may be distant from the hearing room, and an interview room or counsel room may be well used.

A room where the commissioner can relax over lunch and perhaps have a nap or review evidence is of great benefit in helping him stay alert and able to keep up the hectic pace of most inquiries.

The physical set-up should be as informal as possible, while still recognizing that cross-examination and other "court-like" events are to be conducted in that setting. Generally, the commissioner will be at the centre facing the public and participants, perhaps slightly raised. The witness table should also be at the front within easy hearing and viewing distance of the commissioner, also slightly raised. By raising these two tables, the members of the public and the participants are able to see the commissioner and the witnesses without obstruction.

It is strongly suggested that there be a common witness table for all witnesses to use when giving evidence. This allows the press, particularly the television crews, to set up their lighting and equipment so they can take pictures of the commissioner and the witnesses without having continually to change position or move equipment. There is nothing so disconcerting as having television crews and lights moving when a witness is giving evidence.

Cameras and lighting should be set up before the hearing starts or as a new witness is being sworn. They should be focussed on the witness table, the commissioner, and on the lectern or counsel table where counsel will question witnesses. In that way the press need only turn the lights and cameras on as required without scurrying about. In planning the hearing room, the area for the press cameras should be far enough back or to the side so that the participants' view is not disrupted. Also, the area between the counsel table, the commissioner, and the witness table should be out of bounds to even hand-held cameras, thus forcing media to take their pictures from a greater distance, which is much less distracting.

Counsel tables should be set up in rows facing the commissioner. Normally considerable space is required since all participants will need room for documents, and many will require the presence of advisors. The person actually cross-examining or addressing the inquiry should come forward to a designated table so the commissioner is able to communicate with the counsel and the witnesses at close quarters, and cameras can be trained on the counsel without jockeying for position. The cross-examiner should face the commissioner and the witness, which means that he often has his back to the public gallery. Counsel should be able to cross-examine either seated at a table or standing at a lectern in accordance with his personal preference.

Inquiry counsel should have a table at the front, since he is often called upon to comment or intervene in the proceedings as they go along. The media may wish to have him within the lighted area so he can be filmed during these interventions. He should also be within easy sight of the commissioner so that he can be consulted privately should the necessity arise. Finally, the counsel whose witness is on the stand should be seated at a front counsel table because he too may wish to intervene from time to time and this, too, the press may wish to film.

The executive secretary should have a separate table apart from the commissioner–counsel–witness triangle, but not too distant from the commissioner, so that he may locate and provide the commissioner with documents upon request and conveniently swear witnesses. The commissioner should also be able to attract his attention in order to convey messages without disrupting the proceedings. In the area of the secretary's desk, there should be a place where the exhibits, transcripts, and other essential documents can easily be retained and retrieved quickly without anyone's leaving the hearing room.

Also in that area should be a table for those persons transcribing or recording the proceedings. Generally the transcribers will require an unobstructed view of the commissioner and of the locations where people addressing the inquiry are seated.

While the press can be told to use the public gallery, it may be appropriate to set aside specific areas for them. This may be a side position that gives them a clear view of the witnesses and the commissioner, or it may be in the first row behind the participants' tables.

Finally, behind the tables for press or counsel, the inquiry should provide seating for the general public. The rows of seats should be far enough apart to allow people to move easily in and out without disturbing others seated in their row, and the entrance to the hearing room should make it possible for the public to enter and leave the room without disrupting the proceeding.

A sample schematic drawing offering a suggested seating arrangement for formal hearings is shown in Appendix B–16.

Either because of poor acoustics or because the proceedings are being transcribed, microphones are usually required. There should be microphones at the commissioner's table, the cross-examination table, and before inquiry counsel and all of the major participants; at least, there should be microphones before the counsel whose witness is giving evidence. This will ensure that the participants have ready access to a microphone in the event they wish to interject on the record or are called upon to comment.

Finally, there should be a series of microphones at the witness table in the event a panel of witnesses is called.

B. Timing

The hearings should be commenced quickly so the inquiry can develop a momentum and demonstrate that it is getting on with the job. On the other hand, it must not start before important preliminary matters have been resolved. Such matters include appropriate funding and organization of the public participants; completion of any reports, studies, or other materials that are prerequisites for a full inquiry; preparation and distribution of a list of documents (and any other discovery procedures adopted); and an indication by the inquiry staff that key witnesses have been identified and preliminary matters are well enough in hand that the hearings will be meaningful.

Proponents of a project under review generally wish the formal hearings to commence as soon as possible. Besides the fact that delay is costly, the proponent has had the project under review for a considerable time, has retained experts, amassed a number of studies, and now wishes to obtain the regulatory approval for the project. On the other hand, the public participants usually feel that they are poorly informed and ill prepared, and the inquiry staff, depending upon the amount of expertise it can gather through recruitment, may feel that further time is required to review all of the documents and information necessary to understand the project and frame the issues properly. If native people are involved, and especially native people in isolated communities, time will be required to prepare for active participation.

The commissioner should also consider whether there are events going on in other forums (such as established regulatory proceedings), the amount of research available, and the timing of additional research; furthermore, he should consider whether the participants are sufficiently well organized to play the roles assigned them before setting a date for commencement of the formal hearings.

Timing for commencement of hearings may also be dictated by legal requirements concerning adequate notice and the opportunity to prepare adequately for hearings. Physical or logistical constraints, such as engagement of a hearing room and hiring of staff, will also have to be considered.

During the time involved in preparation for the formal hearings, it is possible for the inquiry to hold community hearings (see Section II of this chapter, "Community Hearings").

C. Opening the Formal Hearings

The formal hearings should take place in a friendly but structured atmosphere established by the commissioner. The tone should suggest that there is serious work to be done and that the procedures adopted will be fairly, but firmly, applied.

Because the opening session of hearings is usually well covered by the media, the commissioner will often start the proceedings by making an opening statement describing the inquiry and out-lining any procedural or other rulings he wishes to make widely known. Because of the media attention, the statement should be well thought out and printed for distribution before presentation. The statement should be designed to instil confidence in the partici-pants and the public; it should be carefully written to avoid any appearance of bias or prejudgment of any issues. The commissioner may wish to introduce the executive secretary to the inquiry, inquiry counsel, and senior staff, indicating their responsibilities to the inquiry; describe the transcription system; and establish the rules for the hearings. A checklist for the opening of a formal hear-ing is found in Appendix B-17.

Inquiry counsel has a special responsibility at the opening of the hearing and should be called upon before other participants. Inquiry counsel should begin by tendering a copy of the order in council establishing the inquiry as the first exhibit and should table as subsequent exhibits the oath of the commissioner, a copy of any preliminary rulings, and the notice of hearing for the formal hearings. Counsel should then arrange for the orderly presentation of various other documents that will be required by the inquiry. This includes the list of documents circulated by the various participants, the results of any pre-hearing sessions or applications, and any standard materials that should be made exhibits on the first day.

D. Statements

Inquiry counsel, if he is to play a major role in the proceed-ings, should also make an opening statement. Unless the com-missioner wishes to address them, he can cover a range of preliminary issues. Some of the issues to be addressed are merely housekeeping matters, including the disposition of inquiry transcripts, the handling of exhibits, the use of the inquiry library and facilities, the phasing and timing of the inquiry, the issues arising out of the rules of the inquiry, the significance of any preliminary rulings, and the description of the role of inquiry counsel. He should also indicate something of the nature of the inquiry, such as the procedures adopted to obtain the information the inquiry needs and the role of the inquiry in the total decision-making process of government. Housekeeping matters should also include the role of government and the attendance of government witnesses, arrangements for the attendance of foreign witnesses, and other procedural matters. Inquiry counsel may then go on to discuss many of the substantive issues before the inquiry, either taking a position or setting out a neutral unbiased view and alerting the public to the issues to be considered.

The opening of the formal hearings is a media event. Media coverage, which may be intermittent thereafter, usually overwhelms the opening. All of the participants will want to have an opportunity to participate in the first few days of the inquiry. For that reason, opening statements by each of the major participants may be a good way of introducing the key perspectives before the inquiry to the public. Without an opportunity to give the inquiry their policy perspective, some parties will use every opportunity in the course of the hearings to do so, which is often disruptive. Opening statements may limit this posturing and give the inquiry a policy context for what is to follow. They also serve the useful purpose of explaining to the public who the participants are and the nature of their involvement in the inquiry.

In their opening statements, participants should identify themselves (the history of their organization, their policy perspective), indicate the extent to which they intend to participate in the inquiry, and outline the nature of the evidence they expect to call. Such an opening statement will allow the commissioner to assess the various roles the participants are willing to play. This may be useful in determining which participants are adverse in interest and the extent of participation in various phases of the inquiry.

There is always a concern that certain participants will grab all of the attention at the opening of the inquiry. It is useful to have opening statements by participants limited in time so that each of the participants has a chance to present a position.

E. Calling Witnesses

Calling the first witness should clarify and establish the procedure for participants and witnesses. This should not only set a professional and efficient tone but should also serve as a notice to subsequent witnesses of the level of presentation required. If the first witness is called by inquiry counsel, he will have the opportunity to establish the procedure and level of performance desired by the commissioner. If the first witness is to be called by one of the participants, inquiry counsel should review in detail with the participant's counsel the procedure to be adopted. A sample procedural checklist for calling witnesses is found in Appendix B-18.

Counsel calling a witness should come forward to the designated place. He should indicate the name of the witness and call him forward to take the witness stand. While this can be done by the commissioner or the executive secretary, it is not necessary and often tends to make the proceedings appear too formal. When the witness reaches the witness table, the executive secretary should administer the oath. Taking the oath at the witness table makes it obvious to the commissioner and the public that the witness is giving evidence under oath, and this fact need not be repeated for the record; it should, however, be noted by the court reporter for the purpose of the transcript. It there are a number of witnesses appearing together as a panel, the executive secretary should swear all of them at the same time. A sample form of oath is found in Appendix B-19.

If the appearance of the witness has been proceeded by a filing of his statement of evidence, the secretary will have the correct spelling of the witness's name for use by the commissioner and the court reporters. This information will also have been made available to the press and any participants who are not familiar with the witness. Once the witness has been sworn, counsel calling him should introduce the witness and assist him in the presentation of his evidence. If the inquiry rules require that witnesses file their evidence in writing before appearing, there is little need to repeat the written text. Counsel calling the witness should indicate that a statement of evidence has been filed and introduce it as an exhibit in the usual way; to do this, he requests from the witness confirmation of the fact that the statement of evidence was prepared by him and represents his evidence before the inquiry. The statement of evidence should then be given the next exhibit number and recorded in the exhibit book by the executive secretary.

Counsel calling the witness must also review the witness's qualifications if the witness is being called as an expert. Once the statement of evidence has been filed, the commissioner should be directed to the details of the witness's experience and that experience briefly highlighted, unless another participant wishes to challenge the right of that witness to give evidence as an expert. If his expertise is accepted, depending on the inquiry rules, the witness would adopt the statement of evidence filed as his evidence, make any necessary changes to the filed statement, and either summarize the evidence or agree with his counsel that he is available for cross-examination. If the witness wishes to table any documents or make any clarifying statements, he should do so before being made available for cross-examination.

Many inquiries allow witnesses to appear together as a panel. It is often desirable to have a witness appear with others so that a broader subject area is covered by those most capable of responding, rather than to have one person respond on behalf of other experts, or to call a series of experts one after the other. If each panel member is treated in the same way as if he had appeared alone, the technique of a panel can prove beneficial. Each member should be introduced, qualified, and adopt either a separate statement of evidence or that portion of a longer statement prepared by him.

With a panel of witnesses, it is often useful for at least one of the panelists to be a representative of the organization presenting the evidence. A panel of expert consultants presented by a participant, giving their evidence as to what should be done, may cause everyone erroneously to believe that the consultants' recommendations would be adopted by the participant. It is necessary to have someone from the participant on the panel to confirm that the consultants' evidence is, in fact, the position of the party who retained the consultants or, alternatively, to indicate what the participant proposes to do with each of the recommendations made by the consultants.

Following presentation of his evidence, a witness is usually cross-examined by the other participants, inquiry counsel, and the commissioner. Whatever the order or procedure adopted, it must be perceived to be fair and impartially administered. Courtesy and mutual respect are often the hallmarks of a successful cross-examination process.

Following presentation of evidence and cross-examination by the other participants, inquiry counsel, and the commissioner, counsel calling the witness should be allowed re-examination. The re-examination should be limited to clarification or elaboration of evidence arising out of the cross-examination.

After a witness has presented all of his evidence — that is, has given his statement and answered questions from other participants and the inquiry — the witness can be discharged. Often, counsel calling the witness will ask that his witness be discharged. Before agreeing, the commissioner should be sure the witness's participation in the inquiry has been completed.

If the witness is not discharged — for example, if all cross-examination has not been completed but, for scheduling reasons, other witnesses are to be called — the commissioner should merely ask that witness to stand down. This means that he is entitled to leave the witness stand but his participation in the inquiry is not completed, and he must agree to return to complete his appearance before the inquiry.

In judicial proceedings there is some significance in the distinction between a discharged witness and one who is merely asked to stand down. A witness who merely stands down is still on the witness stand, and counsel cannot speak to him about his evidence or coach him on the presentation of his evidence. While in inquiry proceedings the rule does not have strict application, it is in the interest of the inquiry to have the commissioner remind the witness and his counsel that the witness is still on the stand and, therefore, should not be improperly instructed by counsel.

When a witness is discharged, the commissioner should thank

him for agreeing to attend, particularly if he is appearing as a courtesy, without fee or has travelled a great distance. A few kind words by the commissioner to those who are not appearing as paid consultants indicating the inquiry appreciates their co-operation and assistance will do a great deal to secure future co-operation.

Often a witness is unable to answer a question because he does not have the information with him, but can obtain the information if he can have some time. In those circumstances the commissioner should obtain the undertaking of the witness, under oath and on the official record, or the undertaking of his counsel, to obtain the information and to return for cross-examination on the additional information, if necessary.

In most circumstances it is best to allow cross-examination to continue so that the re-attendance of the witness and the further cross-examination deals only with specific issues on which the witness agreed to present further evidence to the inquiry at a later date.

It is often expedient to ask the witness to provide the additional information in writing. Obtaining the information this way may satisfy the parties and so avoid the re-attendance. In such a case the participant calling the witness should file the reply, in writing, and the commissioner should canvass the other participants, either in the hearing or informally, to see whether it is necessary for the witness to re-attend. If it is not, the commissioner should so indicate on the inquiry record and formally discharge the witness. If re-attendance is required, it should be scheduled at the convenience of the witness and the inquiry; if possible, it should be scheduled at a time when other evidence of a similar nature is to be received.

Because of the interrelated and complex nature of certain evidence and the phasing of formal hearings, it will often be necessary for some witnesses to return a number of times. For example, a witness on the physical environment might be a fisheries biologist to explain the impact on the water quality. His re-attendance might be required at a later stage of the inquiry which examines the impact on the fish themselves or on the fishing potential. With witnesses re-attending, it is possible for questions to be delayed until later phases of the inquiry, without unnecessarily disrupting the proceedings, thus avoiding a special re-attendance.

F. Undertakings

Throughout the hearings witnesses will appear and under-take to provide further information to the inquiry at a later date. While the prime responsibility for following up undertakings rests with the person requesting the information and the participant on whose behalf the witness appears, there is also a responsibility on the inquiry.

Inquiry counsel has a responsibility to establish a complete record, and this further information may greatly assist the inquiry. Therefore, the executive secretary may be asked to note any undertakings and be prepared to follow them up. Because other participants may have an interest in a response, once undertakings are fulfilled, this fact must be communicated to other participants.

Most undertakings can be satisfied by having the counsel for the participant on whose behalf the witness appeared note the undertaking and file, as an exhibit, the documents or further information promised in the undertaking. This would appear in the transcript, and anyone following the proceedings and examining the exhibit list would know when various undertakings had been satisfied. It the undertaking is a major one, such as producing documents hitherto unavailable, the notice that the undertaking has been fulfilled should be made available to all the major participants in a more obvious way such as sending a notice to each of them.

If the further information provided is significant, it must always be possible to have the witness return to be cross-examined on this information. From the inquiry's standpoint the executive secretary, librarian, or person reviewing the transcripts regularly, should keep an undertaking log. If an index to the transcripts is going to be prepared, this person would be the logical one to keep the log since, in going through the transcripts for other purposes, undertakings may be noted. It would be a routine matter for this person to maintain a list of undertakings, indicating the nature of the undertaking, the witness giving the undertaking, the participant on whose behalf the witness appeared, the date and transcript reference for the undertaking, and the disposition. The disposition would record the date the undertaking was satisfied with transcript reference and exhibit number (see sample undertaking log in Appendix B-20).

G. Rulings of the Commissioner

A procedural aspect of hearings that is of particular concern to the commissioner and inquiry counsel is the question of how to handle a request for a formal ruling. A participant may have a disagreement or otherwise require direction and will want an authoritative ruling from the commissioner. This can come up either as a specific request for a procedural ruling or in the course of a heated exchange at the hearings when two parties disagree and turn to the commissioner for a ruling. Whether out of disagreement or confusion, participants may wish to obtain an authoritative ruling, or the commissioner, at his own initiative, may want to establish certain ground rules. Occasional rulings demonstrate that the commissioner is firmly in control of the proceedings.

If there is disagreement among participants, the first impulse of the commissioner should be to ask them to resolve their differences themselves through meetings. This then puts pressure on the participants to establish an effective working relationship informally without continually seeking rulings by the commissioner. The inquiry procedure often cannot be fully bound by strict rules because of the uncertain nature of its activity. It is, therefore, advisable that the commissioner not continually make rulings for the day-to-day operation of the inquiry. It will be almost impossible for him to issue consistent rulings, and this may lead to confusion and even the possibility of a court challenge. Rulings also have the effect of determining matters in a certain way, when a more flexible approach may be preferable. Rather than risk inconsistent or conflicting rulings, the commissioner should direct the participants to attend a meeting chaired by inquiry counsel to attempt to resolve matters; only if a matter cannot be resolved, should it come before the commissioner for a ruling.

Though certain matters may be agreed upon by the participants, there must be no doubt that inquiry procedure is set by the commissioner. Inquiry counsel should attend all participant meetings, report to the commissioner on conclusions reached, and informally advise participants of the commissioner's views. The commissioner should have been previously informed of any disputes or procedural applications so he can agree to the recommended procedure before it is reported out of the meeting. Inquiry counsel should leave no doubt that he will act as a conduit in most cases and that he is there to represent the inquiry's interest.

Disputes arising in the course of the hearing that require resolution before the proceedings continue demand a slightly different procedure. While the commissioner may wish to call a short adjournment to allow the participants to consider how the matter might be dealt with, usually the dispute is of the type that is not amenable to discussion. In situations such as this, the commissioner should listen carefully to the objection presented by a participant and ensure that the nature and significance of the submission, in both the long and short term, is clearly understood. The commissioner should then hear from any party expressing a contrary view.

Depending on the relationship between the commissioner and inquiry counsel, the commissioner may also wish to call on the inquiry counsel to put his views formally on the record. This is often of value since it gives inquiry counsel the opportunity to lay the groundwork for the commissioner's ruling and to put before the commissioner the range of options or the significance of the decision so that all of the parties are aware of the importance of the question raised.

Except in the clearest and most simple situation, the commissioner should call a short adjournment while he considers what has been said before making a ruling. During the adjournment the commissioner is able to consult with his counsel who will, in the role of advisor to the commissioner, indicate the procedural and legal implications of any ruling the commissioner may make. Once the commissioner has decided how he wishes to rule, inquiry counsel may also assist in framing the ruling.

The commissioner should present his rulings in open hearings on the record. He should not permit debate on the ruling but should allow questions of clarification.

If a procedural matter is raised that has profound consequences for the inquiry, and if the issue need not be resolved immediately, the commissioner may indicate to the participants that he is prepared to hear their submissions on the point at a later date. This will give them an opportunity to do the research necessary to present considered views. There may also be circumstances in which the commissioner wants to hear the submissions immediately but may defer making a ruling. In those cases he could advise that he will continue the hearings, consider the submissions, and return with a ruling at a later date. In both situations the commissioner can delay making a ruling and thereby avoid establishing a precedent where it is unnecessary to do so.

While there is a natural tendency to want to make a decision immediately, it is often in the best interests of the participants and the inquiry to avoid a hastily determined ruling. Since a formal ruling of the commissioner governs the proceedings, the long-term implications of any ruling must be considered. For that reason, the prudent course is to hear argument, adjourn to consider the issue, discuss it with inquiry counsel, and then make a formal ruling if it is necessary to do so.

Once a commissioner makes a formal ruling, it must be obeyed. If it is not obeyed, the commissioner's ruling can be made an order of the court; if the court order is not obeyed, the disobedient party can be found in contempt of court and subjected to court-imposed sanctions. In making a formal order that may lead to contempt proceedings, the commissioner should ensure his order is well considered and issued in writing or formally recorded in the transcripts. The party subject to the order and the action required should be clearly set out, as should the method and time limit for compliance. Unless the statute creating the inquiry specifies other-wise, the commissioner's order is made an order of the court according to established rules of practice.

Of course, it is always open to a participant to challenge a commissioner's order in court by launching judicial review proceedings. It is important, therefore, that there be careful consideration and consultation with inquiry counsel before any formal order is issued. For consideration of contempt proceedings, see Chapter VIII, Judicial Review of Inquiries, "Contempt."

H. Order of Presenting Evidence

There is no formula that will determine the order of presenting evidence. Evidence should be presented in a coherent, logical order with the most crucial evidence coming early and being supplemented later by refinements or elaborations. Beyond that, the order of witnesses is a matter of discretion for the commissioner (see Chapter V, The Inquiry Process: Procedural Rules, "Form of Presentation").

If the inquiry is into a proposed project, the proponent often calls his evidence first since he will have done much of the basic research and will be able to put the proposal before the inquiry so that other participants can react to it. Even in these circumstances, however, the proponent's evidence need not necessarily come first. The government may have conducted studies that provide a good backdrop for the more project-oriented evidence of the proponent. In certain phases of the inquiry dealing with, for example, socio-economic impact, it may be appropriate that the evidence of the communities be presented first.

Evidence to be presented and witnesses to be called should be discussed on a regular basis at meetings of participants or reviewed bilaterally by participants and inquiry counsel. On the basis of that information, the commissioner can issue a timetable which will set the order of witnesses. In hearings where evidence must be filed in advance, the commissioner has detailed information on the evidence to be called and can determine the most appropriate order to hear it. However, this information is not available until late in the proceedings, and it may be difficult to reschedule the witnesses if a certain order of presentation commends itself to the commissioner. However the commissioner gets the information he needs, it should be assembled thoroughly and as early as possible for greater flexibility in scheduling.

In deciding the order of witnesses, it is useful for the commissioner to keep in mind the policy positions of the participants. For an inquiry into a development project it may be appropriate to call the witnesses of the participants in support of the project, followed by the witnesses of parties opposed, or vice versa, so that all like-minded evidence is presented together. On the other hand, if two known experts of differing views are to appear, it may prove more stimulating to call the two sequentially, then follow with the evidence of others. Practical considerations should also play a role in scheduling. For example, if witnesses are to be called before a recess in the proceedings, the schedule should be prepared in a way that permits witnesses travelling long distances to complete their testimony, so that re-attendance to complete the evidence affects only the local witnesses.

If, as a result of the inquiry timetable, it is necessary to have a witness re-attend, the inquiry should seriously consider paying for the costs of re-attendance. While some participants may be well enough funded to absorb these costs, they are still costs occasioned as the direct result of the inquiry timetable. If the inquiry will not pay such costs, the scheduling of witnesses should reflect the fact that some parties may not be able to afford the re-attendance of a witness and will abandon the evidence if it cannot be heard at the initial appearance.

Often participants will request an order for calling witnesses that is dictated by events outside the inquiry. As with the order of cross-examination, they may be more influenced by a desire to call the first evidence in an area, to call witnesses early on in the proceedings, to garner initial press coverage, to have a witness appear at a time or day when media coverage is maximized, or to have attendance of a witness coincide with a visit to the area for other purposes. While there is nothing wrong with the inquiry co-operating with such requests, it should be done only if the requested scheduling of witnesses corresponds to the needs of the inquiry. In each case the inquiry should be concerned with the type of evidence being presented and its significance, rather than external issues such as media coverage.

I. Final Submission

Participants may request the opportunity to make a concluding submission or "final argument" to the inquiry after all of the evidence is in but before the commissioner and the inquiry staff retire to prepare the inquiry report. Whether the commissioner agrees to hear final submissions depends very much on the nature of the proceedings.

In order for the final submission to be useful, the commissioner must be prepared to give participants enough time after the end of the hearings to review the proceedings, consider the evidence, and properly present their views as to the conclusions suggested by the evidence. If sufficient time is not provided, the final submissions will be mainly argumentative and will not provide a summary of the evidence before the inquiry. Procedurally this means the commissioner must set aside further hearing days following a period of preparation.

While final argument may be abused by participants who want to make a dramatic gesture for public consumption rather than assist the work of the inquiry, and while it causes some delay in the report-writing phase, there is value in having final submissions. Such submissions force the participants to consider the evidence as a whole; to deal with evidence contrary to their position, suggesting why it should not be adopted; and to make submissions as to why one line of evidence should be preferred over another. Because this is precisely the job the inquiry must do, such creative thinking assists the inquiry by offering insights and different lines of reasoning that may not have occurred to the commissioner. It is also helpful because it requires participants to bring together all of the evidence on a particular issue, evidence that is often presented at different times in the inquiry process. This is a valuable research aid that assists the commissioner in writing his report and allows those with a particular interest in a subject to focus their thinking and substantiate their views.

Final submissions may be oral, written, or a combination of the two. After a short inquiry an oral summation, provided it is recorded in the inquiry transcripts, may be sufficient. If the commissioner does not wish to hold further public sessions once all the evidence is in, he may offer the opportunity for written submissions to be submitted by a certain date. On the other hand, the commissioner may welcome the high public profile that oral summations provide. Since the inquiry is going to go behind closed doors for a period of time while the report is written, the final submissions can be regarded as a public and media send-off to remind the public of the inquiry's work.

The inquiry will usually want a detailed written submission setting out the position of the participant on a number of issues. A public bringing-together of the issues also has a media, public perception, and inquiry morale benefit. A promising compromise is to permit a time-limited oral presentation that may be supplemented by a more detailed written statement. The oral presentations would be a summary of the more detailed written submissions filed with the inquiry. This practice allows the participants to comment on a range of issues in whatever detail they wish, yet gives them an opportunity to present a verbal summary to emphasize certain points and thereby draw public and media attention to their work.

The commissioner may wish to set aside a stated period of time for oral summary and require the more detailed written summary to be submitted by that date as well. He may also require that a copy of the summary be delivered to each of the other participants in advance. This is particularly so if the commissioner wants participants to comment on the conclusions of others at the time of the oral presentation.

The commissioner must also decide whether inquiry counsel, on behalf of the inquiry staff, will submit a final argument. It is often argued that the staff, because they are the resource people who will assist the commissioner in report writing, should not make submissions. To make a submission requires the staff to come to conclusions about the evidence, independent of the commissioner, and to express preferences and biases. That may make it difficult for them to act as impartial advisors to the commissioner during the report writing, and the commissioner may feel he has to treat them as advocates of a position rather than as neutral advisors.

On the other hand, presentation of staff analysis by way of a submission does nothing more than make public the impressions and biases that already exist among the staff, and it puts these views forward in a public way so that they can be criticized and commented upon by other participants. Also, it is often the inquiry staff that has the research capability and knowledge necessary to prepare a detailed summary which will assist all participants in comments they may wish to make. If inquiry staff are to make a final submission, it may be preferable that inquiry counsel file it before the filing dates for submissions by other participants, thereby allowing others to comment on staff positions in the last public session before report writing.

Finally, there should be a provision for rebuttal. Generally, this can be in written form to avoid prolonging the hearings. Rebuttal allows the participants to identify errors or misleading characterizations of the evidence in the conclusions of others and to bring this to the attention of the commissioner. This opportunity is not only fair but is also a valuable research tool in its own right.

IV. SUPPORT SYSTEM FOR HEARINGS

In addition to the proceedings in the hearing rooms, an inquiry may wish to adopt a number of other programs to support the formal hearings. Many of these techniques can, to varying degrees, also be applied to inquiries centred on submissions or community hearings.

A. Index

It should be the responsibility of the inquiry to set up and maintain an index to the inquiry proceedings. While the nature and detail of the index varies, the great amount of information generated by many inquiries would be unmanageable without some form of index to assist in the writing of the report, reviewing the material, preparing final submissions, and generally identifying evidence to document conclusions. Rather than have a number of participants, each attempting to maintain an index, it should be prepared and maintained by the inquiry so that a consistent system is developed and used by all parties.

Preparing an index is a time-consuming and difficult job and, where possible, it should be the responsibility of a specific individual either under contract or on the inquiry staff. Since members of the inquiry staff will use the index extensively at the final report stage, they should be consulted from time to time to ensure that it meets their needs.

The index should record the names of all the witnesses who appeared to give evidence and the transcript reference for their appearance. It should also include a topical index of the subject matter addressed and the witnesses and transcript reference of all those people who gave evidence on each subject. The researchers for the inquiry and the participants should be consulted from time to time to check the appropriateness of subject headings and, generally, whether the index is meeting their needs.

It will be necessary to update the index regularly. It should be made available to all the major participants, libraries, and other centres where research into the transcripts is conducted.

In addition to an index to the materials, an index of undertakings is of assistance to the participants and an effective way of ensuring the inquiry record is complete. If a participant, through its counsel or witnesses appearing on its behalf, agrees to provide information at a later date, this fact is recorded and then followed up if the undertaking is not complied with. A sample form of undertaking index is found in Appendix B-20.

B. Meeting of Participants

An established procedure whereby inquiry counsel and representatives of major participants have an opportunity to meet regularly greatly assists the smooth and efficient operation of the inquiry. Since most inquiries have no established practice, it is sometimes difficult to determine what is expected at various stages without such continuous consultation with inquiry counsel. Consultation also ensures that all the participants understand the issues and are fairly and equally treated.

Participant meetings are designed to deal primarily with the procedural aspects of the inquiry. Such matters as the inquiry schedule, the order for calling witnesses, and problems associated with production of documents may be resolved by agreement at the meetings. As discussed earlier, where agreement cannot be reached, the matter may then be argued before the commissioner and a formal ruling obtained.

These meetings are chaired by inquiry counsel and are generally independent of the commissioner. This allows the participants to explain the nature of the evidence they intend to call, the likely duration of that evidence, and otherwise exchange information that would facilitate the orderly operation of the inquiry without prematurely alerting the commissioner to their evidence or involving him in their disputes with other participants.

There is always the difficulty, especially when there are a number of witnesses to be called, of scheduling. It is very inefficient and expensive to have costly expert witnesses waiting on the sidelines for their opportunity to give evidence merely because the evidence of the panel before them has taken longer than anticipated. This problem can be partially overcome by agreement among the participants as to how long particular evidence will take. This kind of organization is especially critical when participants must file statements of evidence before the witness appears. A serious under-estimation of time required by some witnesses would mean that subsequent witnesses may be called sooner after their evidence is circulated than the rules provide.

If the commissioner makes it clear that he wishes certain procedural matters to be resolved by agreement at meetings of participants, experience indicates that most issues are resolved and few arguments take place before him. On the other hand, if the commissioner is prepared to become involved in every procedural dispute, participants soon realize it is not necessary to make compromises at the meetings of participants and, instead, take every matter to the commissioner for a ruling.

It is preferable to refer matters for resolution than to make a series of rulings. It cuts down on the loss of hearing time and generally results in procedures that work fairly for all participants. In a hearing that by its very nature cannot be rigidly structured, so many compromises must be made that agreement can be reached on most issues if it is clear that agreement, rather than procedural wrangling at the hearing, is the approach preferred by the commissioner.

C. Public Information Program

Generally an inquiry is created in response to public pressure or concern. It is important, therefore, that the public know of the inquiry's establishment, purpose, and the procedure for public participation. Before any hearings are held, there must often be some public education undertaken to ensure that the people know whether they should be interested in the inquiry and how to participate.

As discussed in Chapter III, Establishing the Inquiry, the inquiry must first decide what role, if any, it wishes to play in public education. If it decides to play a role, then it should carefully decide the nature of the public information program it wishes to implement. This program can often be initiated using materials available through government departments or, if the inquiry is into a specific project, the proponents of the project.

In putting together public information, the inquiry must be careful that it does not appear to be passing on information which may be controversial and, in fact, may be the subject matter of the inquiry itself. For example, an inquiry into a development may wish to release information on a project as proposed and indicate the type of impacts it wishes to examine, but information should not include comment on the nature or extent of the impact, nor should it appear to prejudge aspects of the project.

Often at this early stage the government creating the inquiry will agree to make its government press officers available for initial press relations. While such assistance may be useful in the early stages, the inquiry should quickly move away from such a close identification with the government. Because initial media coverage plays such a significant role in the public perception of the inquiry and the commissioner, a public perception that may ultimately determine the success of the inquiry, many commissioners seek out media consultants at an early stage. Depending on the nature and size of the inquiry, such a consultant can be extremely useful. However, the inquiry must be careful that it does not appear too slick or manipulative by engaging in a public relations exercise.

The thrust of the inquiry's activity must be public information and not public relations in the usual sense. Since most media consultants are accustomed to the promotional type of public relations, the commissioner must be careful in his selection of a media adviser and ensure that any and all public relations activities are cleared through him personally until he is satisfied that they are carried out in a manner appropriate to a public inquiry. The inquiry must always be conscious of the judicial aspect of its undertaking and participate in public education and public relations in a restrained and impartial way.

D. Mailing List

As soon as the existence of the inquiry is made known, individuals will communicate with it requesting information or indicating a desire to participate. It is important, therefore, that the inquiry develop a mailing list from the beginning. It is this list that the inquiry will use to communicate with individuals, provide notice of hearings, and indicate how members of the public might participate in the inquiry process.

The inquiry will eventually develop different types of mailing lists for different purposes. The first, and most general, will be the mailing list of all people who have requested to be placed on the mailing list for general communications, such as notices and inquiry documents. This list will also include persons, agencies, or groups that the inquiry has identified as appropriate or useful interests to receive this information.

There will also be a mailing list of persons or groups who actually participate in the inquiry. These persons would receive not only material sent to the general public but also copies of reports and other documentation required for participation in the inquiry. To this list might be added libraries and other community organizations that might be in a position to receive copies of documents on behalf of individuals in their area.

In some cases witnesses appearing before the inquiry or particular groups or agencies will ask that they receive documentation dealing with their subject area. These persons should be added to this list for the purpose of their particular interest only.

A third mailing list will consist of those the inquiry has recognized as major participants. These are the parties who must receive copies of statements of evidence in advance and receive invitations to any meetings of participants and planning sessions. This list is also required by other participants for circulation of statements of evidence, supplementary evidence, and notification of procedural motions.

In addition to these lists, there may also be special lists such as a list of media contacts to whom press releases or notice of press meetings may be sent, a list of affected communities, and other lists designed to meet specific needs.

E. News Coverage

If the inquiry is to play a truly public role, the press must be kept informed of proceedings and procedure.

In most cases there will be an inquiry press officer whose responsibility, in addition to working for the commissioner on any press releases, will be to keep the press informed of the witnesses scheduled to appear, their likely time of attendance, their expertise, and anticipated evidence. All of this information is available before the witness appears either through advance filing of a statement of evidence or, if no such filing is required, by communicating with the parties about their witnesses. If may also be necessary for the commissioner or inquiry counsel to brief the representatives of the press on a regular basis.

So that the inquiry is not viewed as prejudging the issues before it or manipulating the public information about what is taking place, it must be structured in a way that allows for an independent review of the inquiry proceedings. In most major inquiries, there will be regular coverage by daily newspapers with occasional coverage by radio or television in the locality where the hearings are taking place. The inquiry must recognize the important role played by media coverage and structure itself to work with the media as much as possible. The inquiry press office should hold regular briefings and provide daily material at the hearing room press table for use by the media. The inquiry offices should have sufficient space for press conferences.

A system of keeping the media advised of the inquiry activities should be established early and continually reviewed. The commissioner may wish to meet with management of the local media, such as editorial boards and network news executives to advise them of the inquiry and its significance and request advice as to the coverage they intend to provide. The commissioner might request that one individual be assigned to cover the inquiry, whether on a regular or periodic basis, so that person is well briefed and can develop an understanding of the issues. This exercise of encouraging media coverage will pay dividends later when a well-informed public is more usefully able to contribute to the inquiry.

The question of interviews should be considered and guidelines established. For example, the participants may be prepared to agree that no inquiry witnesses will be interviewed concerning their participation in the inquiry until they have actually appeared.

Where statements of evidence are filed, there is the possibility of problems in media coverage. First, the inquiry must be careful that it does not misrepresent the nature of the evidence to be presented. There is always the danger of the inquiry press officer, often unskilled in the technical evidence, extracting parts of the statement for media consumption by reviewing the statement of evidence. The witness may decide to rephrase or express his evidence in a different way. The press officer should only indicate the nature of the evidence to be presented, the expertise of the witness, and who he represents. But he should not go into detail by, for example, selecting quotations from his evidence since they may easily be misinterpreted out of context. Members of the press should be encouraged to review the statement of evidence themselves or wait for the witness to attend before quoting extensively.

It would be unfortunate if the press were to develop the habit of reviewing the statements of evidence before the witness appeared and use that as the basis of the press report, rather than the witness's evidence. Not only would there be confusion if the witness changed his statement, but his evidence would also stand in the media record without contradiction or clarification. Evidence which may have been immediately discredited by cross-examination would have had public exposure because it appeared unchallenged for a considerable period of time. Just as troublesome is the practice of responding to inaccurate press reports with clarifying comments or reaction outside the inquiry before the matter comes up for hearing. The potential for error may encourage the press to agree not to report on a witness's statement until the witness actually appears and gives evidence.

The commissioner may also wish to establish ground rules for the granting of interviews by inquiry staff. In some circumstances only the commissioner should speak on behalf of the inquiry. In other circumstances, however, it would be most inappropriate for the commissioner to discuss an issue, yet the position of the inquiry should be presented. Often it is appropriate for inquiry counsel to act as spokesperson for the inquiry in questions involving inquiry procedures or to provide a public defence of a decision made by the commissioner.

Other inquiry staff members may be asked questions about the technical issues before the inquiry, the structure of community involvement, or other questions within their areas of responsibility. It is often helpful to designate staff members as spokespersons for the various areas of inquiry activity so that these officials can consider the public information role that is appropriate well in advance of media contact.

F. Summary

The commissioner may not be prepared to leave the total responsibility for reporting on the inquiry's activities to the uncertainties of media coverage. Coverage will be sporadic and will usually concentrate on those items that appear newsworthy rather than those that are truly significant. For that reason the inquiry may wish to establish a system of newsletters or other reporting techniques to summarize information presented. If the inquiry regards one of its functions as public information, then such a program is extremely valuable.

Summaries for public consumption are best prepared independently of the inquiry. Since any summary must, of necessity, select certain evidence and exclude the rest, and highlight evidence of certain people to the exclusion of others, it would be unfortunate if the commissioner or the inquiry itself were seen to have made these distinctions before all of the evidence was in. For that reason the inquiry should consider contracting with an independent agency or individual for production of summaries. While the inquiry staff would agree to review the edited version to ensure there are no irregularities, and while the commissioner will always retain a certain residual responsibility, it should be clearly understood that the summary was prepared apart from the inquiry.

Such a summary report should be prepared by someone with some technical knowledge of the information supplied, either pre-existing or through continued exposure to the evidence of the commission. The report would be inexpensively prepared and presented in a readable fashion. Copies should be distributed to those who indicated a desire to be regularly informed of the inquiry's activities. While the form and content of the report is determined by the independent agency, the inquiry should retain residual control over both content and distribution.

G. Transcripts

While summaries are adequate for the needs of most individuals, those wishing to participate may require the actual transcript of the inquiry proceedings to review the evidence in greater detail. A system providing a transcript to various public libraries and public centres should be instituted to ensure transcripts are available at locations where participants or potential participants are able to review them and prepare for the inquiry.

Depending on the procedural rules of the inquiry, it may also be necessary to supplement the transcripts with other documents. For example, witnesses who merely file statements of evidence and do not read the evidence into the record leave serious gaps in the the inquiry record if the total evidence is not available in some other way. The statement of evidence should be filed with the transcript in those cases. While a very expensive activity, broad distribution of the transcripts is essential not only as a tool for research but also to demonstrate that the public inquiry is actually making the information widely available to assist public participation.

H. Inquiry Documents

In the course of the hearings the inquiry may either commission or prepare reports or studies, or it may become aware of significant reports that it feels should be made public. If these reports belong to participants in the hearings, the commissioner may request sufficient copies for public libraries or other centres where they can be used by those intending to participate in the inquiry. If this cost is burdensome, the inquiry may underwrite the cost of making the reports available.

As for its own studies, these have in fact been paid for by the public, and the inquiry will usually make them available to participants. Again, rather than providing copies to everyone, the inquiry may wish to adopt a procedure of depositing significant reports in public libraries and other centres.

Whatever techniques are developed, the goal is to provide all significant documents to the participants in a form and at a time that they can be used effectively to further the work of the inquiry.

VII

Terminating the Inquiry

Most public inquiries are instructed in their authorizing instruments to "investigate and report." The inquiry is, therefore, fully operational from the time the commissioner is appointed until the report is submitted and the inquiry wound up. From the time the public hearings end until the report is submitted to the government, the inquiry still has authority to function in whatever way it considers necessary to fulfil its responsibilities. It can, for example, retain consultants, even new consultants; travel to view areas of interest; and receive new information, which it may adopt for purposes of its report. Therefore, in determining such things as the length of contract for inquiry staff or lease arrangements for premises and equipment, the commissioner must remember that, while the participant involvement may be severely curtailed and the public profile of the inquiry diminished, operations of the inquiry, in this new form, will continue.

While an inquiry may still receive additional information at the end of the public hearings, it must consider very carefully what additional information it will seek out or, if new information comes to its attention, how it will handle this information. Because public hearings are only part of the total inquiry process, there is no requirement that information come to the inquiry solely through hearings. On the other hand, it seriously discredits the process if significant additional information comes before the inquiry outside of the hearings. It also prevents participants from dealing with that information and either supplementing, supporting, or challenging it.

An inquiry that relies on information obtained outside of the public hearing process runs the risk not only of accepting information that could be discredited, but also of losing public support because it will be perceived to have abandoned the public process.

Significant new information that was available during the inquiry process, but not presented, should only be accepted in special circumstances. In those cases the existence of the information should be made known to participants in the inquiry process, who would then be given the opportunity to comment. Often this can be handled by providing the participants with the new information and giving them an opportunity to respond in writing within a stated time. If the information is particularly controversial or if a matter of credibility is involved, the commissioner should seriously consider reconvening the public inquiry for the specific purpose of hearing the new evidence and allowing others to call evidence on only that issue. While reopening the public hearing process is not necessary and would rarely be used, it should be considered in special circumstances.

I. APPROACHING THE EVIDENCE

When the hearings close, the inquiry is faced with the responsibility of reviewing and analysing the information presented and compiling a report, usually with recommendations, to the government. The first thing the inquiry should determine is upon what record should it make its recommendations.

Some aspects of the record are easy to define: transcripts of the public hearings; reports; studies or other material filed with the inquiry; studies undertaken by the inquiry staff and filed; recorded proceedings and information generated through inquiry activity, such as site tours; and generally anything else that was brought before the inquiry and tabled. What other kinds of information may be relied on is less clear. This would include information generally known about the subject matter but not presented to the inquiry (which an inquiry may rely on as a matter of official notice), information presented to the inquiry on a confidential basis, and the technical knowledge of the commissioner himself.

The commissioner and his staff, particularly inquiry counsel, will have satisfied themselves, in the course of the proceedings, that the record was complete. To the extent that this is accomplished, there should be no problem about filling any apparent gaps. However, if serious gaps are found to exist, the inquiry should be prepared to undertake remedial measures such as directing inquiry counsel to call further evidence.

The commissioner should also examine once again some of the general questions raised at the time the inquiry was initiated. Did the inquiry assign an onus to any parties to produce satisfactory evidence in an area? What standard of proof is required? Similarly, it is useful to recall that different evidence should be treated differently. While all evidence relevant to the subject matter before the inquiry may have been admitted, it is useful for the commissioner and staff to recall that the weight given to evidence may vary. So, for example, the views of a recognized expert on a subject may be given more weight than a lay person commenting on the same matters. While the evidence of both individuals should perhaps be brought together for consideration, it is useful to keep in mind, from the beginning, the relative weight that should be attached to the evidence of different individuals.

II. CONFIDENTIALITY

From the time the hearings conclude, a different relationship must exist between the commissioner, his staff, and the public. While an inquiry should be commended for a free and frequent exchange of information with the public during hearings, after that stage of the inquiry is completed, the commissioner has every right to expect that all those still associated with the inquiry will respect the need for confidentiality during the report-writing stage. Disclosure of information during the course of the inquiry deliberations, leaks of portions of the inquiry report, or discussion as to how the inquiry is analysing a matter will lead to speculation and public distrust. Those who agree with the intended report will mount a campaign to press their views; those who do not like the apparent decision will attempt to pressure the inquiry into changing its views before the final report or will work towards discrediting the inquiry. In either case the inquiry process is undermined.

The commissioner should ensure, therefore, that mechanisms are in place to enforce strict confidentiality. The first step is to keep the report-writing stage as short as possible. The inquiry's physical premises should be suitable for report writing. This would mean, for example, that the inquiry has locked filing cabinets and sufficient work area that drafts of the report need not be taken from the inquiry work area or left in public view. Since there may be a desire by researchers and members of the public to continue to consult the inquiry library, public access will have to be limited, for example, by declaring the inquiry library closed except when prior arrangements are made.

Only those staff members that the commissioner is satisfied are trustworthy should be retained. In the course of report writing, responsibility should be sufficiently shared that no one person can claim to know all of the report, except for the commissioner. The commissioner may also want to retain the only copy of the final report and ensure that certain sections, such as the specific recommendations, are not made known to inquiry staff until the last moment. Some commissioners prepare the report by setting out the evidence and leaving a space for the recommendations which are then prepared separately and incorporated into the report at the last minute. Others write the report with alternative recommendations, then select the final recommendations just before the report is printed. Whatever the technique, the report must remain confidential if its release is to be controlled by the commissioner.

III. USE OF INQUIRY STAFF AND COUNSEL

Every commissioner faces the difficult task of deciding who should assist in the writing of the report. On the one hand, the inquiry staff represents a pool of experienced, knowledgeable, and expert persons familiar with the inquiry evidence. On the other hand, some may have played an active role in searching out and presenting certain of that evidence and may have very definite ideas on what should be accepted. For example, should members of the inquiry staff who have advised inquiry counsel be involved in the report where counsel and staff played an active role in the proceedings, calling evidence and cross-examining the witnesses called by others? Can these individuals impartially work with the commissioner in analysing the evidence when, in some cases, they may be asked whether the evidence they helped prepare and call should be preferred to contrary evidence called by others.

While the commissioner has every right to be cautious, previous involvement as advisors should not preclude these individuals from working with the commissioner at the report-writing stage. While the commissioner should avoid retaining anyone who actually appeared before the inquiry to give evidence, there is nothing wrong in having the individuals who prepared and analysed evidence on behalf of inquiry counsel or the commissioner work with the commissioner in writing the report. In fact, there is much to be gained, because these individuals will be familiar with the evidence and can provide the continuity and expertise the commissioner will require.

The same considerations apply when considering the role of inquiry counsel. An active counsel, who presented evidence and cross-examined the witnesses of others, has played a role which may suggest that he will not bring total impartiality to report writing. This appearance of bias is particularly evident if the evidence inquiry counsel was required to call was all on one side of an issue; this could have occurred where there were no participants to call that evidence and, to retain a balance in the information before the inquiry, the counsel appeared as an advocate for a particular point of view. However, counsel is also a professional who can change hats from being an advocate for a particular point of view to someone who, as advisor and counsel to the commissioner, can step back and provide a valuable overview of legal concerns.

The role given to individuals working for the commissioner will vary. Some commissioners retain technical staff to research specific issues based on the inquiry record. When the staff has brought together the evidence and provided an analysis, the commissioner will then write his report on the basis of that information. Other commissioners ask staff members to draft sections of the report for his consideration after giving them some general directions on tentative conclusions he has reached.

Inquiry counsel may be active throughout report preparation, commenting on what constitutes the record, advising on legal concepts such as weight of evidence, and assisting technical advisors in approaching the evidence. Another possibility is that counsel is totally excluded except to review the final report before it is printed for evidentiary errors or potential legal problems, such as defamatory statements. Any report, even one prepared by an expert commissioner, should be reviewed for both technical accuracy and legal correctness before it is printed. More extensive use of both technical and legal assistance is, however, often required.

Commissioners have also treated the work of their staff in different ways. If the inquiry staff is asked to write reports for the commissioner on issues before the inquiry, should these reports also form part of the inquiry record and, more important, should they be made public? Often a commissioner who requests significant staff reports will append such reports to the final report or issue them separately as supporting documents. While such publication has the advantage of making the considered views of the inquiry staff known, it may also detract from the final report, especially if the commissioner comes to conclusions contrary to those of the staff report.

The commissioner should, therefore, carefully consider whether he wishes such reports prepared. If the nature of the evidence does not require this, fewer problems are created if the staff work as a team out of the public eye. On the other hand, if such reports are required, the commissioner may wish to direct that they summarize the information but not include any recommendations or, at least, make it clear when options are available. If such comprehensive reports are prepared, the question still remains whether they should be made public. If they are not to be made public, they can be merely identified in the commissioner's report and left as part of the inquiry documents that may be useful for future research.

IV. THE REPORT

Before setting out on the task of preparing the report, it is useful for the commissioner to consider the form the report is to take. Clearly the commissioner wants a report that accurately brings together and deals with all of the information presented. The ability to bring together information on a subject from widely divergent sources is one of the most important benefits of a public inquiry. The credibility of the inquiry, particularly in the academic or technical communities and government, is often assessed on the basis of how successful the inquiry has been in bringing together all of the essential technical evidence.

On the other hand, the commissioner will want a report that is more than a compendium of technical information. It may have to incorporate some of the local colour, attitudes, and emotions of the people affected and be comprehensible to the general public. To that end he may wish to have a shorter, more succinct, and perhaps more "popular" report than many academic and professional readers would prefer.

To accommodate these considerations, the inquiry can adopt the practice of preparing its report in more than one volume, or it can provide an executive summary. By providing a summary document, the inquiry can widely distribute the substance of its report and recommendations in a format that is reasonably comprehensible and easy to read. The summary volume would be supplemented by graphics, pictures, or other techniques that will make it a readable document. A large number of copies of the abridged form of the report can be distributed at relatively low cost, and the more detailed report, which may be of limited interest, can be produced in smaller bundles.

Any views of the commissioner on the length of the report, whether it should be in separate volumes, and other matters of form should be given to the staff early in the process and reviewed regularly as the documentation comes together. Some direction at the outset assists those working on the report so they can prepare the necessary information in a form that is most useful to the commissioner.

Having determined the form of the final report, the commissioner should ensure that he has a measure of control over the actual preparation. In some cases it is merely a matter of confirming that there are sufficient funds provided in the inquiry budget for a proper report-writing phase. This includes staff, equipment, and facilities, as well as funds for appropriate printing and distribution of the final document, a press release, and a press conference on the day of release. Subsequent travel to present the report to special persons, such as specific ministers or community leaders, should also be budgeted.

The commissioner should control the preparation and distribution of the final report. While, arguably, an inquiry's duty, apart from statutory direction, is merely to report to the government (Cabinet) that created it, in practice commissioners have taken an active role in determining the fate of their report. If the report is a governmental responsibility, it may go unpublished for a period of time or be published in a format or in numbers that are unacceptable to the commissioner. On the other hand, if the commissioner retains control, he can be sure it is attractively printed and contains photographs or coloured graphics to better convey ideas and make it readable for the public. He can have it printed in sufficient numbers to respond to public interest and have it printed and distributed in timely fashion so it is released when the issue is still of public concern.

The commissioner should understand the responsibilities on the inquiry and the government with respect to the public release of the report. Usually the legislation that authorized creation of the inquiry will provide that the report is to be filed with the government. The commissioner must, therefore, structure the report writing to comply with filing requirements specified in legislation. So, for example, if the report is to be tabled in the Legislature or in parliament within a specified period after receipt by the government, it may make sense to provide it to the government while the Legislature or parliament is still in session. Will the report be made available to the public through government book stores and, if so, at what cost? Generally, however, there should be an understanding between the government and the commissioner as to the public distribution of the report.

The government and the commissioner must decide whether copies of the report are to be provided to the government in advance of public release. This is often a sensible gesture since it allows the government officials to review the report and recommendations and to be prepared to comment on them upon public release. If the commissioner decides to have the public release correspond with his filing the report with the government, there is a risk of an uninformed government response or, more likely, no response at all until the report is studied. Similar considerations apply in determining whether a "pre-release" to the major participants in the inquiry is appropriate. An additional problem here is that it is unlikely that the report can be kept confidential for very long once it is given to participants.

In any case the commissioner should ensure that there is a clear understanding as to when and how the inquiry report will be made public and, where possible, he should retain the authority and financial resources to handle the printing and distribution of the report.

V. CLOSING THE INQUIRY

The commissioner should not assume that upon completion of the report there will be no further demands on the inquiry. In the first place the inquiry may require the resources and personnel to ensure that the report, once printed, is appropriately distributed. This may require arrangements whereby the inquiry will distribute the report to the media and those members of the public on the inquiry mailing list. In addition, the commissioner may wish to send copies to government or industry officials with responsibility in the areas covered by the report, key witnesses, and others who assisted the inquiry in its work, personal friends, academics with an interest in the subject area, and other individuals or organizations who may benefit by or be interested in the final report. Both financial resources and staff are needed to carry out an accurate mailing and to respond to the numerous requests for the report that will inevitably follow its release.

At the time the report is released, the commissioner may hold a press conference and arrange adequate media coverage to communicate the key elements of the report to the public. It may be necessary, in some cases, to obtain the services of people experienced in public relations to ensure that this final public act of the inquiry is given the prominence it deserves.

Often it is the commissioner alone who understands the activities to be undertaken and the time left before the report is made public. Based on his assessment of when the report will be completed and the inquiry terminated, the commissioner must arrange for the orderly termination of staff in sufficient time to seek alternate employment, the termination of equipment and space rental agreements, and the preparation of government-supplied equipment for return. He must also arrange for correspondence and inquiries to be forwarded to his home or otherwise re-routed. He should retain a contact within the government so that salaries and other employment benefits are forwarded to the staff after termination and ensure that a recognized line of communications exists for dealing with outstanding matters, such as the payment of late-arriving accounts.

The commissioner himself should assume that he will receive communications from individuals either requesting copies of the report or commenting on the inquiry's work. He should, therefore, have sufficient extra copies of the report or an arrangement whereby copies of the report can be sent at his direction. Even after the inquiry is concluded, there are residual communications, and it is often sensible to retain the executive secretary and secretarial staff to handle the details and properly conclude all physical arrangements for a period after the termination.

VI. DISTRIBUTION OF INQUIRY DOCUMENTS

Under most orders in council establishing an inquiry, the commissioner is instructed to deposit with the government, usually the archivist or librarian, all of the papers and records of the inquiry. This, supposedly, ensures that the inquiry records remain public documents and are kept together in one location. Since this material was assembled largely at government expense, it should be retained by the government for its own use and as a historical record.

The inquiry documents should include the official transcripts and exhibits; any studies or reports commissioned by the inquiry, whether or not they were formally presented as evidence; and any other reports, studies, or works paid for by the inquiry or participants funded for this purpose. Also included should be reports and studies that are background documents, current research by experts not associated with the inquiry, or other like materials obtained by the inquiry staff as part of its research. These reports and studies would normally be part of the inquiry list of documents and are likely to be in the inquiry library.

While the government establishing the inquiry unquestionably has the right to demand the inquiry documents, the commissioner may wish to negotiate a program that will keep some of these documents more accessible and useful as research tools. The basic problem is that most government archives place time restrictions on documents so they do not become public until after a certain period following deposit.

In the case of a public inquiry, paid for by public funds, it seems appropriate the inquiry documents be publicly available from the time the inquiry winds up. There may have been great interest generated in the subject matter of the inquiry, and researchers may want early access to these documents. Undoubtedly, there may be some documents that are of a sensitive nature, but most are not. Some reports are current for only a very short time, and to have them hidden or restricted in use may be a waste of government funds. Unfortunately, most governments do not distinguish between inquiry documents and other government materials, and much valuable work may languish in government vaults for years.

In addition to depositing documents with the government as

required by the order in counsel, it may be appropriate to make certain documents easily available to the public. The commissioner may wish to have some of the studies commissioned by the inquiry more widely available. This can be done by having the evidence or reports put into publishable form and, using recognized publications both within government and the academic community, make this information available to the public and professionals interested in the area through the publications of the authors. Since all studies, reports, and evidence presented to the inquiry are regarded as public, and it is the researcher himself who is publishing, there should be no copyright problems.

Materials collected by the inquiry not part of the inquiry record and duplicates of inquiry material could be made publicly available in the region where the inquiry took place. A substantial portion of the inquiry library and other documents could be retained as resource material in a local, public, or university library, or other such centre of public study. The inquiry library is a public library that can be used for future research if it is readily accessible and is maintained and updated. If arrangements cannot be made to have the inquiry documents accepted as a whole, maintained, and up-dated, the library could be left with the government, though there is a substantial risk that the materials may be neither maintained nor available to the public. If a university or public library in the area is prepared to take the materials, the fact should be advertised.

VII. GOVERNMENT INTERVENTION

Usually an inquiry completes its deliberations, writes its report, then terminates its activities and disappears. There have been occasions, however, where the government that created a public inquiry orders the inquiry to cease its activity and report by a specified date. This may be as a result of changed circumstances such as abandonment of development plans that were the focus of the hearings or an imposed time frame that requires the inquiry to advise the government before a specific date. It may also be occasioned by a desire to curtail the work of the inquiry because of excessive cost or embarrassment to the government. Whatever the reason, such a situation obviously has a dramatic effect on the inquiry.

A commissioner asked to curtail the work of the inquiry voluntarily must consider the effects of such a request both on his personal integrity and on the integrity of the inquiry process. If the commissioner feels he can complete the inquiry within the time frame requested by the government and still fulfil the mandate given him, he may agree to such a government directive. If no change is required in the inquiry procedure to meet the time frame, the commissioner may decide it is not necessary to make this agreement publicly known. However, this is not recommended since, if the existence of the agreement is disclosed and it invariably will be, the commissioner's integrity will suffer tremendously. On the other hand, if the inquiry must curtail the extent of public hearings or the existing relationship between it and the participants, then any such arrangement should be disclosed to the public.

While having a required reporting date causes substantial difficulties for the inquiry process (see Chapter III, Establishing the Inquiry, "Reporting Date"), it may be even more damaging if the date is only made known later. The integrity of the commissioner is put to the test as the public and media speculate about why the reporting date was imposed. For that reason, the commissioner and the government officials should together announce any new schedule and the reasons for it, if possible.

If the commissioner does not feel he can agree to a reporting date, he may be faced with government action which imposes the date on him. In most cases this can only be done by an order in council of the government to amend the order in council that originally established the inquiry by inserting a reporting date. Anything else, such as a ministerial statement or budget limitations, would succeed in building pressure for an early report but would not legally prevent the inquiry from continuing beyond that date and having its expenses paid. A government intent on limiting an inquiry can do so to the extent public opinion permits. A commissioner has a strong argument to make: the imposed time frame so truncates his work that the government is not getting value for the money it has spent and, at the extreme, he is, therefore, forced to resign as commissioner. Once his cards are played, however, the decision goes back to the government, which legally can decide the inquiry's future.

While in most circumstances an order in council is sufficient to terminate an inquiry, there may be exceptions. For example, British Columbia's legislation (B.C. Inquiry Act, section 14(1)) provides that a commissioner must "carry out and complete the Inquiry" entrusted to him and that he "shall report" to the government. There is an argument that, once the order in council creates an inquiry, the Act specifically provides that the officers are to inquire and report, and an order in council cannot override the provisions of the statute by denying the commissioner the opportunity to complete the investigation and report. The argument would be that only an Act of the Legislature could force the commissioner to withdraw from the inquiry or prevent him from reporting when the Inquiry

Act specifically provides that he do so. While this matter has not been judicially determined in Canada, in certain circumstances there may be a legal protection for an independent public inquiry that will enable it to carry out its statutory responsibilities once it is created (see Chapter III, Establishing the Inquiry).

Whether he voluntarily limits the inquiry or is forced to terminate activity, the commissioner should be sure it is clearly understood what termination means. Even if a closing date is specified, the commissioner should determine whether he is expected (and whether he is prepared) to file a report by that date, or whether he is merely required to discontinue his investigations by that date but can file a report soon thereafter. Is he prohibited from filing a report after the report date, or is it only a breach of a government directive, for which there is no penalty, apart from the possibility of judicial review to compel compliance? Even if he reports by that date, the commissioner normally must have a few weeks more to close out the inquiry.

The commissioner must also decide how he wishes to treat the termination for public purposes. If there is sufficient valuable data available, should the commissioner make an interim public report and, to that extent, comply with the government directive? Will the commissioner publicly condemn the government action or merely accept it? Are there extenuating circumstances, such as governmental interference, which should be brought to public attention?

In the final analysis any early termination is best handled by a mutual agreement which the commissioner can publicly defend. If he cannot, he may have no option but to follow directions and limit the scope of the inquiry or resign. The ultimate question here is how independent are our "independent" public inquiries in Canada?

VIII

Judicial Review of Inquiries

The review of alternative procedures in the preceding chapters has focussed largely on "practical" considerations — issues to be considered by the commissioner before deciding on the most satisfactory process for the job at hand. But another consideration has been present. This is the need to establish practices that are fair to the participants and that are within the powers and authority of the inquiry so they cannot be successfully challenged in judicial proceedings.

Apart from statutory procedures, review by the courts of orders and decisions of public inquiries is available only to a limited extent (*Guay v. Lafleur,* [1965] S.C.R. 12). The main basis for intervention by the courts is the time-honoured judicial power to "supervise" the decisions and procedures of "inferior tribunals," that is, all boards, tribunals, commissions, and public officials other than the ordinary courts.

I. REMEDIES

A number of remedies are available in judicial review proceedings, including the basic equitable remedies of declaration and injunction. In addition, special common law remedies known as "prerogative writs" were developed to permit the courts to exercise their supervisory powers effectively and efficiently over administrative bodies. More recently, judicial review remedies have been rationalized and simplified in a number of jurisdictions. For example, judicial review in British Columbia and Ontario is available under the provisions of special judicial review procedure acts. Similarly, the Federal Court of Canada exercises supervisory powers over federal boards and tribunals under the provisions of the Federal Court Act, R.S.C. 1970, c. 10 (2nd Supp.). Some inquiry acts contain special statutory rights of appeal or review for persons affected by the activities of public inquiries.

Only the Manitoba Evidence Act, R.S.M. 1970, c. E150, Part V, contains a "privative clause." Section 97(4) provides that no action lies in relation to anything done or sought to be done by a commissioner, or to restrain, interfere with, or otherwise direct or affect the conduct of a commissioner. Generally, clauses of this type have not been applied by the courts to exclude all judicial review. A tribunal will be protected from review only in relation to matters within its jurisdiction or at least concerning matters that are at the core of its specialized jurisdiction. It is likely that the same approach would be taken to judicial review of Manitoba inquiries. However, there is a serious uncertainty in the law related to privative clauses following the Supreme Court of Canada's suggestion in *Harelkin v. University of Regina*, [1979] 2 S.C.R. 561, 3 W.W.R. 676, that errors concerning procedural fairness are matters within jurisdiction that may be protected from judicial review by a privative clause.

Some inquiry acts also provide a procedure whereby a commissioner of inquiry may state a case for determination by the court. Usually questions referred to the court under these provisions are the result of issues that have been raised in the inquiry by participants. The inquiry concurs in the opinion that the issues raise major uncertainties for the inquiry, so that it is in the interest of the inquiry and all participants that they be resolved by the court. Sometimes, as in the Grange Inquiry into infant deaths at Toronto's Hospital for Sick Children, the issue is raised by the inquiry's proposing a certain interpretation of its terms of reference. (*Re Nelles and Grange* (1984), 9 D.L.R. (4th) 79 (Ont. C.A.); Ontario, Public Inquiries Act, R.S.O. 1980, c. 411, s. 6).

II. GROUNDS FOR JUDICIAL REVIEW

The basic grounds for judicial review include, first, that an inquiry exceeded its jurisdiction, that is, acted beyond its legal authority, either in the course of its process or in its report and recommendations. Constitutional challenges constitute a special jurisdictional ground, since the allegation is that an inquiry exceeds its jurisdiction if the law under which it purports to act is found to be beyond the constitutional powers of the level of government that established the commission.

Apart from lack or excess of jurisdiction, the courts also will review orders or decisions of inquiries to ensure that parties affected by those tribunals are accorded procedural fairness. Historically, these procedural fairness powers were exercised by the court mainly through the doctrine of "natural justice." Natural justice has three main elements: First, tribunal members must be unbiased, in the sense that a reasonable person viewing the proceeding must feel no apprehension of bias. Second, persons affected by a tribunal's process are entitled to an opportunity to be heard on matters affecting them. Third, and closely related to the right to be heard, affected persons must have reasonable notice of decisions or proceedings to permit adequate preparation.

Recently courts have granted remedies for denial of "fairness" in circumstances where the natural justice safeguards had been held not to apply. It is not yet clear whether fairness should be regarded as a doctrine separate from natural justice or merely as the fundamental principle, of which the natural justice safeguards constitute one aspect. These uncertainties concerning natural justice and procedural fairness are reviewed more fully below.

A number of judicial review grounds are based on matters related to the production and presentation of evidence, including discovery, privilege, and the "legal" rules of evidence. Although these practices were considered earlier in discussing alternative methods for receiving evidence (see Chapter V, The Inquiry Process: Procedural Rules), they can equally be regarded as aspects of the natural justice/fairness and jurisdiction grounds for judicial review.

A. Characterization

The principles of natural justice have been held by the courts to apply only to tribunals whose functions may be characterized as "judicial" or "quasi-judicial." This characterization is made by the court in light of the nature and process of the tribunal and, in particular, whether or not it makes "adjudications" that affect the rights of persons in a substantial manner. If its process and decisions are not of this character, then the principles of natural justice do not apply, and judicial review of the tribunal is not available on the basis that there was a denial of any of the elements of natural justice.

The functions of public inquiries have been characterized in a number of judicial decisions. These authorities suggest that commissions of inquiry generally speaking exercise administrative rather than quasi-judicial functions. Consequently, inquiries are not subject to the rules of natural justice in the strict sense. The reason is that inquiries are primarily investigatory in nature and function. Commissioners make recommendations that are neither binding nor conclusive. These recommendations do not in law have a direct effect on the rights of individuals. There is no final adjudication of disputes between parties involving findings of fact and application of established legal principles. The process and recommendations of commissions of inquiry are in the policy-making, rather than legal decision-making, realm.

The Supreme Court of Canada has not definitively stated that the principles of natural justice do not apply to commissions of inquiry. However, in *Guay v. Lafleur*, [1965] S.C.R. 12, the court held that an investigator appointed under the Income Tax Act exercises a purely administrative function. The investigation merely results in a recommendation to the deputy minister and makes no final determinations concerning the legal rights of the persons under investigation. In *Bisaillon v. Keable*, [1983] 2 S.C.R. 60, 51 N.R. 81, the Supreme Court agreed with the Quebec court of appeal's conclusion that the natural justice bias rules do not apply to a commission of inquiry because it makes no decision but merely inquires and reports. However, the court did not provide a thorough analysis of the legal character of commissions.

Several trial and appeal level decisions do deal with public inquiries. The trial division of the federal court has held that commissions of inquiry into certain specific matters concerning the federal Department of Manpower and Immigration (*B. v. Department of Manpower and Immigration*, [1975] F.C. 602, 60 D.L.R. (3d) 339 (T.D.), and into RCMP wrongdoing (*Re Copeland and McDonald*, [1978] 2 F.C. 815, 88 D.L.R. (3d) 724 (T.D.)), exercise neither judicial nor quasi-judicial functions. In the case of the McDonald Commission's RCMP inquiry, the result was that the principles of natural justice or procedural fairness did not apply to the commission and, consequently, a claim of apprehended bias could not be raised by an inquiry participant.

However, procedural fairness requirements have been imposed on commissions of inquiry. This was done in circumstances in which the inquiry was aimed at investigation of allegations against individuals that could result in criminal proceedings (*Saulnier v. Quebec Police Commission*, [1976] 1 S.C.R. 572, 57 D.L.R. (3d) 545)) as opposed to inquiries directed toward gathering information for the purpose of making recommendations to government concerning matters of policy or statute reform. Thus, in one case (*Re Ontario Crime Commission; Ex parte Feeley and McDermott*, [1962] O.R. 872 (C.A.)) an affected individual was permitted to examine and cross-examine witnesses and required to be furnished with a transcript of previous evidence that had been heard by the commission *in camera*. A second case (*Re Public Inquiries Act and Shulman*, [1967] 2 O.R. 375 (C.A.)) resulted in a senior government official under investigation being accorded the privilege of having his evidence on allegations made against him elicited by his own counsel rather than commission counsel. The court held that he should also be subject to cross-examination by commission counsel and by any other person affected by his evidence.

In a judicial review application arising out of an Alberta public inquiry into police wrongdoing, the Alberta supreme court held that, generally, the court does not have supervisory jurisdiction over the proceedings of public inquiries (*Anderson v. Laycraft, Commissioner of Inquiry* (1978), 5 Alta. L.R. (2d) 155, 88 D.L.R. (3d) 706 (S.C.) (*sub nom. Re Anderson and Royal Commr. into Royal American Shows Inc.*)). Inquires are not decision-making bodies but are merely authorized to investigate and report on certain matters. However, Mr. Justice Miller stated that there are four exceptional situations in which judicial review may be available. These are:

1. Where the report of the commission of inquiry, although in the form of recommendations that need not be accepted by and need not form the basis of a decision to be made by a higher body, directly affects the rights of any person;
2. Where the commission in the exercise of its auxiliary powers, such as citing for contempt or imposing any penalty, wrongfully impairs the liberty or goods of a person;
3. Where the area of investigation is not a matter within the jurisdiction of the provincial legislature, and;
4. Where the commissioner seeks to inquire into matters outside his terms of reference.

The Supreme Court of Canada has taken a stronger position. In *A.G. Quebec v. A.G. Canada*, [1979] 1 S.C.R. 218, 24 N.R. 1 (*sub nom. Keable v. A.G. Canada*), with reference to a commission under the Quebec Public Inquiry Commission Act, Pigeon J. said at 36 N.R.:

> The commissioner does not enjoy the status of a superior court, he has only a limited jurisdiction. His orders are not like those of a superior court which must be obeyed without question; his orders may be questioned on jurisdictional grounds because his authority is limited. Therefore his decisions as to the proper scope of his inquiry, the extent of the questioning permissible, and the documents that may be required to be produced, are all open to attack.

. . . and further at 37 N.R.:

> Because a commissioner has only limited authority he enjoys no inherent jurisdiction, unlike superior courts which have such jurisdiction in all matters of federal or provincial law unless specifically excluded.

The Privy Council has held that in a New Zealand inquiry by a single judge, the commissioner, in drawing certain conclusions and making certain remarks in his report, failed to adhere to those rules of natural justice that are appropriate to inquiries (*Mahon v. Air New Zealand*, [1984] A.C. 808 (P.C.)). The commissioner said, in effect, that certain clearly identifiable persons were party to a plan of deception and conspiracy to commit perjury and complained that he had to "listen to an orchestrated litany of lies."

Two relevant procedural fairness rules taken from *R. v. Deputy Industrial Injuries Commissioner; Ex parte Moore,* [1965] 1 Q.B. 456, 488, 490 (C.A.), were adopted by the Privy Council. These are, first, that a commissioner, in making a finding, must base the decision on evidence that has some probative value, that is, on some material that tends logically to show the existence of facts consistent with the finding. Any reasoning shown in support of the finding must not be logically self-contradictory. Secondly, a commissioner must listen fairly to any relevant evidence or logical arguments contrary to the finding by persons, represented at the inquiry, whose interests (including career or reputation) may be adversely affected. Similar rights are available to persons who would have wished to respond in this way had they been aware of the risk of the finding being made by the commissioner.

B. Summary

Generally, then, commissions of inquiry have been characterized as administrative bodies to which the procedural safeguards embodied in the natural justice principles do not apply. However, to the extent that inquiries directly investigate the activities of individuals, certain procedural safeguards are available. This is so because inquiry functions, in circumstances where individual rights are directly affected, can be characterized as quasi-judicial and not merely administrative.

C. Fairness

Even if it is assumed that public inquiry functions will be characterized as administrative, the cases suggest that the courts will enforce certain minimum procedural requirements. The basis for the court's actions may be application of the emergent doctrine of procedural "fairness." Fairness imports certain fundamental procedural safeguards even in circumstances in which the tribunal's function would be characterized as purely administrative and, therefore, not subject to the principles of natural justice.

The substantive content of the doctrine of fairness is not yet clear. However, it appears that, while the requirements may be less rigorous than the rules of natural justice, nevertheless, natural justice will serve as a guideline. Therefore, understanding of natural justice principles is essential, even on the assumption that natural justice does not, strictly speaking, apply to commissions of inquiry.

One case (*Re Copeland and McDonald,* [1978] 2 F.C. 815; 88

D.L.R. (3d) 724 (T.D.), suggests that even fairness may not be applicable to commissions of inquiry. However, it is unlikely that this trial-level opinion will be upheld by higher courts. (One judge held that fairness applied to a commission of inquiry in *Fraternité Inter-Provinciale des Ouvriers en Électricité v. Office de la Construction du Québec* (1983), 148 D.L.R. (3d) 626 (Que. C.A.).) In any event, even without the doctrine of fairness, there is still some minimum procedural standard that is likely to be applied to the proceedings of commissions of inquiry. In these circumstances the natural justice principles will serve as a guideline, or at least a starting point in determining specific procedural requirements.

D. Natural Justice

Natural justice principles are judge-made and operate in the absence of statutory procedural safeguards. They may, however, be supplemented, supplanted, or even excluded (subject to the Canadian Charter of Rights and Freedoms. See Chapter II, Constitutional Position of Public Inquiries, "Canadian Charter of Rights and Freedoms") by statute. Basically, there are three natural justice "rules":

1. The tribunal or official shall be unbiased;
2. Affected persons shall receive reasonable notice of proceedings; and
3. Affected persons shall be given a fair opportunity to be heard.

1. Bias

The principle here is not concerned with bias in fact. Rather, the court considers whether a reasonable person, who knows something of the circumstances, will be suspicious or apprehensive that the tribunal or official is biased. The standard is objective rather than subjective. Thus, a ruling that particular circumstances suggest a "reasonable apprehension" or a "real likelihood" of bias does not impute an actual bias to the official in question. The distinction may be subtle, but it is important that the essential integrity and honesty of an official is not necessarily impugned by allegations or findings of legal bias.

A somewhat clearer situation is one in which a hearing officer has an actual pecuniary interest in the subject matter of a proceeding. Such an interest must be reasonably direct.

Employment by or participation in the affairs of parties in a proceeding may raise a reasonable apprehension of bias. For example, the Supreme Court of Canada ruled that a member of the National Energy Board was disqualified from hearing a pipeline certificate application by a consortium in which he was involved before his appointment to the board (*Committee for Justice and Liberty v. National Energy Board*, [1978] 1 S.C.R. 369; 68 D.L.R. (3d) 716).

There are no examples of commissioners being disqualified on bias grounds. In *Re Copeland and McDonald*, [1978] 2 F.C. 815; 88 D.L.R. (3d) 724, Mr. Justice David C. McDonald and two other commissioners, appointed under Part I of the federal Inquiries Act to conduct an investigation into alleged RCMP wrongdoing, were challenged on the ground of bias. The federal court action was brought by participants in the inquiry.

It was alleged that all three commissioners were political partisans of the Liberal Party of Canada, which formed the government that had made the appointments. Mr. Justice McDonald had been president of the Liberal Association of Alberta and had accompanied the Prime Minister on a trip to the Orient following his appointment as commissioner. The other two commissioners were alleged to have close business and personal relationships with federal Cabinet ministers, including the Solicitor General who is responsible for the RCMP. An apprehension of bias arose, it was argued, because the commission was charged with determining whether any Cabinet ministers were involved in or had knowledge of any illegal RCMP activities.

The federal court decided the case on the preliminary characterization issue. Mr. Justice Cattanach reasoned that, for a reasonable apprehension of bias to exist, there must be an issue to be decided by the commission. Here he concluded there was no such dispute between parties to be decided by the commission. Consequently, the commission's function was neither judicial nor quasi-judicial but purely administrative. Thus, the natural justice rules, including the bias principles, did not apply.

This does not mean that the bias principles are not relevant to public inquiries. It is significant that the parties alleging bias were not themselves the subject of investigation. Also, it may be significant that the *Copeland* case was decided before the Supreme Court's decision in the *Nicholson v. Haldimand–Norfolk Police Commissioners Board*, [1979] 1 S.C.R. 311, 88 D.L.R. (3d) 671, which established a duty of procedural fairness even where a purely administrative function is carried out. But it is now clear, as the Supreme Court of Canada confirmed in *Bisaillon v. Keable*, [1983] 2 S.C.R. 60, 51 N.R. 81 at 107–108, that the bias principles do not apply, at least with the same rigour, to inquiries which, unlike courts or tribunals, make no decisions, but merely inquire and report.

2. *Notice*

Any person affected by tribunal proceedings must be given reasonable notice of commencement of those proceedings so that there is a proper opportunity to prepare. The appropriate form of notice is a question of fact in each case. Usually newspaper or other media advertisement by public inquiries will suffice. But there may be cases in which affected parties are so well known to hearing officers that personal service will be required.

Notice must be given of matters or issues to be raised that may affect a party's rights or interest. Thus, it was held that a commission established to investigate the dealings of an individual with a certain utility failed to notify him adequately that it was also considering other charges against him (*Landreville v. R. No. 2*, [1977] 2 F.C. 726; 25 D.L.R. (3d) 380 (T.D.)). It was not until release of the commission's report that included a finding that he was "in gross contempt of other tribunals", that the individual was aware of this charge. A declaration was issued that the commissioner had failed to follow the federal Inquiries Act, and particularly s. 13, which states that:

> 13. No report shall be made against any person until reasonable notice has been given to him of the charge of misconduct alleged against him and he has been allowed full opportunity to be heard in person or by counsel.

Other authoritative cases suggest that the result would have been the same even in the absence of this statutory provision. (See *Fraternité Inter-Provinciale des Ouvriers en Électricité v. Office de la Construction du Québec.*)

3. *Fair Opportunity to Be Heard*

(a) Disclosure

In a sense, the requirements for notice are merely one element of the more general principle that all affected parties be given a fair opportunity to be heard by the inquiry. Any affected person is entitled to know enough about the matters in issue before the inquiry to be able to decide whether to participate and, if so, on what matters to make representations. This disclosure principle permits parties to prepare the most effective interventions possible. Several inquiry acts specifically provide for reasonable notice to "persons charged" with misconduct, and an opportunity to be heard before the making of any report (Canada, Inquiries Act, s. 13; P.E.I., Public Inquiries Act, s. 7).

But this does not mean that the inquiry is obliged to disclose any and all information that it has initially or that it acquires through commissioners, inquiry counsel, and staff in the course of the inquiry. Disclosure does not necessarily require detailed information; it requires notice, perhaps in a summary form, of matters to which the inquiry will direct its attention. In practice, this notice is provided by the formal terms of reference. Where these are broad or ambiguous, however, clarification may be required, particularly where, as in the *Landreville* case, *supra,* matters of individual rights are involved. There may even be circumstances in which an inquiry will be justified in holding *in camera* hearings, though this may depend on the existence of specific statutory powers *(Fraternité Inter-Provinciale des Ouvriers en Électricité v. Office de la Construction du Québec, supra).*

(b) Hearing

The inquiry is obliged to give all affected parties a reasonable opportunity to make representations. This "opportunity to be heard" does not necessarily mean an opportunity to be heard orally. Certainly, as a general rule, no person has an absolute right to appear before an inquiry except persons summoned to the inquiry *(Re Ontario Crime Commission,* [1962] O.R. 872, 888 (C.A.)). Some inquiry acts specify an opportunity to be heard in person or by counsel for persons "charged" with misconduct before any report is made against them (Canada, Inquiries Act, s. 13; P.E.I. Public Inquiries Act, s. 7). It has been held in the context of an investigative inquiry, that persons or organizations suspected of wrongdoing are entitled to be present and represented by counsel *(Fraternité Inter-Provinciale des Ouvriers en Électricité v. Office de la Construction du Québec).*

However, in the absence of statutory requirements, written representations may, in many circumstances, be properly considered a fair and reasonable means to present evidence. Everything depends on the circumstances, and particularly on whether the matters in issue are such that it can fairly be said that oral representations are not essential.

Other key elements of this right to be heard include a reasonable opportunity to consider and prepare and, generally, equal treatment of parties. Thus, parties cannot fairly be expected to file or present evidence within a few days of disclosure of extensive and complex technical or financial proposals or reports. Time limits must be applied equally and, in the absence of statutory distinctions (*e.g.,* the specifications in inquiry acts for persons "charged" with misconduct), similar opportunities to be heard must be accorded all parties. An inquiry may not, for example, be able to establish a firm rule that some parties will be heard orally, while others will be permitted only to file written representations. Nor, particularly where individual rights are involved, can it permit some parties but not others to file information in confidence.

Generally, there is an equal treatment principle that must be observed. Unfairness is produced if, in any material sense, the inquiry distinguishes in a definitive way between first class and second class participants, except in the case of a narrow investigative inquiry, where the alleged wrong-doing of specific persons is the main object of the inquiry. In this latter case, even apart from statute, the procedural fairness rights of persons directly affected stand on a higher footing than those of other parties *(Re Ontario Crime Commission, supra)*. Also, this equal treatment principle should not be taken to deny inquiries the authority to recognize major participants on the basis of commitment to participate regularly in the inquiry process. This is a matter of choice for participants. But this classification cannot be inflexible so that, for example, changed circumstances or new information should permit a participant to obtain major participant status at a later stage or for certain phases only.

After a hearing has been completed, parties as a general rule should not be permitted to file new or additional information unless other parties are notified and given an opportunity to respond. An inquiry also errs if it declines to accept representations relevant to matters within its terms of reference *(Re Restrictive Trade Practices Commission,* [1983] 1 F.C. 520 (T.D.), rev'd on other grounds, [1983] 2 F.C. 222 (C.A.); *Re Bortolotti and Ministry of Housing* (1977), 15 O.R. (2d) 617, 76 D.L.R. (3d) 408 (C.A.)). This may require that it permit representations from parties to counter statements of policy filed by government officials or agencies *(Re Township of Innisfil v. Township of Vespra,* [1981] 2 S.C.R. 145). Where the circumstances suggest that interrogation is the only fair method of stating views, then the inquiry may be obliged to permit questioning or cross-examination of presenters *(Re Public Inquiries Act and Shulman,* [1967] 2 O.R. 375 (C.A.); *Fraternité Inter-Provinciale des Ouvriers en Électricité v. Office de la Construction du Québec).*

(c) Questioning or Cross-Examination

Section 5(1) of the Ontario Public Inquiries Act gives a right to cross-examine to persons with a "direct and substantial interest" in the subject matter of the inquiry. Generally, however, the subject of procedural fairness is the appropriate context for consideration of whether inquiries are required, as a matter of law, to permit cross-examination. First, cross-examination is merely the formal court-room term for questioning of witnesses by parties opposed in interest. The issue is not whether cross-examination is a legal requirement. The common law answer to this question is no (*Re Ontario Crime Commission,* [1962] O.R. 872, 888 (C.A.)). Rather, the question is whether a fair opportunity to be heard demands an opportunity to question other parties and their witnesses.

The Supreme Court of Canada has taken this a step further, holding in *Township of Innisfil v. Township of Vespra,* [1981] 2 S.C.R. 145, that, where a hearing is required by statute, the hearing tribunal must "follow the traditional adversarial road." This means that affected parties are entitled to cross-examine, unless there is a clear statutory curtailment or abridgment of the right to meet the case of parties adverse in interest. The inquiry acts provide no general rights to be heard. But the *Innisfil* case suggests that the courts now consider cross-examination to be an important safeguard in hearings. Thus, denial of cross-examination or questioning by an inquiry where rights of parties are directly affected, or perhaps generally where an inquiry is conducted in a formal, court-like way, may be taken to produce unfairness in law. (*Fraternité Inter-Provinciale des Ouvriers en Électricité v. Office de la Construction du Québec*).

In the case of investigative inquiries directed to the actions of certain individuals or bodies, as opposed to inquiries with more general information-gathering and reporting duties, it has been held in a number of cases that affected persons have a right to cross-examine and to be represented by counsel. Several of the inquiry acts specifically confirm the right to counsel (P.E.I., Public Inquiries Act, s. 6; Canada, Inquiries Act, s. 12; Yukon, Public Inquiries Act s. 7).

This cross-examination must not be limited, and may extend to "all matters relevant to eliciting the truth or accuracy of the allegations or statements made" (*Re Public Inquiries Act and Shulman, supra,* at 378 O.R.). The Ontario court of appeal has clearly stated that the absence in an inquiry Act of an express right to cross-examine by persons affected is not significant, particularly where a broad scope for judicial review can be established (*Re Ontario Crime Commission,* [1962] O.R. 872 at 894 (C.A.)).

E. Evidence

Whether or not any particular inquiries Act so provides, inquiries are not bound by the legal rules of evidence used in the courts (*Re Children's Aid Society of the County of New York,* [1934] O.W.N. 418, 420 (C.A.)). This means, for example, that hearsay — one person reporting statements of another person in order to establish the truth of the other's statements — may be received and considered. Similarly, there will be no formal exclusion of "opinion evidence", that is, conclusions on the ultimate issues before the inquiry.

In courts or formal administrative tribunals, this opinion evidence prohibition on second guessing the tribunal's conclusions is handled through the device of "expert" witnesses. "Experts" are formally qualified by the tribunal to speak to matters within their expertise, and they may draw considered conclusions. The technique used is to pose hypothetical questions to the expert witness who then gives conclusions in the form of a professional opinion.

Strictly speaking, neither the opinion evidence exclusion nor the expert witness exception applies to inquiries as a matter of law. Thus, opinions of lay persons will not be excluded. However, it is natural that considerable weight is likely to be attached to the opinions of qualified, experienced professionals on matters within their particular areas of expertise. Also, legally trained commissioners are familiar with the opinion evidence rules and are likely to be influenced by them even though they may understand and acknowledge that they are not binding. It is important, however, that evidence of lay "experts" has even been admitted by courts in certain cases, such as air or water pollution prosecutions (*R. v. Cherokee Disposals and Const. Ltd.*, [1973] 3 O.R. 599, 13 C.C.C. (2d) 87 (Prov. Ct.).

On the other hand, if evidence is excluded which, according to the rules of evidence, is reasonably relevant and should have been admitted, this may be a basis for characterizing the action as unfair or "contrary to law." The inquiry would then be said to have declined or exceeded its jurisdiction (*Re Bortolotti and Ministry of Housing* (1977), 15 O.R. (2d) 617, 76 D.L.R. (3d) 408 (C.A.)).

Similarly, if evidence is relied upon that has no cogency — *i.e.*, that is so tenuous that no reasonable person would rely on it — this may produce unfairness. Alternatively, it may be concluded that the inquiry exceeded its proper legal authority, namely, to obey the law and base its conclusions on cogent evidence. The weight of evidence is strictly a matter for the commissioner in forming his conclusions. The courts will not attempt to second guess the inquiry. A majority of the commissioners has the authority to bind the inquiry on questions of admissibility of evidence. (*Re Bortolotti and Ministry of Housing, supra*, at 421 D.L.R.)

1. *Written Evidence*

Inquiries will often stipulate that evidence must be filed in writing within a specified time before oral presentation (see Chapter V, The Inquiry Process: Procedural Rules). There are no fairness problems with this procedure, so long as it is applied equally to the parties and so long as time limits are reasonable and do not inhibit adequate preparation.

2. Order of Presentation

Problems are often associated with the order of presenting evidence that is established by the inquiry. In project-oriented inquiries, there is no unfairness in permitting the proponent to go first. However, a sense of unfairness may develop among parties if the proponent is permitted to introduce all of its evidence initially in great detail and over a long period of time. Unless the proponent is permitted to be essentially the sole participant for unreasonably long periods of time, however, it is unlikely that there is any legally recognizable unfairness so long as all parties are ultimately permitted adequate opportunity to respond.

As a practical matter, however, since the inquiry is a public process as well as a legal institution, these concerns must be recognized. Often the problem is handled by dividing the inquiry into phases according to issues or subjects and by permitting all parties to make opening statements (see Chapter IV, The Inquiry Structure).

Arguably, fairness requires that parties similar in interest should be grouped in the inquiry's order of presentation to at least make "friendly cross-examination" under the appearance of adverse interests more difficult. However, in a case arising out of National Energy Board proceedings, the court did not consider that failure to group parties apparently (but not obviously) similar in interest, produced grave unfairness (*Union Gas Ltd. v. Trans Canada Pipelines Ltd.*, [1974] 2 F.C. 313 (T.D.).

3. Discovery

Procedures to compel disclosure of relevant information controlled by other parties are merely a means of clarifying how the inquiry will exercise its statutory power to require disclosure by parties. Inquiries, as opposed to courts, have no such common law power: *A.G. Quebec v. A.G. Canada*, [1979] 1 S.C.R. 218, 24 N.R. 1 at 31 *(Sub nom. Keable v. A.G. Canada)*. Inquiry acts give commissioners the procedural powers of superior courts or, more specifically, the power to summon witnesses before the inquiry and to require them to produce such documents or things as the commissioner considers necessary for the full investigation of the issues before him. Included are items in the possession or under the control or power of any party. Thus, documents and reports prepared by and in the possession of consultants or controlled corporations would be subject to discovery. Some of the inquiry acts spell out the possession or control criteria (*e.g.*, federal Inquiries Act, s. 8), but, even where this is not the case, it is likely that these traditional tests, developed in the courts, would be applied.

This power of the commissioner to compel production is also the basis for interrogatory procedures. Failure to respond or to respond adequately to such interrogatories will result in the request being brought before the inquiry for a specific ruling that would compel a response.

A ruling by the inquiry that a party is not required to produce particular documents or to respond to particular interrogatories may be challenged in the courts in judicial review proceedings. The basis will be that denial of such information results in inadequate notice or opportunity to be heard contrary to the procedural fairness principles.

4. Privilege

Another legal concept that is often troublesome in the inquiry context is the notion of "privilege." The idea is that information communicated in certain circumstances and relationships should not be subject to disclosure. Where, for example, the relationship is priest–penitent or lawyer–client, the public interest in preserving the integrity of these relationships is said to outweigh the public interest in compelling disclosure.

Solicitor–client privilege is the most common problem. The privilege is limited to communications directed to or in anticipation of litigation. It appears that, in the case of information prepared for several purposes, legal professional privilege will be accorded only if the dominant purpose in preparation was submission to a legal advisor for advice and litigation use (*Waugh v. British Railways Board*, [1979] 2 All E.R. 1169 (H.L.)).

In the case of inquiries the question, in the absence of clear legislation (*e.g.*, Ontario, Public Inquiries Act, s. 11; see *Re Bortolotti and Ministry of Housing* (1977), 15 O.R. (2d) 617, 76 D.L.R. (3d) 408 (Ont. C.A.)), is whether the inquiry process should be characterized as "litigation." There are no cases on whether solicitor–client privilege is available in administrative tribunals or inquiry proceedings of a quasi-adversarial character. The question is open but, in the case of information-gathering inquiries, it is difficult to describe the proceedings as litigation in the traditional adversarial sense, even though elements of adversarial procedure such as cross-examination may be used.

It has been suggested that the rules concerning legal privileges apply to tribunals which by statute are given the powers, rights, and privileges of a superior court for the purpose of obtaining information (I. Blue, "The Protection of Confidential Information in Tribunal Proceedings," Law Society of Upper Canada C.L.E.,

Emerging Issues in Administrative Law and Administrative Law Practice (September, 1983), 42). However, in the case of inquiries this information-acquisition process is not directed toward a decision or adjudication. One consequence is that the principles of admissibility of evidence applicable to courts of law do not necessarily apply to the proceedings of commissions of inquiry (*Re Commission of Inquiry Concerning Certain Activities of the RCMP* (1979), 94 D.L.R. (3d) 365, 376 (commission ruling *per* D.C. McDonald J.). This suggests the inappropriateness of the privilege doctrine for inquiries.

Very likely a court would conclude that there is no solicitor-client privilege in inquiry proceedings except where the proceeding is narrowly investigative, and individual rights are in issue. This view tends to be confirmed by cases such as *Di Iorio v. Montreal Jail Warden*, [1978] 1 S.C.R. 152, 8 N.R. 361, at 403, which have held that the self-incrimination protections under the Evidence Act are available to witnesses before commissions of inquiry.

Also relevant is the privilege against self-incrimination, which prevents a person being compelled to give self-incriminating evidence. In *R.L. Crain Inc. v. Couture* (1983), 6 D.L.R. (4th) 478, 30 Sask. R. 197 (Q.B.), it was held that a provision of the Combines Investigation Act which empowered the Restrictive Trade Practices Commission to summon persons suspected of unlawful activity to testify at an inquiry was contrary to the Canadian Charter of Rights and Freedoms. Specifically, it was held to infringe the s. 7 right to "security of the person", which the court found included the right not to be required to give self-incriminating evidence (see Chapter II, Constitutional Position of Public Inquiries, "Canadian Charter of Rights and Freedoms"). This conclusion differs from that of Dickson J. (now Chief Justice) in *Di Iorio v. Montreal Jail Warden, supra*, who held that though s. 5 of the Canada Evidence Act (and provisions of the inquiry acts) may compel a person to assist in the investigation of his own criminal activity. These provisions are nevertheless valid. However, the *Di Iorio* case was decided prior to the coming into force of the Charter.

Section 13 of the Charter establishes a right in witnesses not to have their own evidence used to incriminate them in subsequent proceedings. This resembles s. 5(2) of the Canada Evidence Act, but it is a positive right only and includes no compulsion to testify in the first instance.

(a) Public Interest Privilege

The law also recognizes another form of privilege, often termed "public interest" privilege or immunity. In certain circumstances the harm to the public interest caused by disclosure of particular facts or material is said to outweigh the benefits available from making such information public. Application of this doctrine usually involves the weighing of two competing public interests. Most commonly this kind of privilege problem arises in relation to matters of high government policy. This is the doctrine known as "Crown privilege."

Until recently this was an absolute privilege whereby specified government information would be excluded from judicial or tribunal proceedings upon the responsible Minister's filing a certificate in the court. The court would decline to review the basis for the privilege claim.

However, more recent English and Canadian cases, as well as statutory amendments, have changed the law of Crown privilege. Now ministerial certificates claiming privilege are not necessarily accepted without question. If it is reasonably probable that the information is relevant to the proceeding and if review of the ministerial certificate suggests a doubt that the balance of the public interest is against disclosure, then the court will review the Crown's claim. It will consider whether the balance of public interest lies in preventing frustration of the judicial or inquiry process, or in preventing harm to national or provincial interests likely to result from disclosure. However, the court will not necessarily review the material in question. It has been held to be a matter of judicial discretion. (*Re Goguen and Albert and Gibson* (1984), 7 D.L.R. (4th) 144 (Fed. C.A.): objection to disclosure by government official under ss. 36.1 and 36.2 of the Canada Evidence Act, R.S.C. 1970, c. E-102, enacted 1980-81-82-83, c. 111, s. 4).

These common law principles have been largely codified in sections 36.1 and 36.2 of the Canada Evidence Act. Where objection to disclosure is based on grounds that disclosure would be injurious to international relations or national defence or security, the objection will be heard in closed court and, at the request of the person objecting to disclosure, will be heard in Ottawa. The predecessor of this provision (s. 41 of the Federal Court Act) was held applicable to all "courts," federal or provincial, including inquiry commissioners, who are given the powers of a court for the purpose of production of documents (*A.G. Quebec v. A.G. Canada,* [1979] 1 S.C.R. 218, 24 N.R. 1 *(sub nom. Keable v. A.G. Canada))*.

Special disclosure rules for Cabinet "confidences" were enacted by parliament in 1983. Section 36.3 of the Canada Evidence Act establishes an absolute privilege in relation to confidences of the Privy Council. Where a Minister or the clerk of the Privy Council objects by filing a certificate in writing to disclosure of such confidences before any body, including a public inquiry, with power to compel production of information, disclosure must be refused without examination or hearing of the information. Cabinet "confidence" is defined to include Cabinet memoranda (for presentation of proposals or recommendations to Cabinet), discussion papers, minutes, or records of Cabinet decisions, records of communications between ministers, briefing materials, and draft legislation. There is a general twenty-year confidentiality time limit and a special limit for discussion papers of four years following decisions.

A common law doctrine known as Cabinet solidarity is also relevant to Cabinet information. Cabinet solidarity protects information likely to disclose the views of individual ministers in relation to policy decisions reached by Cabinet. However, the courts have ruled that this confidentiality, designed to maintain the joint responsibility of Cabinet, may lapse in relation to particular information after a reasonable period of time (*A.G. v. Jonathan Cape Ltd.*, [1976] Q.B. 752)).

Thus, apart from Cabinet confidences, there must be some reasonably compelling basis for non-disclosure, such as national security or federal–provincial relations effects, before non-disclosure will be permitted. The present law is likely to make sensitive government officials wary of claiming Crown privilege in all but the most compelling circumstances. Certainly no blanket privilege claims will be permitted. Given the relatively precise definition of Cabinet confidences, it will be difficult to bring most information generated by government departments or agencies within this exception.

The RCMP Commission took the position that the legal rules of evidence, including the privilege doctrines, do not strictly apply to commissions of inquiry. However, McDonald J. stated that the commission was not prepared to apply to its proceedings a rule more absolute than the flexible approach taken to the Cabinet solidarity rule in the *Jonathan Cape* case. He suggested that, when faced with an objection to public disclosure, the commission must consider a number of factors including:

1. The role of commissions of inquiry;
2. The rationale of any privilege asserted in relation to government documents;
3. The public interest in preventing government malfeasance;
4. The status of the possessor or originator of the information;
5. The interest of persons who may potentially be "charged" by a commission in hearing the testimony of superiors for whom they acted.

It was also noted that disclosure of particular documents may result in a breach of the federal Official Secrets Act, R.S.C. 1970, c.0-3. This would depend on the inquiry's authority, based on its empowering statute and terms of reference, to disclose such information to the public. There is also a question of whether the disclosure is not "in the interest of the state" according to section 4(1)(a) of the Act. McDonald J. suggested, in effect, that the interest in maintaining public confidence in the proceedings of an inquiry into the conduct of high officials may be an important factor in this determination (*supra*, 382).

There is also a rule concerning secrecy of the identity of police informers that is closely related to Crown privilege. This rule has been held applicable to commissions of inquiry (*Bisaillon v. Keable*, [1983] 2 S.C.R. 60; 51 N.R. 81; *Solicitor General of Canada v. Royal Commission of Inquiry into the Confidentiality of Health Records in Ontario*, [1981] 2 S.C.R. 494; *Fraternité Inter-Provinciale des Ouvriers en Électricité v. Office de la Construction du Québec* (1983), 148 D.L.R. (3d) 626 (Que. C.A.)). In *Bisaillon v. Keable* the court pointed out that the informers rule is not to be confused with Crown privilege. Although the two doctrines have several points in common, the public interest bases are different. In the case of Crown privilege, the public interest rationale is national security or effective conduct of government, whereas police informer secrecy is based on the public interest in maintaining police efficiency and effective enforcement of the criminal law (at 125 N.R.).

(b) Commercial Information

Another form of public interest privilege or immunity is nongovernmental information that may nevertheless have substantial public interest significance. An example may be certain forms of private industrial or commercial information, disclosure of which would arguably cause public economic harm that would outweigh the benefits of disclosure. The greater public benefit from nondisclosure, however, must be clearly shown. If there is a doubt, disclosure will be ordered (*D. v. National Society for the Prevention of Cruelty to Children*, [1977] 2 W.L.R. 201, 232 (H.L.); *Norwich Pharmacal Co. v. Commissioners of Customs and Excise*, [1973] 2 All E.R. 943 (H.L.)).

Trade secrets are sometimes accorded a separate privilege, but the test and evaluation scale is similar to that for public interest privilege generally (*Forestral Automation Ltd. v. R.M.S. Industrial Controls Inc.* (1977), 4 B.C.L.R. 219, 231 (S.C.)).

It is clear that the public interest in open and complete disclosure, which is the essence of the inquiry process, will be given considerable weight by the courts. Little weight has been given to factors such as future loss of candour by the class of persons required to disclose information (*Blais v. Andras*, [1973] F.C. 182, 30 D.L.R. (3d) 287 at 292 (C.A.).

Although the courts have often stated that there is no general privilege protecting communications given in confidence, nevertheless there are conditions under which a privilege against disclosure of communications can be established. Four basic conditions have been held necessary to establish a privilege against disclosure of confidential communications:

1. The communication must be made in a confidence that it will not be disclosed;
2. This element of confidentiality must be essential to the full and satisfactory maintenance of the relationship between the parties;
3. The relationship must be one that the community considers ought to be fostered;
4. The injury to the relationship that would result from disclosure must be greater than the benefit from the correct conclusion of the proceedings (*Slavutych v. Baker*, [1976] 1 S.C.R. 254, 260 citing *Wigmore on Evidence* 3rd ed., McNaughton Revision, 1961, para. 2285).

(c) Access to Information

A further aid to production of government information is the federal Access to Information Act (S.C. 1980-81-82-83, c. 111, Sched. I). Any Canadian citizen or permanent resident has a right, upon request, to be given access to information under the control of government institutions. This right is subject to a range of exemptions, including information received in confidence from another governmental body; information that may reasonably be considered injurious to Canadian international relations, federal-provincial relations, national defence, or control of subversive or hostile activities; information related to law enforcement; trade secrets; certain scientific information, personal information, and third party information; and certain information concerning the operations of government (ss. 13-24).

Commissions of inquiry appear not to be subject to the public access to information process established by the Act. The public right of access to information extends only to the "government institutions," including departments, ministries, and agencies listed in a schedule to the Act. Commissions of inquiry are not included, though the federal Cabinet is empowered to amend the schedule by adding "any department, ministry of state, body or office of the government of Canada" (s. 77(2)). Particular inquiries, as bodies established by the government of Canada, could thus be made subject to the access to information requirements.

(d) Subpoena

The legal power to issue subpoenas requiring the attendance of witnesses and the production of evidence before the inquiry is conferred on commissioners by the inquiry acts. Several acts refer specifically to subpoenas. However, there is no magic in the term subpoena, and the remaining acts clearly empower the commissioners to compel witnesses to attend and give evidence.

A party may request the commissioner to issue a subpoena to any person. The commissioner has a discretion on such requests. Under the rules of most courts, the issue of subpoenas is a purely administrative act (*Restrictive Trade Practices Commission v. Director of Investigation and Research*, [1983] 2 F.C. 222, 230 (C.A.)). As the federal court of appeal has pointed out, however, this is because the courts have adopted rules providing for the issue of subpoenas on demand by officers of the court, including lawyers. Unless inquiries adopt similar rules, the commissioners retain a discretion.

However, commissions have a duty not to use this discretionary subpoena power in an unfair and oppressive manner (*Restrictive Trade Practices Commission v. Director of Investigation and Research, supra*). If the evidence that the subpoena target is likely to present is relevant to the tasks of the inquiry, refusal to issue the subpoena may, notwithstanding the *Restrictive Trade Practices Commission* case, be the subject of successful judicial review. This could be on the basis that failure to place the evidence in question on record, or lack of opportunity to question the proposed witness, will result in a denial of procedural fairness to some party.

Another judicial review ground may be that failure to issue subpoenas could result in total exclusion of evidence on certain relevant matters. This amounts to the inquiry's declining to examine subjects that, under its terms of reference, it has a duty to consider and, consequently, a declining of its jurisdiction. See *Re Restrictive Trade Practices Commission*, [1983] 1 F.C. 520, 524 (T.D.) rev'd on other grounds, [1983] 2 F.C. 222 (C.A.); *Furniture Workers Union v. Board of Industrial Relations* (1969), 69 W.W.R. 226 (Alta. T.D.), an administrative tribunal case; and *dicta* in *Cotroni v. Quebec Police Commission*, [1978] 1 S.C.R. 1048 *per* Pigeon J.). The requirement that the proposed evidence be shown to be relevant is fundamental in any action to require issue of a subpoena (Hon. Mr. Justice R.F. Reid, "The Right to Subpoena

and Challenge Witnesses and Documents Before Tribunals," Law
Society of Upper Canada C.L.E., *Emerging Issues in Administrative
Law and Administrative Law Practice* (September 1983), 10-17).

The self-incrimination privilege and the effects of the Charter
of Rights and Freedoms should also be recalled. It has been held that
statutory provisions authorizing commissioners to subpoena witnesses whose own conduct is under investigation are of no force
and effect by reason of inconsistency with s. 7 of the Charter (*R.L.
Crain Inc. v. Couture, supra*. See Chapter II, Constitutional Position of Inquiries, "The Canadian Charter of Rights and Freedoms").

5. Record

It is not clear whether or to what extent the idea of a record
applies to commissions of inquiry. Certainly commissioners have
authority to conduct their investigations personally or with the
assistance of staff and may even, in some circumstances, dispense
with hearings altogether. Nevertheless, recommendations, if they
affect the rights of persons, must have some evidentiary basis. This
is because they must have some basis in law and because, otherwise,
unfairness is produced in affected persons. In this sense the commissioners may be required to follow the record of evidence. This
is even clearer where public hearings are held. If findings are
based on facts not established in the record of the proceedings,
then it will be clear that affected parties had no notice or opportunity to respond and, consequently, were treated unfairly (see
Mahon v. Air New Zealand, [1984] A.C. 808 (P.C.)).

6. Official Notice

A final factor is the administrative counterpart of "judicial
notice." Tribunal members, including inquiry commissioners, are
entitled to take "official notice" of facts that are broadly within
public knowledge. The scope of this doctrine is considerably wider
than judicial notice since tribunal members are often chosen for
their particular expertise. Thus, official notice may be taken of basic
technical and economic matters. This wide scope of official notice
appears to apply to inquiries as well. Commissioners are often
chosen for their particular expertise, and this expertise is enhanced
and complemented by that of the inquiry staff.

F. Jurisdiction

A court may intervene in the proceedings of a public inquiry
if the court is satisfied that the inquiry either lacked proper legal

authority initially, or that in one of several ways it lost or exceeded its legal authority in the course of its inquiry.

1. *Appointment*

A court may, in effect, order an inquiry halted if one or more of the commissioners are not properly appointed according to the requirements of the relevant Inquiry Act or other authorizing statute.

Thus, the jurisdiction of a provincial inquiry was successfully challenged by means of the historic writ of *quo warranto*, which has the effect of requiring the commissioner to show cause why the appointment was lawful (*Sargent v. McPhee* (1967), 60 W.W.R. 604 (B.C.C.A.)). It was held that the terms of reference of the inquiry, appointed to investigate alleged wire-tapping activities in the context of a labour dispute, were outside the scope of the general terms of reference in the B.C. Inquiries Act which specified matters "connected with the good government of the Province or the conduct of any part of the public business thereof . . . or the administration of justice therein. . . ."

2. *"Special Law"*

Some of the inquiry acts provide for appointment of commissioners by the Lieutenant Governor in Council provided the inquiry is not regulated by any "special law" (Ontario, Public Inquiries Act, s. 2; Nova Scotia, Public Inquiries Act, s. 2; Manitoba Evidence Act, Pt. V, s. 85). This means inquiries that are authorized under special statutes and not merely inquiries that may be affected by other statutes (*Re Commission of Inquiry into Police Department of Charlottetown* (1977), 74 D.L.R. (3d) 422 (P.E.I.C.A.)). There must be some action, such as an application, or circumstances to trigger proceedings under statutes other than the inquiries Act before the inquiry will be considered to be "regulated by . . . [a] special law" (*Re Canadian Environmental Law Assn. and Pitura* (1979), 26 O.R. (2d) 488, 102 D.L.R. (3d) 674, 9 C.E.L.R. 41, aff'd. 32 O.R. (2d) 605, 122 D.L.R. (3d) 492, 10 C.E.L.R. 80 (C.A.)).

An inquiry may also be restrained if its terms of reference exceed the legislative authority of the government from which it ultimately draws its authority. This may, as already indicated, be a matter of constitutional division of federal and provincial powers or infringement of rights or freedoms protected by the Canadian Charter of Rights and Freedoms.

Jurisdictional limitations may also arise where the inquiry's terms of reference extend beyond the specific matters for which commissions of inquiry may be established under the relevant statute (*Sargent v. McPhee, supra*); *Hydro Electric Commission of Mississauga v. City of Mississauga* (1975), 13 O.R. (2d) 511, 71 D.L.R. (3d) 475 (Div. Ct.)). Similarly, an inquiry may be restrained or directed as to its legal authority if it considers matters clearly beyond any reasonable interpretation of its terms of reference (*Re Bortolotti and Ministry of Housing* (1977), 15 O.R. (2d) 617; 76 D.L.R. (3d) 408 (C.A.)).

3. Terms of Reference

If an inquiry's terms of reference are too generally stated, it may be considered so vague as to constitute an unlawful subdelegation of the executive power to define the objects of the inquiry (see *Bisaillon v. Keable*, [1983] 2 S.C.R. 60, 51 N.R. 81 at 102–106). The clearest case is that in which the terms of reference state a general subject matter but then give the commissioner a discretion to determine the precise subjects for inquiry (*Ratnagopal v. A.G.*, [1970] A.C. 974 (P.C.)).

In *Re Nelles and Grange* (1984), 9 D.L.R. (4th) 79 (Ont. C.A.), an Ontario royal commission of inquiry was appointed to investigate thirty-four infant deaths that occurred during an eight-month period in the cardiac ward of a major public hospital. Murder charges had been laid against a nurse in relation to four of the children. The nurse was discharged following a preliminary inquiry, though the judge found that some of the children had died as a result of deliberate drug overdoses.

Mr. Justice Grange, the commissioner, was authorized by his terms of reference to inquire into, report on, and make recommendations with respect to how and by what means the children died, and with respect to the circumstances surrounding the investigation, institution, and prosecution of charges arising out of the infant deaths. It was specified in the terms of reference that the commissioner was to carry out these duties, "without expressing any conclusion of law regarding civil or criminal responsibility."

The question posed for the court was whether the commissioner was right in determining that he was entitled in his report to express an opinion as to whether the death of any child was a result of the action, accidental or otherwise, of any named person. This question was answered in the affirmative by the divisional court. However the court of appeal allowed the appeal, holding that the commissioner lacked authority to "name names."

The court expressed the view that public inquiries are not the means for investigating commission of particular crimes. Such an investigative inquiry would be a coercive procedure, incompatible with Canadian notions of justice in the investigation of particular crimes and the determination of criminal or civil responsibility. It was held that the commissioner was prohibited by the terms of reference from expressing conclusions of law regarding civil or criminal responsibility. This includes findings of fact which, when found against a named person, would, without more, constitute conclusions of criminal or civil responsibility.

Thus, a finding that a named person deliberately administered a toxic dose of digoxin amounts, in the circumstances, to a finding that the person acted with intention to cause death and is a conclusion of law as to civil or criminal responsibility. Similarly, a finding that a named person accidently administered a fatal overdose would also amount to a conclusion of civil or criminal responsibility since it is tantamount, in these particular circumstances, to a finding of negligence.

In addition, though the commissioner's conclusions are not final and binding, the public would consider them to be a determination to the serious prejudice of the named persons in subsequent proceedings. Even if no further proceedings were taken, there would be prejudice since the persons named would have no opportunity to clear themselves.

4. Investigation of Criminal Offences

Apart from interpretation of an inquiry's terms of reference, as in the case of the Grange Commission, there is no indication that Canadian inquiries are limited in their authority to investigate whether or not a criminal offence has been committed. It has been held that provincial inquiries in both Manitoba and British Columbia were validly authorized to investigate and report on alleged unlawful acts with a view to enabling the respective governments to initiate criminal or civil proceedings (*Kelly v. Mathers* (1915), 25 Man. R. 580; 23 D.L.R. 225 (C.A.); *Re Public Inquiries Act* (1919), 48 D.L.R. 237 (B.C.C.A.)).

The High Court of Australia has held that, since any individual is free to make any inquiry he chooses, so long as there is no interference with the liberty or reputation of persons or with the course of justice, the Crown, through a commission of inquiry, is not precluded from doing the same thing (*Clough v. Leahy* (1905), 2 C.L.R. 139 (H.C.). Accord *Ex parte Walker* (1924), 24 S.R. (N.S.W.) 604 (C.A.); *McGuinness v. A.G. Victoria* (1940), 63 C.L.R. 73 (H.C.)). A different view was taken by the New Zealand Court of Appeal in *Cock v. A.G.* (1909), 28 N.Z.L.R. 405. The court noted that the English statute which abolished the Court of Star Chamber recognized that no man is to be put to answer except in the manner prescribed by law. This meant only by the ordinary criminal law with the protections that it accords to persons accused of criminal offences. Subsequently, the opposite conclusion was reached by the court of appeal in *Re Royal Commission on the Thomas Case*, [1982] 1 N.Z.L.R. 252. It was held that a 1970 amendment to the Commissions of Inquiry Act authorized appointment of commissions with terms of reference that include jurisdiction to investigate crimes, provided such investigation is necessarily incidental to the subject matter of the inquiry.

5. *Reporting*

Commissions are directed by their authorizing orders in council to inquire and report, normally in writing. Often the order in council specifies that the inquiry is to report to a particular Minister. In the absence of such specification, the report should be submitted directly to Cabinet, the original appointing authority (L.A. Hallett, *Royal Commissions and Boards of Inquiry* (Sydney: Law Book Company, Agincourt: Carswell (1982)), 297.

Strictly speaking, in the absence of a special statutory provision, the decision whether or not to make an inquiry report public is a matter within the discretion of Cabinet (L.A. Hallett, *supra*, 299). However, in practice, overwhelming pressure for publication of inquiry reports can be produced by the public nature of the inquiry process, the development of expectations in the public, and the potential for adverse public and parliamentary reaction if disclosure is refused.

However, in England, inquiry reports have not been published as a result of government's concern that the right to a fair trial of persons charged with offences arising from inquiry issues would be prejudiced. The main legal basis for this position is that disclosure would either prejudge the issue or cause public prejudgment of the issue and, consequently, would constitute contempt of court *(A.G. v. Times Newspapers*, [1974] A.C. 273 (H.L.); see "Contempt", *infra)*. But courts have also pointed out that there is an important competing public interest, namely, publication of information and comment on current issues *(A.G. v. Times Newspapers, supra)*. An Australian judge has stated that public comment cannot be "stifled merely by the issue of a writ" *(Egan v. Commonwealth Minister for Transport (No. 2)* (1976), 15 S.A.S.R. 408, at 444 *per* Bright, J.; L.A. Hallett, *Royal Commissions and Boards of Inquiry, supra*, 301–308).

Generally, however, apart from constitutional authority and mandatory statutory procedural requirements, jurisdictional grounds for judicial review of public inquiries are less important than procedural fairness grounds. The reason is that inquiry terms of reference are often relatively broadly and imprecisely stated. Except in the unlikely event that an inquiry proceeds into matters outside any rational scope of its terms of reference, the courts are likely to be very reluctant to hinder the inquiry in what it considers to be its task. Because, strictly speaking, the inquiry does not decide issues, the case law that permits judicial intervention when administrative tribunals "ask the wrong question," base decisions on incorrect "collateral or jurisdictional facts," or "fetter their discretion" by applying rigid self-made rules or by following without question the decision of some other body, becomes largely irrelevant. There is also the general principle that the courts will not attempt to second guess the inquiry in matters where it is relatively clear inquiry has been authorized.

6. Relationship with Natural Justice/Fairness

In many circumstances the jurisdiction principles and the fairness concept are either closely related or form two sides of the same coin. For example, if only two members of a three-member commission hear evidence but all three take part in considering the evidence and formulating the inquiry's recommendations, a court may restrain the inquiry from proceeding further. If there are provisions as to quorum in the Inquiry Act, or perhaps in the relevant Interpretation Act, that have been breached, then the commission has failed to comply with mandatory procedural requirements and has, thereby, exceeded or lost its jurisdiction (*Re Bortolotti and Ministry of Housing* (1977), 15 O.R. (2d) 617; 76 D.L.R. (3d) 408 (C.A.)).

Another approach to this problem is to consider whether a party is treated unfairly if a commissioner considers and weighs but does not actually hear the evidence of that party. There is natural justice/procedural fairness case law that suggests a "whoever decides should also hear" principle. The cases are not completely clear, but it is likely that, where a commissioner considers, weighs and perhaps even discusses with the other commissioners evidence that he has not heard, the offending commissioner may be disqualified and the inquiry restrained by the court (*Re Ramm and Public Accountants Council of Ontario*, [1957] O.R. 217 (C.A.)).

G. Contempt

1. Contempt of Inquiries

Certain inquiry acts confer on commissioners specific powers to punish for acts of contempt in refusing to appear or to produce evidence when so ordered (New Brunswick, Inquiries Act, s. 6; Quebec, Public Inquiry Commissions Act, ss. 11, 12; Manitoba Evidence Act, Pt. V, s. 93). Several acts also contain general powers to punish for contempt, presumably including the power to punish actions calculated to lower the reputation of the inquiry as well as more direct actions of obstruction (New Brunswick, Inquiries Act, s. 7; B.C., Inquiry Act, s. 16; Alberta, Public Inquiries Act, s. 5).

Since commissions of inquiry, unlike courts of law, have no inherent common law powers, powers in relation to contempt must be conferred by statute (*C.B.C. v. Quebec Police Commission,* [1979] 2 S.C.R. 618). It appears that the powers found in all inquiry acts concerning summoning and compulsion of witnesses and evidence implicitly carry the powers to impose the normal contempt sanction in the event of failure to comply (*Re Hawkins and Halifax County Residential Tenancies Board* (1974), 47 D.L.R. (3d) 117, 125 (N.S.S.C.) (see Nova Scotia, Public Inquiries Act, s. 4; Saskatchewan, Public Inquiries Act, s. 4; P.E.I., Public Inquiries Act, s. 4; Canada, Inquiries Act, s. 5). However, this implied contempt power is limited to punishing contempts committed in the face of the inquiry. Unless the inquiry is found to have the procedural powers of a superior, as opposed to an inferior, court of record (*Re Hawkins, supra,* 129) or has express statutory contempt powers, there is no authority to punish for acts committed outside the presence of the inquiry (*C.B.C. v. Quebec Police Commission, supra,* 638). In *C.B.C. v. Quebec Police Commission,* the contempt powers conferred on inquiries by the Quebec Public Inquiry Commission Act were construed as not extending to contempt outside the presence of the inquiry.

A provision giving commissioners "with respect to the proceedings upon the hearing, all the powers of a judge of the Supreme Court" was held to be limited to those powers concerning procedure for the examination of witnesses. The Supreme Court stated that the power to punish contempts committed outside its presence was not necessary for the exercise of the functions of the police commission, as it is for protection of the superior courts' judicial function (*C.B.C. v. Quebec Police Commission, supra,* 642-44). Moreover, provinces lack the constitutional authority to confer power on inquiries to punish contempt committed outside the inquiry's presence. To do so would be to grant powers limited to superior courts, and the appointment of members of such courts is governed by s. 96 of the Constitution Act, 1867, which provides for appointment only by the federal government (*C.B.C. v. Quebec Police Commission, supra,* at 639-42).

Under the Ontario Public Inquiries Act (s. 8), where contemptuous acts are committed "without lawful excuse," the inquiry may, by stated case, place the matter before the court, and the latter may punish the contempt. Refusal by a witness to answer on the ground that he has applied to state a case for decision by the court is not "without lawful excuse" until the court has decided the stated case (*Re Yanover and Kiroff* (1974), 6 O.R. (2d) 478, 483-84 (C.A.)). Even without a statutory provision of this type, it appears that commissions of inquiry, like inferior courts, are entitled to apply to the appropriate superior court and ask that contempt outside the presence of the inquiry be found and punished (*C.B.C. v. Quebec Police Commission, supra,* 638).

2. Contempt by Inquiries

It is also possible that inquiries themselves, by their proceedings, may be in contempt of related judicial proceedings. An inquiry is noι in contempt merely because it inquires into the correctness of a decision of a court (*Clough v. Leahy* (1905), 2 C.L.R. 139 (H.C.)). Generally, however, any act of an inquiry that can be said to prejudice a fair trial of either criminal or civil matters may be considered contempt. This may include inquiry into the same matter that is the subject of current civil or criminal litigation (*McGuinness v. A.G. Victoria* (1940), 63 C.L.R. 73, 85 (H.C.)), refusal to accede to a subpoena in relation to documents required in court proceedings, and publication to the general public of inquiry findings or recommendations on matters then before a court (*Johns & Waygood Ltd. v. Utah Australia Ltd.,* [1963] V.R. 70, 75 S.C.; L.A. Hallett, *Royal Commissions and Boards of Inquiry, supra,* 237-39). However, the affected legal proceedings must be *bona fide* (*Johns & Waygood, supra,* 76). The mere issue of a writ will not immediately curtail an inquiry's public inquiry and public discussion.

III. STANDING

Several of the inquiry acts (Canada, Inquiries Act, s. 13; P.E.I., Public Inquiries Act, s. 7; Alberta, Public Inquiries Act, s. 12) contain provisions designed to guarantee persons "charged" with misconduct in inquiry proceedings an opportunity to be heard in their defence. However, only the Ontario and Alberta acts contain general criteria for determining what persons beyond those directly "charged" have standing to participate (Ontario, Public Inquiries Act, s. 5(1); Alberta, Public Inquiries Act, s. 11). The Ontario section uses the term "substantial and direct interest" in the subject matter of the inquiry, words very similar to the common law standing test traditionally applied in the courts. Section 11 of the Alberta Public Inquiries Act refers to persons whose interest may be "adversely affected" by evidence in the inquiry. It must be asked whether, in the absence of clear statutory criteria, the judicial standing test, which has been interpreted as largely restricted to economic interests, applies to commissions of inquiry in the other jurisdictions.

There are very few cases concerning the question of standing before administrative tribunals generally. However, these suggest that the narrow economic interest test from the judicial context will not govern. Rather, a broader public interest approach will be taken to accommodate groups or persons who lack direct economic interests, but who demonstrate by activity or orientation their interest or concern.

This broader approach is apparent in a recent Ontario commission of inquiry case (*Re Royal Commission on the Northern Environment and Grand Council of the Treaty 9 Bands* (1983), 144 D.L.R. (3d) 416 (Ont. Div. Ct.)). The Royal Commission on the Northern Environment denied a native organization the opportunity to cross-examine other parties that made submissions to the commissioner. In judicial review proceedings by the Grand Council of the Treaty 9 Bands, the issue turned on the interpretation of s. 5(1) of the Ontario Act which reads as follows:

> 5(1) A commission shall accord to any person who satisfies it that he has a substantial and direct interest in the subject matter of its inquiry an opportunity during the inquiry to give evidence and to call and examine or to cross-examine witnesses personally or by his counsel on evidence relevant to his interest.

It was held that the grand council was entitled to cross-examine witnesses. In effect, it had to be determined whether the grand council had standing to cross-examine witnesses or, as Linden J. put it, whether there was an entitlement to "full participation rights." He concluded that the subject matter of the inquiry is a significant factor, and continued as follows at 419:

> Obviously, the more general, theoretical and abstract the subject of an inquiry is, the more difficult it would be to find that a person has a substantial and direct interest in it. The more specific, practical and concrete the subject of an inquiry is, the more likely it would be that the property or individual rights of a person are affected, and hence, he would have a substantial and direct interest. The potential importance of the findings and the recommendations to the individual involved would have to be considered; if a particular person would be greatly affected by a recommendation or a finding in relation to him or his interests, then that would be taken into account in deciding whether he had a substantial and direct interest. Obviously, individual property interests have to be taken into account: see *Re Royal Com'n. on Conduct of Waste Management Inc. et al.* (1977), 17 O.R. (2d) 207, 80 D.L.R. (3d) 76, 4 C.P.C. 166. If a person has vital information to give or has made the charges that the commission is inquiring into,

then that person may be considered to have a substantial and direct interest, whereas others might not: see *Re Public Inquiries Act and Shulman,* [1967] 2 O.R. 375, 63 D.L.R. (2d) 578. It seems to us that the value of the potential interest that is being affected would have to be considered in arriving at its conclusion. Similarly, if one person is potentially affected, that might be viewed differently than if 100 or 1,000 or more persons may be affected. None of these specific items would be controlling; it is necessary to look at all of these factors as well as any others in the context of each inquiry. The decision must be made after examining all of the circumstances. Essentially, what is required is evidence that the subject-matter of the inquiry may seriously affect an individual. If this is the case, then that individual is entitled to full participation rights pursuant to s. 5(1).

It was significant that the grand council represented approximately two-thirds of the people in the area in question — people with a different culture and lifestyle — and that a central theme of the inquiry was addressing the position of native people in the area. The commissioner should not have been unduly influenced by his concern that to grant standing to the grand council would make it impossible to prevent any other group in the area from participating and thus slow down the work of the commission. Linden J. concluded by observing that the grant of standing does not confer unconditional cross-examination rights. The commissioner remains in charge of the inquiry and is empowered to determine the relevance of any questions.

In practice, commissions of inquiry, like other Canadian administrative tribunals, have rarely denied standing to participate. This approach appears to be based on the principle that the proceedings involve an important public interest element that may override the interests of particular parties (A. Roman, "Locus Standi: A Cure in Search of a Disease," in J. Swaigen, ed., *Environmental Rights in Canada* (Toronto: Butterworths 1981), 11, 31). Arguably, the courts will also be guided by this principle if matters of standing before commissions of inquiry are brought before them.

Even though Linden J., in the *Royal Commission on the Northern Environment* case, concluded by emphasizing the criterion of serious effects on individuals, his other criteria, including potential importance of recommendations and whether or not a person has vital information, suggest that wider public interest was also a factor. It should also be remembered that he was not considering whether the Grand Council of the Treaty 9 Bands had standing to participate at all, but whether it was entitled to cross-examine according to the statutory criteria of "substantial and direct interest." The result in the case may also be seen as influenced by considerations of procedural fairness (though the term fairness is not mentioned), given that the grand council was already an inquiry participant for the purpose of making submissions.

IV. DEFAMATION

Since commissions of inquiry are not courts, commissioners are not necessarily protected from defamation actions by the absolute privilege that applies to courts. In *O'Connor v. Waldron*, [1935] A.C. 76 (P.C.), a commissioner under the federal Combines Investigation Act was held liable in defamation to a lawyer who had appeared before the inquiry. The court concluded that the commissioner, in conducting the investigative inquiry, acted as part of the administrative arm of government and was not and did not function as a court. However, Lord Atkin suggested that bodies with a duty of inquiry may be protected by absolute privilege because they act in a manner similar to a court. (See also *Royal Aquarium and Summer and Winter Garden Society Ltd. v. Parkinson*, [1892] 1 Q.B. 431 (C.A.)).

Thus, it is possible that a more formal court-like inquiry, particularly one established to investigate alleged wrongdoing, may be entitled to claim absolute privilege. Otherwise, there is only a qualified privilege, which requires that an otherwise defamatory statement be fairly made in the discharge of some public or private duty related to the conduct of those affairs. However an Australian commissioner and his commission counsel were held not to be protected by absolute privilege (*Bretherton v. Kaye and Winneke*, [1971] V.R. 111 (S.C.)), as was a New Zealand commissioner (*Jellicoe v. Haselden* (1902), 5 N.Z.L.R. 207 (S.C.)). Statutory absolute privileges for inquiries, like that provided by s. 21A of the state of Victoria's Evidence Act, added in 1971 (see Hallett, *supra*, 309ff), are found in s. 12 of the British Columbia Inquiry Act, s. 12 of the New Brunswick Inquiries Act, and s. 89 of Part V of the Manitoba Evidence Act.

Even if inquiries have absolute privilege of the kind enjoyed by courts, commissioners may still be subject to certain legal actions. If a commissioner acts in circumstances that suggest a lack of *bona fides* in the exercise of his function, and in careless disregard of whether he is within his legal authority, an action by affected persons based on abuse of power may lie (see *Tampion v. Anderson*, [1973] V.R. 715 (S.C.); L. Hallett, *Royal Commissions and Boards of Inquiry*, *supra*, 316–18). Damages, injunctive remedies, or both would be potentially available. However, since this duty applies only to public officers, no action of this kind may be available against either inquiry staff or inquiry counsel.

Postscript for Participants

The earlier chapters set out the considerations for the creation, operation, and termination of a public inquiry. The comments are designed to benefit those who are directly involved in the inquiry as commissioner, staff, or counsel and those who will be participants or will represent participants. In setting out the reasons for and against the inquiry's adoption of a particular course of action, participants in the inquiry process will develop their own ideas of the kinds of arguments they may wish to address to the commissioner.

Participants have their unique concerns, which must be considered in the course of establishing their approach to and involvement in the public inquiry process. Since the successful participation of all segments of the public is essential for the full and fair operation of the public inquiry process, some comments on these unique issues facing participants, particularly those representing public interest of groups, are included.

1. Be sure your facts are correct. Before launching into participation (particularly criticism) of an inquiry, its processes, or the position of other participants, make sure you understand all the necessary facts. Consult the source documents. These include the order in council appointing the commissioner, any press statements or other documents issued by the inquiry, and whatever further information — even articles in the press — that will acquaint you with the commissioner and the inquiry. As the inquiry proceeds, you will have to retain copies of all preliminary rulings, key documents (both yours and other participants), inquiry transcripts, and the various other sources of information on the inquiry and the substantive issues necessary for effective participation. Set up separate binders holding all of this relevant documentation so it can be easily consulted to verify information. When presenting information to the inquiry, document facts to the fullest extent possible.

2. Know the people involved. Get to know the commissioner, inquiry counsel, the executive secretary, and the head of the technical staff, along with the key representatives of all of the other major participants. Knowing these individuals on a personal basis means that you are able to exchange information, or otherwise deal with the inquiry's business, informally without procedural comments at the hearings. This personal relationship is especially important in a long inquiry, where interrelationships are generally informal and most problems are best resolved through mutual agreement.

3. Contact the inquiry early. Participants can play a creative role in structuring the inquiry through recommendations and submissions on procedure, timing, and other issues of concern. At the initial stages most participants know more about the issues than the inquiry, and demonstration of a helpful attitude and commitment to the inquiry could pay dividends later. Any major decisions made informally should be confirmed in writing or stated on the record later.

4. Establish the scope of the inquiry. There should be guidelines, in the form of rulings or statements of the commissioner on the inquiry record, which set out the limits of the inquiry's mandate. Help to shape this mandate, then ensure that your research and preparation fits within the inquiry's terms of reference. The inquiry should then refrain from considering extraneous matters that come as a surprise to you and for which you are not prepared.

5. Make sure you understand what the commissioner and the inquiry expect from you. Often participants are expected to play certain roles in the inquiry or to represent certain interests, and it is valuable to determine this early. If there will be participant funding, any application for funds should reflect the role that the inquiry has requested you to play.

6. Define your goals. Participants should consider what recommendations they want the commissioner to make and what intermediate steps they have to take to achieve that objective. As an applicant, what must be established to obtain regulatory approval, and what is required to satisfy the inquiry? Is there an onus on you to prove anything? Is this onus placed by other participants, by the inquiry, or is it self-imposed?

As a public interest intervenor, are you attempting to prevent a certain action from taking place? If so, what do you have to prove or disprove to succeed? Do you carry responsibilities beyond those assigned by the inquiry, such as conducting a public education or public relations program in the course of representing a particular interest at the inquiry? Do you also want to establish precedents for other public inquiries so that the next hearing will be conducted in a way more sympathetic to your interests? Do you want to support this form of inquiry or to demonstrate its weaknesses and, thereby, create pressure for reform?

As counsel to an inquiry, are you a participant or counsel to the impartial hearing officer? Do you perform your functions as an adversary, or do you reflect the range of interests appearing before the inquiry and represent those public interests not represented?

All participants should not only set goals within the confines of the inquiry but also beyond. For example, if it is clear that the inquiry's recommendations are only part of the advice that will be considered by the elected officials who will make the ultimate decision, how can the inquiry process be most effectively used to establish a climate that will be favourable to your position? How can you use the inquiry to mould public opinion to put political pressure on the government to support your position? How do you keep the people you represent well enough informed to retain their support? Most public inquiries serve a multitude of purposes, and participants bring a variety of goals, many conflicting. In this confusion it is important to keep your ultimate objects in mind at all times.

7. Take a position. One fundamental aspect of defining goals is to learn from your clients whether they wish to take a position on the key issues before the inquiry or whether they merely wish counsel to ensure that the evidence is thoroughly presented and tested without coming to any final conclusions until all of the evidence is in.

8. Define your turf. Based on the goals you wish to achieve and a decision on whether the role the inquiry wants you to play is acceptable, are there others with similar goals or responsibilities? Are you able to form a coalition of like-minded interests to share responsibility for participation. How can these participants split up responsibility so their resources are most efficiently used?

9. Understand the role of the inquiry officers. The role of inquiry counsel, whether advisor to the commissioner or participant in the proceedings and the role of technical staff, whether advisors or expert witnesses may shape your approach. Also, you should find out what assistance you can expect from the staff regarding participant funding, identifying witnesses, and sharing research.

10. Evaluate the role of other participants. It is important to understand the role and objectives of other participants in the proceedings to determine whether they are allies so that you might share research and the burden of participation, whether they are opposed in interest so that you will cross-examine their witnesses as adversaries, or whether they are somewhere in between. It is particularly important to determine the role of governments. Is it their intention to become active participants or, if not, what arrangements have been made for their staff expertise to be brought before the inquiry?

11. Contact support organizations. Contact public interest advocacy centres and other such organizations, which provide resource material for intervenors in public inquiries and sometimes counsel.

12. Use inquiry resources. Use the inquiry library, government witnesses, inquiry research documents, and other resources that are usually made available to participants during a hearing before spending your limited resources on such services, facilities, or expertise. If you do not mind who gets the credit, there is a lot that can be accomplished by using the resources of others.

13. Consider fund raising. Is it proper to use the inquiry process to assist in fund raising? As counsel, what role do you play in preparing budgets, fund raising, and otherwise supporting activities aimed at financing the objectives of the interest you represent?

14. Consider media and public relations. Because inquiries are often only advisory to politicians, the effect of the inquiry on the political process becomes a dominant concern of many participants and, consequently, their relationship with the media is important. The media also plays an important role if there is a public education function to be performed. As a participant in the proceedings, what approach do you take in defining your relationship with the media? What techniques are properly available to ensure that evidence favourable to your position is given media coverage? Should you advise media in advance of your witnesses, prepare press releases based on your witness's evidence, or hold press conferences or interviews? What authority or scope does your counsel have to comment on inquiry issues on your behalf or on related political or regulatory developments, beyond the inquiry itself?

15. Get instructions. When representing public interest groups, particularly coalitions of public interests, or government, it is important that a clear line of communications is established so that counsel knows the source of his instructions. It must be possible to obtain quick and authoritative instructions when necessary.

16. Make a complete disclosure. Demonstrate to the inquiry and the other participants that you can be trusted and are operating in the best interests of the inquiry as well as your own client. When you are obliged to provide information, take care and do a professional job. By being thorough, you will avoid being embarrassed at the hearing by unexpected disclosures and will demonstrate your good faith.

17. Select expert witnesses with care. First determine what you have to prove, then who can best provide the evidence. Witnesses can include in-house experts, government officials, academics, world authorities, or knowledgeable local residents. Cost, availability, and potential impact will all determine which type of witness is required. Find out what evidence is likely to be called by others, select your vital interests and orient your research and witnesses to meet your specific needs. Make many of these decisions early so that all of your funds are not spent in the early phases of the inquiry, and important evidence (to you) is left out at later hearings.

18. Consider the priorities. Public groups often concentrate on having representatives at all hearings to observe and ask questions, often at the cost, because of limited funds, of research and preparation for those areas of vital concern. It may be better to form loose coalitions of like-minded interests and have fewer counsel and more researchers. Competent research and preparation ultimately are more important than having broad "representation" at the hearings.

19. Prepare your witnesses carefully. The preparation of evidence is a difficult and time-consuming operation. If you lack time and resources, concentrate on your key witnesses to make sure their evidence is well presented. It is better to present a few well-prepared witnesses than to try to cover a broad range of issues. It is good practice to obtain a prepared written statement for the witness, whether this is required by the inquiry or not. The witness's statement should be reviewed before his appearance with respect to both substance and presentation. Counsel should satisfy himself that the evidence is sufficient to prove the point and does not contain anything that might be improper. To the extent possible the witness should be made familiar with the project and the evidence of others who will be appearing on the same issue. Adequate preparation is very important to demonstrate competence and to assist in the efficient operation of the inquiry.

Witnesses should also be briefed on the procedure, demeanour, and style used in presenting evidence (speak clearly, answer only the questions that are asked, speak to the commissioner, do not indulge in personality clashes, be respectful toward the other participants). If possible, witnesses should attend some hearings or review transcripts to get a feel for the process. If witnesses are to appear in panels, their interrelationship should be discussed so that each panel member understands what is expected.

20. Cross-examine effectively. Again, preparation is the key. With a variety of participants and different levels of experience with inquiry processes, the commissioner is likely to give more attention to someone whose cross-examination is concise, to the point, and carried out in a respectful and competent manner. It is often advisable to let the people you are cross-examining know generally the issues to be covered so they can bring reports that may be needed as references, unless the element of surprise is important to the cross-examination. Since many of these experts have given evidence on previous occasions, your technical expert should, if possible, be with you during the cross-examination and should have reviewed the witness's evidence given at earlier hearings.

21. Concentrate on the final submission. Participants should remember that the final submission is their last opportunity to convince the commissioner of their point of view. Since it is the document that stays with the commissioner as he writes his reports, it should be designed not only to present the participant's point of view but also to assist the commissioner in his report writing. A tightly written, well documented, and well presented final argument may be reproduced, with appropriate changes, in the final report. The goal should be to present something to the inquiry that could, properly, form part of the final report. Summaries or extracts can be used for other purposes such as media information.

One approach is to indicate the conclusions to be drawn from the evidence, then present the information and argument to show the commissioner why he should want to reach those conclusions, and finally set out the evidence that will allow the commissioner to come to those conclusions. This evidence should be well documented with direct transcript references and other aids that will help the commissioner or his staff document these conclusions and, if they wish, incorporate them into the inquiry report. The distinction between evidence and the conclusions that should be drawn from that evidence must be kept clear, and great care must be taken that the inquiry is not misled by suggesting unwarranted conclusions from evidence.

22. Be fair and respectful. Even though inquiries are often informal, non-judicial proceedings, they should be approached with respect and a sense of fairness. Not only will the inquiry process work better and gain public support and confidence, it will, at the same time, better serve your own interests as well.

Appendices

A-1

Federal, Provincial, and Territorial Inquiry Act Citations

Canada: Inquiries Act, R.S.C. 1970, c. I-13.
Alberta: Public Inquiries Act, R.S.A. 1980, c. P-29.
British Columbia: Inquiry Act, R.S.B.C. 1979, c. 198.
Manitoba: Manitoba Evidence Act, Part V, R.S.M. 1970 (C.C.S.M., c. E-150).
Newfoundland: Public Enquiries Act, R.S.N. 1970, c. 314.
New Brunswick: Inquiries Act, R.S.N.B. 1973, c. I-11.
Nova Scotia: Public Inquiries Act, R.S.N.S. 1967, c. 250.
Ontario: Public Inquiries Act, R.S.O. 1980, c. 411.
Quebec: Public Inquiry Commissions Act, R.S.Q. 1977, c. C-37.
Prince Edward Island: Public Inquiries Act, R.S.P.E.I., 1974, c. P-30.
Saskatchewan: Public Inquiries Act, R.S.S. 1978, c. P-38.
Northwest Territories: None.
Yukon: Public Inquiries Act, C.S.Y.T., c. P-8.1.

Federal Inquiries Act

CHAPTER I-13

An Act respecting public and departmental inquiries

SHORT TITLE

1. This Act may be cited as the *Inquiries Act.*

PART I
PUBLIC INQUIRIES

2. The Governor in Council may, whenever he deems it expedient, cause inquiry to be made into and concerning any matter connected with the good government of Canada or the conduct of any part of the public business thereof.

3. Where an inquiry as described in section 2 is not regulated by any special law, the Governor in Council may, by a commission in the case, appoint persons as commissioners by whom the inquiry shall be conducted.

4. The commissioners have the power of summoning before them any witnesses, and of requiring them to give evidence on oath, or on solemn affirmation if they are persons entitled to affirm in civil matters, and orally or in writing, and to produce such documents and things as the commissioners deem requisite to the full investigation of the matters into which they are appointed to examine.

5. The commissioners have the same power to enforce the attendance of witnesses and to compel them to give evidence as is vested in any court of record in civil cases.

PART II
DEPARTMENTAL INVESTIGATIONS

6. The minister presiding over any department of the Public Service may appoint at any time, under the authority of the

Governor in Council, a commissioner or commissioners to investigate and report upon the state and management of the business, or any part of the business, of such department, either in the inside or outside service thereof, and the conduct of any person in such service, so far as the same relates to his official duties.

7. The commissioner or commissioners may, for the purposes of the investigation, enter into and remain within any public office or institution, and shall have access to every part thereof, and may examine all papers, documents, vouchers, records and books of every kind belonging thereto, and may summon before him or them any person and require him to give evidence on oath, orally or in writing, or on solemn affirmation if he is entitled to affirm in civil matters; and any such commissioner may administer such oath or affirmation.

8.(1) The Commissioner or commissioners may, under his or their hand or hands, issue a subpoena or other request or summons, requiring and commanding any person therein named to appear at the time and place mentioned therein, and then and there to testify to all matters within his knowledge relative to the subject-matter of such investigation, and to bring with him and produce any document, book, or paper that he has in his possession or under his control relative to any such matter as aforesaid; and any such person may be summoned from any part of Canada by virtue of the subpoena, request or summons.

(2) Reasonable travelling expenses shall be paid to any person so summoned at the time of service of the subpoena, request or summons.

9.(1) If, by reason of the distance at which any person, whose evidence is desired, resides from the place where his attendance is required, or for any other cause, the commissioner or commissioners deem it advisable, he or they may issue a commission or other authority to any officer or person therein named, empowering him to take such evidence and report it to him or them.

(2) Such officer or person shall, before entering on any investigation, be sworn before a justice of the peace faithfully to execute the duty entrusted to him by such commission, and, with regard to such evidence, has the same powers as the commissioner or commissioners would have had if such evidence had been taken before him or them, and may, in like manner, under his hand issue a subpoena or other request or summons for the purpose of compelling the attendance of any person, or the production of any document, book or paper.

10.(1) Every person who

(a) being required to attend in the manner provided in this Part, fails, without valid excuse, to attend accordingly, (*b*) being commanded to produce any document, book or paper, in his possession or under his control, fails to produce the same,

(*c*) refuses to be sworn or to affirm, as the case may be, or

(*d*) refuses to answer any proper question put to him by a commissioner, or other person as aforesaid,

is liable, on summary conviction before any police or stipendiary magistrate, or judge of a superior or county court, having jurisdiction in the county or district in which such person resides, or in which the place is situated at which he was so required to attend, to a penalty not exceeding four hundred dollars.

(2) The judge of the superior or county court aforesaid, shall, for the purposes of this part, be a justice of the peace.

PART III
GENERAL

11.(1) The commissioners, whether appointed under Part I or under Part II, if thereunto authorized by the commission issued in the case, may engage the services of such accountants, engineers, technical advisers, or other experts, clerks, reporters and assistants as they deem necessary or advisable, and also the services of counsel to aid and assist the commissioners in the inquiry.

(2) The commissioners may authorize and depute any such accountants, engineers, technical advisers, or other experts, or any other qualified persons, to inquire into any matter within the scope of the commission as may be directed by the commissioners.

(3) The persons so deputed, when authorized by order in council, have the same powers that the commissioners have to take evidence, issue subpoenas, enforce the attendance of witnesses, compel them to give evidence, and otherwise conduct the inquiry.

(4) The persons so deputed shall report the evidence and their findings, if any, thereon to the commissioners.

12. The commissioners may allow any person whose conduct is being investigated under this Act, and shall allow any person against whom any charge is made in the course of such investigation, to be represented by counsel.

13. No report shall be made against any person until reasonable notice has been given to him of the charge of misconduct alleged against him and he has been allowed full opportunity to be heard in person or by counsel.

PART IV
INTERNATIONAL COMMISSIONS AND TRIBUNALS

14. (1) The Governor in Council may, whenever he deems it expedient, confer upon an international commission or tribunal

all or any of the powers conferred upon commissioners under Part I.

(2) The powers so conferred may be exercised by such commission or tribunal in Canada, subject to such limitations and restrictions as the Governor in Council may impose, in respect to all matters that are within the jurisdiction of such commission or tribunal.

Order in Council for Mackenzie Valley Pipeline Inquiry

P.C. 1974-641 — March 21, 1974

WHEREAS proposals have been made for the construction and operation of a natural gas pipeline, referred to as the Mackenzie Valley Pipeline, across Crown lands under the control, management and administration of the Minister of Indian Affairs and Northern Development within the Yukon Territory and the Northwest Territories in respect of which it is contemplated that authority might be sought, pursuant to paragraph 19(f) of the Territorial Lands Act, for the acquisition of a right-of-way;

AND WHEREAS it is desirable that any such right-of-way that might be granted be subject to such terms and conditions as are appropriate having regard to the regional social, environmental and economic impact of the construction, operation and abandonment of the proposed pipeline;

THEREFORE, HIS EXCELLENCY THE GOVERNOR GENERAL IN COUNCIL, on the recommendation of the Minister of Indian Affairs and Northern Development, is pleased hereby, pursuant to paragraph 19(h) of the Territorial Lands Act, to designate the Honourable Mr. Justice Thomas R. Berger (hereinafter referred to as Mr. Justice Berger), of the City of Vancouver in the Province of British Columbia, to inquire into the report upon the terms and conditions that should be imposed in respect of any right-of-way that might be granted across Crown lands for the purposes of the proposed Mackenzie Valley Pipeline having regard to

    (a) the social, environmental and economic impact regionally, of the construction, operation and subsequent abandonment of the proposed pipeline in the Yukon and the Northwest Territories, and

    (b) any proposals to meet the specific environmental and social concerns set out in the Expanded Guidelines for

Northern Pipelines as tabled in the House of Commons on June 28, 1972 by the Minister.

HIS EXCELLENCY THE GOVERNOR GENERAL IN COUNCIL is further pleased hereby

1. to authorize Mr. Justice Berger
   (a) to hold hearings pursuant to this Order in Territorial centers and in such other places and at such times as he may decide from time to time;
   (b) for the purposes of the inquiry, to summon and bring before him any person whose attendance he considers necessary to the inquiry, examine such persons under oath, compel the production of documents and do all things necessary to provide a full and proper inquiry;
   (c) to adopt such practices and procedures for all purposes of the inquiry as he from time to time deems expedient for the proper conduct thereof;
   (d) subject to paragraph 2 hereunder, to engage the services of such accountants, engineers, technical advisers, or other experts, clerks, reporters and assistants as he deems necessary or advisable, and also the services of counsel to aid and assist him in the inquiry, at such rates of remuneration and reimbursement as may be approved by the Treasury Board; and
   (e) to rent such space for offices and hearing rooms as he deems necessary or advisable at such rental rates as may be approved by the Treasury Board; and

2. to authorize the Minister of Indian Affairs and Northern Development to designate an officer of the Department of Indian Affairs and Northern Development to act as Secretary for the inquiry and to provide Mr. Justice Berger with such accountants, engineers, technical advisers, or other experts, clerks, reporters and assistants from the Public Service as may be requested by Mr. Justice Berger.

HIS EXCELLENCY THE GOVERNOR GENERAL IN COUNCIL is further pleased hereby to direct Mr. Justice Berger to report to the Minister of Indian Affairs and Northern Development with all reasonable despatch and file with the Minister the papers and records of the inquiry as soon as may be reasonable after the conclusion thereof.

HIS EXCELLENCY THE GOVERNOR GENERAL IN COUNCIL, with the concurrence of the Minister of Justice, is further pleased hereby, pursuant to section 37 of the Judges Act, to authorize Mr. Justice Berger to act on the inquiry.

Documents Establishing West Coast Oil Ports Inquiry

P.C. 1977-2149 — July 28, 1977

Note: Underlining indicates the changes made to the original order in council (P.C. 1977-597, March 10, 1977) following receipt of a second proposal for a west coast tanker terminal after the inquiry was established.

WHEREAS a proposal has been made by Kitimat Pipe-Line Ltd. for the construction of a marine terminal at the Town of Kitimat in the Province of British Columbia to form part of a new pipeline system for the transmission of oil from Kitimat to the City of Edmonton in the Province of Alberta;

WHEREAS the marine terminal proposed from Kitimat will receive oil shipped to Kitimat by tankers from Alaska and other points;

WHEREAS proposals have been made to receive oil shipped by tankers moving along Canada's West Coast for transmission in other pipeline systems, including a proposal by Trans Mountain Pipe Line Company Ltd.;

AND WHEREAS it is expedient that inquiry be made into and concerning the environmental and social impact and navigational safety aspects of the construction and operation of a marine terminal at Kitimat on Canada's West Coast designed to receive oil shipped by tanker from Alaska and other points.

THEREFORE, the Committee of the Privy Council, on the recommendation of the Minister of Fisheries and the Environment and the Minister of Transport, advise that, pursuant to Part I of the Inquiries Act, a Commission do issue under the Great Seal of Canada, appointing Dr. Andrew R. Thompson, of the City of Vancouver in the Province of British Columbia a Commissioner

(*a*) to inquire into and concerning and to report upon

    (i) the social and environmental impact regionally (including the impact on fisheries) that could result from

the establishment of a marine tanker route and construction of a marine terminal (deep water oil port)
at Kitimat, B.C.;

(ii) navigational safety and related matters associated with
the establishment of a marine tanker route and construction of a marine terminal at Kitimat, B.C.;

(iii) the broader <u>Canadian</u> concerns and issues related to
oil tanker movements on the West Coast as might be
affected by the <u>Kitimat Pipe-Line Ltd., Trans Mountain Pipe Line Company Ltd.</u>, and other proposals;
and

(*b*) to report upon representations made to him concerning
the terms and conditions which should be imposed, if
authority is given to establish a marine terminal at Kitimat,
on the size, construction and operation thereof and on the
size, construction and operation of tankers in the approaches thereto.

The Committee is further pleased to advise that Dr. Thompson
be authorized

(*a*) to hold hearings pursuant to this Order at such places in
the Province of British Columbia and at such times as he
may decide from time to time;

(*b*) to adopt such practices and procedures for all purposes of
the inquiry as he from time to time deems expedient for
the proper conduct thereof;

(*c*) for the purposes of the inquiry, to engage the services of
such accountants, engineers, technical advisers, or other
experts, clerks, reporters and assistants as he deems
necessary or advisable and also the services of counsel to
aid and assist him in the inquiry, at such rates of renumera-
tion as may be approved by the Treasury Board;

(*d*) to exercise all the powers conferred upon him by section 11
of the Inquiries Act and be assisted to the fullest extent by
Government departments and agencies; and

(*e*) to rent such space for offices and hearings as he deems
necessary at such rental rates as may be approved by the
Treasury Board.

The Committee further advise that Dr. Thompson be directed
to report to the Minister of Fisheries and the Environment and the
Minister of Transport before the end of the current year and to file
with the Dominion Archivist the papers and records of the inquiry
as soon as may be reasonable after the conclusion thereof.

The Committee further advise that Orders in Council P.C.
1977-597 of 10th March, 1977 and P.C. 1977-1890 of 30th June,
1977 be revoked.

COMMISSION

appointing

Doctor Andrew R. Thompson

to be Commissioner under Part I of the Inquiries Act to inquire into the establishment of a marine tanker route and construction of a marine terminal at Kitimat, British Columbia.

DATED .... 12th April, 1977
RECORDED .... 12th April, 1977

TO ALL TO WHOM these Presents shall come or whom the same may in anyway concern,

GREETING:

WHEREAS pursuant to the provisions of Part I of the Inquiries Act, chapter I-13 of the Revised Statutes of Canada, 1970, His Excellency the Governor General in Council by Order in Council P.C. 1977-597 of the tenth day of March in the year of Our Lord one thousand nine hundred and seventy-seven, has authorized the appointment of Our Commissioner therein and hereinafter named

(a) to inquire into and concerning and to report upon

(i) the social and environmental impact regionally (including the impact on fisheries) that could result from the establishment of a marine tanker route and construction of a marine terminal (deep water oil port) at Kitimat, British Columbia,

(ii) navigational safety and related matters associated with the establishment of a marine tanker route and construction of a marine terminal at Kitimat, British Columbia, and

(iii) the broader concerns and issues related to oil tanker movements on the West Coast as might be affected by the proposal; and

(b) to report upon representations made to him concerning the terms and conditions which should be imposed, if authority is given to establish a marine terminal at Kitimat, British Columbia, on the size, construction and operation thereof and on the size, construction and operation of tankers in the approaches thereto;

and has conferred certain rights, powers and privileges upon Our Commissioner as will by reference to the said Order more fully appear.

NOW KNOW You that, by and with the advice of Our Privy Council for Canada, We do by these Presents nominate, constitute and appoint Doctor Andrew R. Thompson, of the City of Vancouver, in the Province of British Columbia, to be Our Commissioner to conduct such inquiry.

TO HAVE, hold, exercise and enjoy the said office, place and trust unto the said Andrew R. Thompson, together with the rights, powers, privileges and emoluments unto the said office, place and trust of right and by law appertaining during Our Pleasure.

AND WE DO hereby authorize Our said Commissioner to hold hearings at such places in the Province of British Columbia and at such times as he may decide from time to time.

AND WE DO further authorize Our said Commissioner to adopt such practices and procedures for all purposes of the inquiry as he from time to time deems expedient for the proper conduct thereof.

AND WE DO further authorize Our said Commissioner to engage the services of such accountants, engineers technical advisers, or other experts, clerks, reporters and assistants as he deems necessary or advisable, and also the services of counsel to aid and assist him in his inquiry at such rates of remuneration and reimbursement as may be approved by the Treasury Board.

AND WE DO further authorize Our said Commissioner to rent space for offices and hearings as he deems necessary at such rental rates as may be approved by the Treasury Board.

AND WE DO hereby require and direct Our said Commissioner to report to the Minister of Fisheries and the Environment and the Minister of Transport before the end of the current year and to file with the Dominion Archivist the papers and records of the inquiry as soon as may be reasonable after the conclusion of the inquiry.

IN TESTIMONY WHEREOF, We have caused these Our Letters to be made Patent and the Great Seal of Canada to be hereunto affixed.

WITNESS:

Our Right Trusty and Well-beloved Jules Léger, Chancellor and Principal Companion of Our Order of Canada, Chancellor and Commander of Our Order of Military Merit upon whom We have conferred Our Canadian Forces' Decoration, Governor General and Commander-in-Chief of Canada.

AT OUR GOVERNMENT HOUSE, in Our City of Ottawa, this twelfth day of April in the year of Our Lord one thousand nine hundred and seventy-seven and in the twenty-sixth year of Our Reign.

Order in Council for McDonald Commission on the RCMP

P.C. 1977-1911

WHEREAS it has been established that certain persons who were members of the RCMP at the time did, on or about October 7, 1972, take part jointly with persons who were then members of la Sûreté du Québec and la Police de Montréal in the entry of premises located at 3459 St. Hubert Street, Montreal, in the search of those premises for property contained therein, and in the removal of documents from those premises, without lawful authority to do so;

WHEREAS allegations have recently been made that certain persons who were members of the RCMP at the time may have been involved on other occasions in investigative actions or other activities that were not authorized or provided for by law;

WHEREAS, after having made inquiries into these allegations at the instance of the Government, the Commissioner of the RCMP now advises that there are indications that certain persons who were members of the RCMP may indeed have been involved in investigative actions or other activities that were not authorized or provided for by law, and that as a consequence, the Commissioner believes that in the circumstances it would be in the best interests of the RCMP that a Commission of Inquiry be set up to look into the operations and policies of the Security Service on a national basis;

WHEREAS public support of the RCMP in the discharge of its responsibility to protect the security of Canada is dependent on trust in the policies and procedures governing its activities;

AND WHEREAS the maintenance of that trust requires that full inquiry be made into the extent and prevalence of investigative practices or other activities involving members of the Royal Canadian Mounted Police that are not authorized or provided for by law.

THEREFORE, the Committee of the Privy Council, on the recommendation of the Prime Minister, advise that, pursuant to the

Inquiries Act, a Commission do issue under the Great Seal of Canada, appointing

Mr. Justice David C. McDonald of Edmonton, Alberta

Mr. Donald S. Rickerd of Toronto, Ontario

Mr. Guy Gilbert of Montreal, Quebec

to be Commissioners under Part I of the Inquiries Act:

(a) to conduct such investigations as in the opinion of the Commissioners are necessary to determine the extent and prevalence of investigative practices or other activities involving members of the RCMP that are not authorized or provided for by law and, in this regard, to inquire into the relevant policies and procedures that govern the activities of the RCMP in the discharge of its responsibility to protect the security of Canada;

(b) to report the facts relating to any investigative action or other activity involving persons who were members of the RCMP that was not authorized or provided for by law as may be established before the Commission, and to advise as to any further action that the Commissioners may deem necessary and desirable in the public interest; and

(c) to advise and make such report as the Commissioners deem necessary and desirable in the interest of Canada, regarding the policies and procedures governing the activities of the RCMP in the discharge of its responsibility to protect the security of Canada, the means to implement such policies and procedures, as well as the adequacy of the laws of Canada as they apply to such policies and procedures, having regard to the needs of the security of Canada.

The Committee further advise that the Commissioners:

1. be authorized to adopt such procedures and methods as the Commissioners may from time to time deem expedient for the proper conduct of the inquiry;

2. be directed that the proceedings of the inquiry be held in camera in all matters relating to national security and in all other matters where the Commissioners deem it desirable in the public interest or in the interest of the privacy of individuals involved in specific cases which may be examined:

3. be directed, in making their report, to consider and take all steps necessary to preserve

(a) the secrecy of sources of security information within Canada; and

(b) the security of information provided to Canada in confidence by other nations;

4. be authorized to sit at such time and at such places as they may decide from time to time, to have complete access to personnel and information available in the Royal Canadian Mounted Police and to be provided with adequate working accommodation and clerical assistance;

5. be authorized to engage the services of such staff and technical advisers as they deem necessary or advisable and also the services of counsel to aid them and assist in their inquiry at such rates of remuneration and reimbursement as may be approved by the Treasury Board;

6. be directed to follow established security procedures with regard to their staff and technical advisers and the handling of classified information at all stages of the inquiry;

7. be authorized to exercise all the powers conferred upon them by section 11 of the Inquiries Act; and

8. be directed to report to the Governor in Council with all reasonable dispatch and file with the Privy Council Office their papers and records as soon as reasonably may be after the conclusion of the inquiry.

The Committee further advise that, pursuant to section 37 of the Judges Act, His Honour Mr. Justice McDonald be authorized to act as Commissioner for the purposes of the said Commission and that Mr. Justice McDonald be the Chairman of the Commission.

A-6

Order in Council for British Columbia Uranium Mining Inquiry

O.C. 442/80

On the recommendation of the undersigned, the Lieutenant-Governor, by and with the advice and consent of the Executive Council, orders that Whereas, by order 170/79, Commissioners were appointed to make an inquiry into and concerning the adequacy of existing measures providing protection as the result of uranium mining in British Columbia and in particular,

(1) to examine the adequacy of existing federal and provincial requirements for the protection of the health and safety of workers associated with exploration, mining and milling of uranium in British Columbia, and for the protection of the environment and of the public,

(2) to receive public input on these matters, and,

(3) to make recommendations for setting and maintaining standards for worker and public safety and for the protection of the environment as a result of the exploration for the mining and milling of uranium ores;

And whereas it has been decided that there shall be no locating and recording of mineral claims in the Province for the purpose of development of uranium deposits on existing mineral claims for a period of seven years and that therefore there is no necessity for the continuation of the activities of the Commissioners at this time;

And whereas the Commissioners have held a number of hearings and received representatives and submissions and information as the result of those hearings and generally as the result of their appointment;

The Commissioners appointed by order 170/79 shall report their findings and recommendations to date to the Lieutenant-Governor in Council on or before the 31st day of May, 1980;

And further orders that for the purpose of preparing that report:

(a) the Commissioners may continue to engage necessary professional, secretarial, consultative and administrative services, and

(b) the Commissioners shall be paid living and travelling expenses and remuneration prescribed heretofore by order of the Lieutenant-Governor in Council;

And further orders that, except as otherwise provided in this order, the powers and duties conferred and imposed by order 170/79 are rescinded.

And further orders that, effective the 31st day of May, 1980, orders 400/79, 449/79, 944/79, 1281/79, 1521/79, 2013/79, 2214/79 and 6/80 are rescinded.

B-1

Oath of Commissioner

IN THE MATTER OF THE PUBLIC INQUIRIES
ACT, _____, CHAPTER _____.
AND
IN THE MATTER OF A COMMISSION APPOINTED
BY ORDER IN COUNCIL THE _____ DAY OF
_____, 19____, TO INQUIRE INTO

OATH OF COMMISSIONER

    I, _____, do swear [or affirm, as the case may be] that I will truly and faithfully execute the powers and trusts vested in me by His Honour the Lieutenant-Governor, under and pursuant to the Public Inquiries Act, according to the best of my knowledge and judgment. [So help me God].

SWORN before me at the City)
of _____, this _____)
day of _____, 19____.)
)
_____)   _____
A Judge of the Supreme Court   COMMISSIONER
of _____

B-2

Letter of Disclosure of Interest

TO: THE COMMISSIONER

By agreement dated _____ between the _____ Inquiry and [the consultant or his consulting firm] I was retained by the inquiry, for the period of _____ to _____, as an advisor on [short statement of scope of contract]. During the term of the agreement, I have agreed to avoid conflict of interest situations and to promptly, fully, and frankly disclose any actual or possible conflicts.

Pursuant to those obligations, I wish to advise as follows:

1. Office, property, membership, or interest I, or any member of my family, or business associate holds whereby directly or indirectly, a duty or interest may be created in conflict with my duty to the inquiry.

_____

_____

2. Nature and extent of any interest I, my family, or business associate have or may have, directly or indirectly, in any current or proposed contract or transaction with the inquiry or with any present or potential participants in the inquiry.

_____

_____

3. In the past, I, my family, or business associate had the following involvement or interest in matters likely to come before the inquiry or with any present or potential participant in the inquiry.

_____

_____

I DECLARE this to be a full, frank, and honest disclosure of any duties or interests that may directly or indirectly create a conflict with my duties to the inquiry and further promise to file a further statement should there be a material change in circumstances.

Yours truly,

_____

CONSULTANT

B-3

Major Consulting Agreement

Note: Most personal service contracts are documented in some form of consulting agreement. The precedent set out here is a comprehensive contract for major consulting services (such as a major engineering study) and can be shortened or amended as required.

CONSULTING AGREEMENT

_____ INQUIRY

Name and address of Consultant:

_____

_____

_____

_____

    The undersigned hereby agree as follows with respect to the supplying by the Consultant of certain services to _____ Inquiry (the "Inquiry").

1. SERVICES

    Subject to the terms of this Agreement, the Consultant shall provide to the Inquiry the services listed in Schedule A and all such other services as are necessarily incidental thereto, including appearing as a witness in the Inquiry (collectively called the "Services") in connection with the [briefly set out Inquiry terms of reference] (the "Project").

2. QUALIFICATIONS AND SPECIFICATIONS

    The Consultant represents and warrants to the Inquiry that it and its personnel listed in Schedule B have the respective qualifications, experience and capabilities described in Schedule B and that the Services will be performed to the standard of care, skill, and diligence of an experienced professional in the Consultant's field, and in a competent and efficient manner. Without restricting the foregoing, the Consultant shall meet the specifications and performance standards set forth in Schedule C (herein collectively called the "Specifications") and provide the Inquiry with such evidence thereof as the Inquiry considers necessary from time to time to determine whether the Specifications are being met.

3.   COMMENCEMENT AND COMPLETION DATE

The Consultant shall commence its Services not later than the commencement date set forth in Schedule A and shall complete each stage of the Services on or before the respective completion date or dates specified in Schedule A (the "Completion Dates"). The Consultant shall notify the Inquiry if and as soon as it becomes aware or has reasonable grounds to expect that it will be unable to achieve any Completion Date and shall plan and schedule its activities so as to achieve all Completion Dates.

4.   PERSONNEL

If specified in Schedule B, the Consultant's personnel listed in Schedule B shall report to the Inquiry from and after the respective commencement dates and shall serve during the respective periods (each of which is herein called a "Service Period") specified in Schedule B, subject to any extension or termination required under the terms of this Agreement.

5.   INSURANCE

5.1   If the Consultant is supplying architectural or engineering services, the Consultant shall purchase and maintain group professional insurance in the amount and on the terms set forth in Schedule F.

5.2   The Consultant will ensure that all its employees engaged in performing the Services shall be covered by Worker's Compensation and that it shall obtain comprehensive general liability or other insurance to indemnify and save harmless the Inquiry in respect of any accident or death for which the Inquiry or the Consultant may be liable.

6.   STATUS REPORTS

The Consultant shall provide the Inquiry with status reports regarding the performance of the Services by the Consultant at such intervals as the Inquiry may direct. Each such report shall be in a form acceptable to the Inquiry.

7.   SUPERVISION

7.1   The Inquiry shall designate from time to time one of its staff having authority to deal with the Consultant in connection with the Services and to make decisions binding on the Inquiry falling within the scope of this Agreement (such staff and any successor being herein called the "Supervisor"). Unless the Inquiry otherwise notifies the Consultant, the Supervisor shall be authorized to determine whether Completion Dates and Specifications have been met and to require that the Consultant carry out such investigations as the Supervisor may deem necessary to ensure the performance of the Services by the Consultant. The Supervisor may require that the Consultant replace or re-assign employees engaged in supplying the Services on behalf of the Consultant where the Supervisor reasonably objects to their performance; but except for such changes and for voluntary departures or dismissal for cause, the Consultant shall not during the currency of this Agreement change the employees or their respective work assignments respectively set forth in Schedule B.

7.2 The Consultant shall carry out, and cause its personnel to carry out, the duties assigned to them in accordance with the standards, specifications and requirements set forth in this agreement and in accordance with the internal policies and procedures of the Inquiry. Those employees (if any) of the Consultant listed on Schedule B who are specifically designated as subject to the Inquiry's supervision shall be subject to the control and supervision of the Inquiry during their respective Service Periods.

8. FACILITIES

Except for the facilities, if any, listed in Schedule D to be provided by the Inquiry, the Consultant shall provide its own facilities (including office space, typing, drafting, reproduction, and other clerical assistance) as may be necessary to perform the Services.

9. APPROVAL

The Inquiry shall at all times have the right of control, review and prior approval of all reports, terms of study, drawings, and other documents prepared by the Consultant in connection with the Services and may from time to time impose specific requirements and general procedures delineating items which the Consultant must submit to the Inquiry for specific review and approval. Without restricting the foregoing, the Inquiry may require that its approval of any particular stage of the Services be obtained before the Consultant continues to the next stage.

10. DRAWINGS AND COPYRIGHT

Unless otherwise agreed in writing by the Inquiry, all drawings, plans, models, designs, reports, specifications and other documents, and all concepts, products and processes prepared or produced by or at the direction of the Consultant directly or indirectly in connection with the Project or otherwise developed or first reduced to practice by the Consultant in performing the Services (collectively called "Work Product") shall belong exclusively to the Inquiry, which shall be solely entitled to all patents, copyright and trademark rights in respect thereof; provided that the Consultant is hereby granted a non-exclusive licence to prepare and use the Work Product in performing the Services. Such licence shall terminate on the termination of this Agreement. No copies, plans, diagrams or other reproductions of any Work Product, shall be made by the Consultant or any agent or employee thereof without the express permission of the Inquiry and the Consultant shall deliver to the Inquiry immediately upon its request all Work Product in the possession of the Consultant or any employee or agent thereof notwithstanding any termination of this Agreement.

11.   PATENT AND COPYRIGHT INFRINGEMENT

Unless otherwise agreed in writing by the Inquiry, all Work Product shall be developed by the Consultant specifically for the performance of the Services and shall not infringe any patent, copyright, trade secret or other property right of any third party. The Consultant shall indemnify and hold the Inquiry free and harmless from any cost, expense, loss, obligation or damage suffered or incurred by the Inquiry in any suit, proceeding or otherwise so far as the same is based on any claim that the use of any Work Product for the performance of the Services infringes any copyright, patent, licence, trade secret or other property right.

12.   NOTICE ON DRAWINGS

Unless otherwise agreed in writing by the Inquiry, all drawings, plans and designs required to be prepared by the Consultant hereunder shall be prepared in the form designated by the Inquiry and shall contain the following notice:

> "This drawing/plan/design and all copyright therein are the sole and exclusive property of _____
> Inquiry. Reproduction or use of this drawing/plan/ design in whole or in part by any means or in any form whatsoever without the prior written consent of the Inquiry is strictly prohibited."

13.   CONFIDENTIALITY AND CONFLICTS OF INTEREST

13.1   The Consultant shall not disclose any information, plans or documents to which the Consultant may have access by virtue of its connection with the Project (unless such information plans or designs are already publicly available or were disclosed to the Consultant by a third party in a non-confidential capacity), or disclose Work Product or information developed by the Consultant in connection with the Project, to any person not expressly authorized by the Inquiry to receive such information, plans, designs or Work Product. The Consultant shall comply, and shall cause its agents and employees to comply, with such directions as the Inquiry may make to ensure the safeguarding or confidentiality of all such information, plans, designs and Work Product, which directions may include imposition of procedures to ensure confidentiality, both prior to and subsequent to the termination of this Agreement.

13.2 The Consultant shall avoid circumstances where a duty owed to, or an interest in, an outside business enterprise, will conflict directly or indirectly with the duties owed by the Consultant to the Inquiry.

13.3 The Consultant, in performing the Services, shall at all times act in the best interests of the Inquiry, without regard to the interests of, or any duty owed to, an outside enterprise.

13.4 Where the duties of the Consultant to the Inquiry hereunder might possibly conflict with the Consultant's duty to, or interest in, an outside enterprise, the Consultant shall immediately notify the Inquiry in writing and disclose fully and frankly the nature and extent of the possible conflict. Upon receiving such a notice from the Consultant, the Inquiry shall either:

    (a) determine that the possible conflict is acceptable to the Inquiry, in which event this Agreement shall remain in full force and effect; or

    (b) determine that the possible conflict is unacceptable to the Inquiry, in which event the Inquiry may, in its discretion, either:

        i. stipulate terms with respect to the conflict which are to be incorporated as additional terms of this Agreement, as condition of the continuation of this Agreement by the Inquiry; or

        ii. terminate this Agreement.

14. RESPONSIBILITY FOR INQUIRY PROPERTY

The Consultant shall indemnify and save the Inquiry harmless from and against all loss of or damage to any property of the Inquiry (including Work Product, equipment and supplies) while in the custody of the Consultant for work to be performed pursuant to this Agreement, resulting in whole or in part from the negligent act or omission of the Consultant or any agent or employee thereof and shall pay and discharge all costs, expenses, losses, damages or obligations suffered or incurred by the Inquiry in connection therewith.

15. LIABILITY OF CONSULTANT

The Consultant shall indemnify and save the Inquiry harmless from and against all costs, expenses, losses, damages and obligations it may suffer or incur as the result of the breach of any covenant or warranty on the part of the Consultant set forth in this Agreement. Any work or services outside the scope of this Agreement performed by the Consultant without prior written approval of the Supervisor shall be deemed to be gratuitous effort on the Consultant's part and the Inquiry shall have no liability therefore.

16. REMUNERATION OF CONSULTANT

In consideration of the performance of the Services in accordance with this Agreement, the Inquiry shall pay the Consultant the amount or amounts at the time or times, and in the manner set forth in Schedule E. Subject to such restrictions or requirements as the Inquiry may impose from time to time, out-of-pocket expenses of the kind listed in Schedule E properly and necessarily incurred by the Consultant or its employees in providing the Services shall also be reimbursed by the Inquiry upon receiving such vouchers, receipts or other evidence as it may require.

17. BOOKS AND RECORDS

The Consultant shall keep proper accounts and records of all expenditures made in connection with the Services, and all invoices, receipts and vouchers relating thereto. Such accounts, records, invoices, receipts and vouchers shall at all times be open to audit and inspection by the authorized representative of the Inquiry with all such information as they may from time to time require in connection therewith.

18. CONSULTANT NOT AGENT OR EMPLOYEE

Unless specifically agreed to in writing by the Inquiry, the Consultant shall not be the employee or agent of the Inquiry and accordingly, shall not purport to enter into any contract or sub-contract on behalf of the Inquiry, or otherwise act on its behalf; and the Consultant hereby acknowledges that the Inquiry shall not be required on its behalf to make remittances, filings, or payments required by statute of employers.

19. INQUIRY'S OBLIGATIONS

The Inquiry shall make available to the Consultant such information and data, and shall permit the Consultant, its agents and employees to have access to such sites or locations, as are reasonably necessary to enable it to perform the Services. In addition, the Inquiry shall give prompt consideration to all sketches, drawings, specifications, proposals and other documents produced by the Consultant and whenever prompt action is necessary, shall inform the Consultant of the Inquiry's decision in such reasonable time so as not to delay the performance of the Services.

20. CHANGES IN SERVICES

20.1 The Inquiry shall by giving written notice to the Consultant be entitled to order changes in or deletions from the Services as set forth in Schedule A without invalidating this Agreement. If the Consultant is being remunerated hereunder on a lump sum basis, the parties shall at the time of such change or deletion agree on a revised lump sum or other means of remuneration.

20.2 If the inquiry wishes to make additions to the Services not within the scope of those activities set forth in Schedule A, it shall so notify the Consultant and the Consultant shall, unless it objects in writing within five (5) days, be deemed to be included in the Services for the purposes of this Agreement. If the Consultant is being remunerated hereunder on a lump sum basis, the parties shall at the time of the addition to the Services agree on a revised lump sum or other means of remuneration.

21. SUSPENSION

21.1   The inquiry may by notice in writing to the Consultant suspend the performance of the Services at any time and from time to time. After a period of directed suspension, the Consultant shall resume the performance of the Services if and when directed to do so by the Inquiry.

21.2   In the event the Services are suspended:

    (a) by the Inquiry pursuant to paragraph 21.1 and are thereafter resumed at the Inquiry's direction, or

    (b) by order of any court of competent jurisdiction or by order or ruling of any governmental authority having jurisdiction (except where due to the negligent act or omission of the Consultant or its failure to carry out any of its obligations hereunder) and are thereafter resumed upon any such order or ruling being withdrawn or modified,

then any Completion Date or Dates set forth in Schedule A shall be extended to the extent the Consultant can demonstrate that the occurrence of such suspension has delayed the achievement of such Completion Date or Dates. The Consultant shall have no claim against the Inquiry for any costs, expenses, damages or other liabilities suffered or incurred by the Consultant as a result of any suspension hereunder, unless otherwise agreed by the Inquiry in writing.

22. COMPLETION BY OTHER PARTIES

If and so often as the Inquiry determines that the Consultant has not achieved or is not likely to achieve one or more Completion Dates, the Inquiry may terminate the Services by whatever means it deems expedient. In such event, the Inquiry may withhold any further payments to the Consultant until the Services are complete, and upon completion charge the Consultant the amount by which the full cost of completing the Services exceeds any unpaid balance owing to the Consultant hereunder and set-off such amount against the balance. Nothing herein contained shall be deemed to restrict the right of the Inquiry to seek such other remedies and relief as are available to it under this Agreement or otherwise.

23. TERMINATION BY INQUIRY

23.1   The Inquiry shall be entitled to terminate this Agreement, prior to completion of the Services as follows:

    (a) if the Inquiry in its absolute discretion decides to alter the project on which the Consultant has been working, such that the Services will no longer be required;

    (b) if the Inquiry in its absolute discretion elects to terminate this Agreement and gives 30 days prior written notice to the Consultant; or

(c) immediately upon the Inquiry giving written notice to the Consultant of the occurrence of an Event of Default (as hereinafter defined).

In addition, this Agreement shall terminate automatically upon the dissolution or winding up of the Consultant unless the Consultant is a joint venture or partnership, in which even the obligations of the joint venture or partnership and the surviving member or members thereof shall continue as joint and several obligations notwithstanding the dissolution or winding up of a member.

23.2 Upon the termination of this Agreement, the Inquiry shall pay to the Consultant all amounts accruing hereunder up to and including the effective date of termination; provided that if the Consultant is being remunerated on a lump sum basis, the Inquiry shall pay to the Consultant only the actual cost of services performed and not previously paid for hereunder and the Inquiry may take such steps (including the engagement or employment of outside parties) as it deems necessary to remedy any default and to complete or assist in the completion of the Services. The cost of such steps may be deducted or withheld from any amount that would otherwise have been payable by the Inquiry to the Consultant. Nothing herein contained shall be deemed to limit the right of the Inquiry to seek damages against the Consultant for failing to fulfil or observe any obligation or covenant hereunder or to seek specific performance of this Agreement. Except as expressly provided in this paragraph 23.2, the Inquiry shall have no further obligation or liability to the Consultant in connection with this Agreement or its termination.

23.3 For the purposes hereof, "Event of Default" shall be deemed to occur if:

(a) the Consultant is in breach of any covenant, obligation or warranty hereunder and such breach continues for a period of 7 days after written notice thereof has been given to the Consultant;

(b) the Inquiry acting reasonably determines that the Consultant will not achieve one or more Completion Dates;

(c) the Consultant becomes insolvent or unable to discharge its liabilities as they become due, makes an assignment for the benefit of its creditors, or a petition in bankruptcy is made against him; or

(d) the Inquiry acting reasonably determines that the Consultant or any agent or employee thereof has acted, is acting or is likely to act in a manner detrimental to the Inquiry or has violated or is likely to violate the confidentiality of any information, plans, designs or Work Product.

24. EXPIRATION OF AGREEMENT

Unless sooner terminated in accordance with paragraph 23, this Agreement shall be deemed to be completed when the Inquiry determines that the Services have been completed. All obligations of the Consultant to ensure that the Specifications have been met and the Services have been performed in accordance with this Agreement shall survive any termination or completion.

25. FORCE MAJEURE

Notwithstanding anything herein to the contrary, neither party hereto shall be deemed in default with respect to the performance of the terms, convenants and conditions of this Agreement if the same shall be due to any strike, lock-out, civil commotion, invasion, rebellion, hostilities, sabotage, governmental regulations or controls, or acts of God.

26. NON-ASSIGNABILITY

The Consultant shall not assign this Agreement or subcontract to any person any right, duty or obligation hereunder without the prior written consent of the Inquiry and any attempt to so assign or subcontract without such consent shall be null and void and of no effect. Where the Inquiry's consent is so obtained, any assignment or subcontract shall be made subject to the terms of this Agreement and the Consultant shall require the assignee or subcontractor, as the case may be, to acknowledge such terms in writing at the time the assignment or subcontract agreement is executed. No such assignment or subcontract shall derogate from any obligation or liability of the Consultant to the Inquiry hereunder and any assignee or subcontractor shall, as between the Inquiry and the Consultant, be deemed to be the agent of the Consultant.

27. COMPLIANCE WITH LAWS AND CO-OPERATION

27.1 In carrying out its obligations hereunder, the Consultant shall familiarize itself with and comply with all applicable laws and regulations and obtain at its own expense all necessary licences, permits and registrations as may be required by law. The Consultant shall also co-operate with other parties engaged or employed by the Inquiry on the Project from time to time, and co-ordinate its activities with the activities of such parties as and when requested by the Inquiry.

27.2 The Consultant shall pay and discharge all wages, salaries, charges, costs and expenses due and accruing due to any of its employees and shall make and remit to the proper authorities all deductions therefrom required by law.

28. JOINT VENTURE OR PARTNERSHIP

If a joint venture, the Consultant represents and warrants that all members of the joint venture are as indicated on the execution page of this Agreement and have duly executed same and that a true and complete copy of any written joint venture agreement has been delivered to the Inquiry. The obligations and liabilities of each member of a joint venture or parntership executing this Agreement as Consultant shall be joint and several with all other members thereof.

29. GOVERNING LAW

This Agreement shall be governed by and in accordance with the laws of the Province of _____.

30. NOTICE

All notices, demands and payments required or permitted to be given hereunder shall be in writing and may be delivered personally, sent by telegram or telex or may be forwarded by first class prepaid registered mail to the addresses set forth below. Any notice delivered or sent by telegraph or telex shall be deemed to have been given and received at the time of delivery. Any notice mailed as aforesaid shall be deemed to have been given and received on the expiration of 72 hours after it is posted, addressed as follows:

IF TO THE INQUIRY

_____

_____

_____

IF TO THE CONSULTANT:

_____

_____

_____

or at such other address or addresses as may from time to time be notified in writing by the parties hereto.

31. ENTIRE AGREEMENT

The provisions herein contained constitute the entire agreement between the parties and supersede all previous communications, representations and agreements, whether oral or written, between the parties with respect to the subject matter hereof.

32. REMEDIES CUMULATIVE

All rights and remedies of either party hereunder are cumulative and are in addition to, and shall not be deemed to exclude, any other right or remedy allowed by law. All rights and remedies may be exercised concurrently.

33. NUMBER AND GENDER

All references to any party to this Agreement shall be read with such changes of number and gender as the context hereof or reference to the parties may require.

34. FURTHER ASSURANCES

Each party shall execute such further and other documents and instruments and do such further and other acts as may be necessary to implement and carry out the intent of this Agreement.

35. ENUREMENT

This Agreement shall enure to the benefit of and be binding upon the parties hereto and their successors and permitted assigns.

EXECUTED ON BEHALF OF THE
————————————————— INQUIRY
BY:

—————————————————————————

Authorized Signatory

AGREED AND ACCEPTED BY:

—————————————————————————

(the "Consultant")

To be signed if Consultant is a Joint Venture:
NAME OF JOINT VENTURE:
—————————————————————————

Agreed to and Accepted on behalf of
the Joint Venture by:

—————————————————————————

(Authorized Signatory of Joint Venture)

Agreed to and accepted by the
undersigned members of the Joint Venture:

Name: ————————————————————
—————————————————————————
(signature)

Name: ————————————————————
—————————————————————————
(signature)

SCHEDULE A

TO

CONSULTING AGREEMENT

(Paragraphs 1 and 3)

Description and Scope of Services to be Supplied by Consultant:

Date by which Services are to be Commenced:

_____ , 19 ____

Completion Dates:

Description of Stage of Services   Completion Date

SCHEDULE B

TO

CONSULTING AGREEMENT

(Paragraphs 2, 4 and 7)

Qualifications and Capabilities of Consultant or Consultants' Agents or Employees:

List of Consultant's Personnel who shall be Subject to Corporation's Control and Supervision:

SCHEDULE C

TO

CONSULTING AGREEMENT

(Paragraph 2)

Specifications and Performance Standards
to be met by Consultant

SCHEDULE D

TO

CONSULTING AGREEMENT

(Paragraph 8)

Facilities to be Provided by Corporation:

SCHEDULE E

TO

CONSULTING AGREEMENT

(Paragraph 17)

Compensation Arrangements:

Reimbursement of Expenses:
Types of reimbursable expenses:

Requirements and procedures to be followed for
reimbursement of claims:

B-4

Letter of Formal Introduction

Dear Minister:

_____ Inquiry
By Order in Council No. _____ dated _____
_____, the Government of _____ established the
_____ Inquiry under the _____ Act to inquire
into [terms of reference]. A copy of the Order in Council is enclosed.

The inquiry's preliminary work suggests that your department, in the exercise of its statutory responsibilities, has available
to it reports, studies and other documents that would greatly assist
the work of the inquiry and that certain of your officials have
information in areas of direct concern to us.
[If appropriate, the general areas of interest can be briefly outlined.]

In order that the inquiry may fulfil its mandate, I will be
asking Mr. _____, executive secretary to the inquiry,
to communicate with your office and, working with whatever
official you designate, establish an effective and co-operative working relationship.

Thank you for your anticipated assistance. If you require any
further information on the inquiry, I would be pleased to discuss
the matter further with you.

Yours truly,

_____

COMMISSIONER

Inquiry Budget

A. OPERATING COSTS

    Hearing facilities   _____
    Transcripts   _____
    Travel and accommodation   _____
    (staff and witnesses)
    Rent and office overhead   _____
    Media relations   _____
        Advertising   _____
        Fees and expenses   _____
    Community relations   _____
        Staff   _____
        Travel   _____
        Community information
        (newsletter; radio summary)

B. CAPITAL COSTS

    Furniture and equipment   _____
    Books, maps, etc.   _____

C. STAFF

    Research staff   _____
    Support staff   _____

D. PROFESSIONAL SERVICES
    Commissioner   _____
    Legal counsel   _____
    Staff consultants   _____
    Outside consultants   _____
    Professional witnesses   _____

E. INTERVENORS' FUNDING

F. REPORT

Preparation, printing   _____
Translation   _____
TOTAL   ════════════════

B-6

Notice of
Preliminary Hearing

_____ INQUIRY

NOTICE OF PRELIMINARY HEARING
LOCATION:
DATE:
TIMES:

The government of _____ has appointed [commissioner] to inquire into [terms of reference]

The purpose of this preliminary hearing is to receive representation from interested persons on the following matters:

- the terms of reference and scope of the inquiry
- procedures to be followed
- the structure, timing, and location of hearings
- funding of interested parties

Those wishing to make statements about the issues or submit evidence will be provided an opportunity to do so at a later stage in the inquiry.

For further information contact:

Executive Secretary
[address of inquiry]

_____

COMMISSIONER

B-7

Inquiry Counsel
Submission on Procedure

TO: THE COMMISSIONER

INQUIRY COUNSEL
SUBMISSION ON PROCEDURE

Enclosed is the submission of proposals which I, as inquiry counsel, propose to put before the preliminary hearings of the inquiry on _____ .

The enclosed submission is being circulated to the participants who have so far indicated an intention to appear before the inquiry and will be made available to the public at large to provide an advance indication of the position inquiry counsel will be putting before you so that others may consider these proposals and respond to them at the preliminary hearing.

As inquiry counsel and the inquiry staff are themselves reviewing and re-examining these proposals we reserve the right to vary or amend them prior to formally presenting them to you.

A. LOCATION OF HEARINGS

1. The formal hearings of the inquiry should be held in _____ and _____ . In addition, the inquiry should hold hearings in a number of communities in the affected area to allow residents of these communities to take their submissions. The inquiry should also accept written submissions at any time.

B. ORDER AND PHASING OF HEARINGS

2. The formal hearings should be phased into the following subject matter areas:

PHASE I: [describe generally the evidence to be covered]

PHASE II: and so on

3. The inquiry should regularly advise the public of the relevant subject areas to be addressed at any particular phase of the hearing. Inquiry counsel will invite the participants to consult with him to determine the desirability of a further breakdown of evidence within the subject areas as the hearings progress.

4. Because of the necessary interrelationship of the various subject areas, the right to recall witnesses will, generally speaking, be available upon it being demonstrated to the commissioner that it is desirable or necessary.

C. PARTICIPANTS

5. Any person or group of persons shall be deemed a participant

   if he appears at any formal hearings of the inquiry (including preliminary hearings) and gives his name and address to the inquiry, or if he advises the inquiry in writing of his intention to appear. The inquiry shall maintain a list of all participants which shall be available for inspection by any person at the offices of the inquiry in _____ or any regional office.

6. Those participants who intend to appear on a regular basis before the inquiry to call evidence and cross-examine the evidence of other parties shall be identified as "major participants" and their participation shall be governed by the procedural rules of the inquiry as determined by the commissioner.

D. PRODUCTION OF DOCUMENTS

7. All major participants before the inquiry shall, at an early date as determined by the commissioner, file with the inquiry

   and circulate to the other major participants a list of reports, studies or other documents within their possession or power which are relevant to the subject matter of the inquiry, including those for which privilege may be proposed to be claimed.

8. The list of documents shall be available for inspection by any participant before the inquiry and, upon notice to inquiry counsel and to the participant filing the list, any participant may demand production of any document on the list.

9. Upon reasonable notice being given to the inquiry and to inquiry counsel, any participant may bring before the commissioner an application for production of any listed document if production has been refused or for a further or better list of documents. The participants may, in addition to the above, request production of any particular report, study or document known to him and in the possession or power of any other participant.

10. Inquiry counsel shall solicit and file the list of documents on behalf of the governments of _____ and _____.

E. DISCOVERY OF WITNESS

11. Every participant before giving evidence or calling witnesses on his behalf at the formal hearings shall file with the inquiry and circulate to the major participants at least two weeks before giving evidence or calling such evidence, a text or full synopsis of that evidence together with a list of any reports, studies or other documents to which the witness may refer or upon which he may rely and a biographical note on the witness. If the witness is to be offered as an expert the biographical note should be sufficient to qualify him as such.

F. ORDER OF EXAMINATION

12. At the formal hearings, as a general rule, [the proponent; a government; or major participant] will lead its evidence first followed by [any other project proponents], the other major participants and, finally, by inquiry counsel. The order of calling evidence may be varied from time to time as the nature of the evidence and the particular situation requires.

13. With respect to the witnesses, the participant calling the witness shall be permitted to examine him in chief. The witness will then be cross-examined by the various counsel for the other major participants and by inquiry counsel. The participant calling the witness shall be entitled to re-examine the witness. In certain circumstances, by agreement, or as may be directed by the commissioner, the evidence of a particular matter, from whatever source, may be presented by inquiry counsel on behalf of all of the participants to enable varied and perhaps conflicting evidence to be presented together before any cross-examination by any of the parties.

G. APPLICATION

14. Any application made by a participant to the commissioner for any relief whatsoever shall be made upon reasonable notice to the commissioner, inquiry counsel and the major participants as well as any other participants that may be directly affected.

H. SUBPOENA

15. The issue of a subpoena shall be at the discretion of the commissioner upon application by a participant or inquiry counsel according to the rules of the inquiry. These rules should provide that where a participant considers it necessary to have a subpoena issued and served upon a witness the attendance of that witness shall, in any event, be in accordance with the inquiry rules. If any witness should refuse to comply with the inquiry procedure, as, for example refusing to file a statement of evidence two weeks in advance of attendance, the participant shall so advise the inquiry at the time the subpoena is sought (or as soon as such refusal is made known to him) and, in addition, shall comply with the rules to the greatest extent possible and, in any event, shall file with the inquiry a summary of evidence which the participant intends to adduce from that witness.

I. COMMUNITY HEARINGS

16. In addition to the formal hearings, the inquiry shall conduct community hearings in all of the communities requesting such hearings where, in the view of the commissioner, there is evidence that should properly come before the inquiry. The community hearings shall not commence until the formal hearings are well underway.

17. The timing, format and structure of the community hearings will be determined by the commissioner following discussion with the various major participants and the communities themselves. The formal rules of evidence and procedure will not apply with respect to the community hearings. Witnesses should be encouraged, wherever possible, to file a written submission with the inquiry. All evidence will be presented orally and will not be subject to cross-examination.

J. WRITTEN SUBMISSIONS

18. Any person or group of persons may file a written submission in person at any formal or community hearing, by

leaving a copy with the commissioner or executive secretary or by sending a copy to the _____, office of the inquiry. Each written submission will be given a number and a list of submissions will be maintained by the executive secretary. Any one may review a written submission at the inquiry office.

K. COMMENCEMENT DATE

19. It is proposed that the formal hearings commence at _____ on _____ .

All of which is respectfully submitted.

_____

INQUIRY COUNSEL

Participant Funding

PARTICIPANT FUNDING

The inquiry has been provided with limited funds for interested groups to assist them in participating in the inquiry.

Guidelines

The guidelines for funding of participants before the inquiry are as follows:

(a) There should be a clearly ascertainable interest that ought to be represented at the inquiry.
(b) It should be established that separate and adequate representation of that interest will make a necessary and substantial contribution to the inquiry.
(c) Those seeking funds should have an established record of concern for, and should have demonstrated their own commitment to, the interest they seek to represent.
(d) It should be shown that those seeking funds do not have sufficient financial resources to enable them adequately to represent that interest, and will require funds to do so.
(e) Those seeking funds should have a clear proposal as to the use they intend to make of the funds, and should be sufficiently well organized to account for the funds.

In order to avoid duplication, various groups of similar interests are encouraged to jointly prepare their presentation.

APPLICATION FOR FUNDS

Application for funding should be made in writing to the executive secretary at the address below, and should provide the following information:

(a) A statement of how the applicant satisfies the guidelines for funding.

(b) A description, including a detailed budget, of the purposes for which the funds are required, how the funds will be disbursed and how they will be accounted for.

(c) A statement of the extent to which the applicant will contribute its own funds and personnel to participate in the inquiry.

(d) The name, address, telephone number and position of the individual within the group who will be responsible for administering the funds.

The deadline for submitting an application will be _____, 19_____.

_____

On behalf of the inquiry;
[address]

B-9

Inquiry Procedural Rulings

_____ INQUIRY

PRELIMINARY RULINGS
[Commissioner]
[dated]

NOTE: Before preparing rulings the commissioner should bring together all of the submissions on procedure, terms of reference, funding and so on presented by participants, inquiry staff and inquiry counsel and address each of the significant issues in order.

I have been appointed by the government of _____ by order in council dated _____ to conduct an inquiry as commissioner under _____ Act into [terms of reference].

The order in council refers to [set out the facts that gave rise to the inquiry being established and place the inquiry into context — what proposals gave rise to the inquiry, what government or regulatory action is underway, the events to be investigated].

The inquiry's mandate is to conduct a fair and thorough investigation. To do this I am authorized to hold hearings, and adopt such practices and procedures as I deem expedient, with the powers of compelling the production of documents and the attendance of witnesses.

A. TIMING
   Comments on the timetable for the inquiry and the inquiry report.

B. TERMS OF REFERENCE OR SCOPE OF THE INQUIRY
   An elaboration of the inquiry terms of reference. In particular rule on what specific items are within the terms of reference and what are not, especially if these issues were raised by participants in preliminary submissions.

C. FORM OF PARTICIPATION

Where will hearings be held and what form of hearings (formal, community) will be adopted. Will hearings begin with overview sessions. Describe the procedures to be followed in the different form of hearings.

D. GENERAL PRACTICE AND PROCEDURE

Using the inquiry counsel submission on procedure, consider:
- Who will be participants
- Phases of the formal hearings
- Timing of the phases
- Discovery/production of documents
- Subpoena

E. PROCEDURE AT HEARING

Set out, in the form of a series of succinctly stated rules, the procedure to be followed, including:
- Opening statements
- Order of presenting evidence
- Appearance of witnesses
  Oath
  Filing statement in advance
  Cross-examination
- Applications to the commissioner

F. INTERVENOR FUNDING

Comments on criteria for funding and any decisions made regarding level and recipients of funding.

COMMISSIONER

List of Documents

List of Documents of
[Participant]

The following is a full and complete list of reports and other documents in the possession or power of [participant] relevant to the matters within the terms of reference of the _____ Inquiry.

The documents are all located at [address and location] and are available for inspection Monday through Saturday between the hours of 9:00 a.m. and 6:00 p.m.

Access to the documents and, where appropriate, copies or extracts made by contacting, in advance, the librarian [name; address; phone number;].

_____

On behalf of participant

A. List of documents in the possession or power of _____
    _____ and which [the participant] is prepared to produce.

    _____
    _____
    _____

B. List of documents in the possession or power of [the participant] but which the participant objects to produce as being privileged.

    _____
    _____
    _____

B-11

Statement of Evidence

STATEMENT OF EVIDENCE OF [Witness]

A. STATEMENT
[Evidence of the witness set out in question and answer or simple narrative format.]

B. LIST OF REPORTS AND DOCUMENTS REFERRED TO OR RELIED UPON
[List each report or document in the order referred to in the statement.]

C. STATEMENT OF QUALIFICATION
[Set out the witness's academic and other qualifications, experience and other relevant information necessary to qualify the witness as an expert or at least properly introduce the witness to the inquiry.]

Number all pages consecutively. Number all paragraphs and documents on the list so each can be referred to and identified easily and accurately.

B-12

Form of Subpoena

SUBPOENA

IN THE MATTER OF THE PUBLIC INQUIRIES
ACT, _____, CHAPTER _____.
AND
IN THE MATTER OF A COMMISSION AP-
POINTED BY ORDER IN COUNCIL THE _____
DAY OF _____, 19____, TO INQUIRE INTO
_____

TO:

BY VIRTUE of the powers vested in me by the _____
Act and by Order in Council No. _____, I do hereby order that
you and each of you, do personally be and appear before the
_____ Inquiry at _____
_____ on _____ day, the _____ day of
_____, 19____ at _____ o'clock in the _____
noon and thereafter as long as your attendance shall be required
to testify the truth according to your knowledge.

AND that you bring with you and then and there produce
before the said _____ Inquiry those documents,
reports and materials in your possession or power relevant to the
matters before the inquiry, and show all and singular those things
which you know, or which the said paper writing imports, concerning the issues before the said inquiry.

WITNESS the commissioner of the _____
Inquiry at _____ the _____ day of _____, 19____.

_____

COMMISSIONER

B-13

Request for Subpoena

A. REQUEST FOR SUBPOENA WHERE INQUIRY RULES WILL BE COMPLIED WITH

REQUEST FOR SUBPOENA

TO: THE COMMISSIONER
         [address]

FROM: [Participant]
         [address]

[The participant] is a participant before the _____ inquiry and requests a subpoena be issued ordering the attendance of the following:

> Peter Parker
> Director
> Clean Water Section
> Department of the Environment
> Government of Canada
> 123 West Street
> Ottawa, Ontario
> (hereinafter the "witness")

1. The witness would be required to appear before the inquiry on _____ day, _____, 19____, or thereafter as the schedule of the inquiry demands.

2. The witness will be appearing according to the procedures established by the inquiry as to filing a statement of evidence and otherwise.

3. The witness advises that he cannot be authorized to appear unless ordered to do so by the inquiry and the participant believes, therefore, that a subpoena is necessary to ensure the attendance of the witness.

This REQUEST FOR SUBPOENA is presented at ＿＿＿＿＿＿,
this ＿＿＿＿＿ day of ＿＿＿＿＿, 19＿＿.

PARTICIPANT

A copy of this request for subpoena has been provided to:
[list other participants]

B. REQUEST FOR SUBPOENA WHERE INQUIRY RULES CANNOT BE COMPLIED WITH

REQUEST FOR SUBPOENA

TO: THE COMMISSIONER
           [address]

FROM: [Participant]
           PEOPLE FOR AND AGAINST COMMITTEE
           [address]

[The participant] is a participant before the ＿＿＿＿＿＿＿
inquiry and requests a subpoena be issued ordering the attendance
of the following:

     Peter Parker
     Director
     Clean Water Section
     Department of the Environment
     Government of Canada
     123 West Street
     Ottawa, Ontario
     (hereinafter the "witness")

1. The witness would be required to appear before the inquiry on ＿＿＿＿＿ day, ＿＿＿＿＿＿＿＿, 19＿＿, or thereafter as the schedule of the inquiry demands.

2. The witness will be requested to give evidence on the following:
   (i) the structure and operation of the Clean Water Section on the west coast of Canada;
   (ii) a description of the contingency plans of the Clean Water Section as they related to west coast oil tanker traffic;
   (iii) details of the action taken by the Clean Water Section at the time of the oil tanker spill in Vancouver Harbour on March 1, 1984;
   (iv) His personal advice and opinion on the adequacy of contingency plans and recommendations as to further changes in legislation or practice.

3. The witness will be requested to produce and comment upon the following reports listed in the list of documents of the government of Canada, Department of the Environment:
   (a) Contingency planning on the west coast of Canada (Parker 1982);
   (b) Clean-up operations in the Vancouver Harbour spill, March 1, 1984 (Parker and Brown, 1984);

4. The Participant has written to the witness requesting his voluntary attendance pursuant to the rules of the inquiry on _____, 19____, and _____, 19____, without response. The participant believes that the witness's voluntary attendance pursuant to the rules of inquiry cannot be obtained and therefore requests this subpoena.

This **REQUEST FOR SUBPOENA** is presented at _____, this _____ day of _____, 19____.

_____
COUNSEL/PARTICIPANT

A copy of this request for subpoena has been provided to:
[list other participants]

B-14

Statement of Evidence of Witness Appearing by Subpoena

INTENDED EVIDENCE
OF
[Witness]

A witness appearing under subpoena
prepared by [participant]

1. A request for subpoena was filed with the inquiry on _____, 198__ (copy attached).

2. The request for subpoena was heard by the commissioner of the _____ Inquiry on _____, 19__. (Transcript reference volume _____ page _____) and was granted by the commissioner _____, 198__. (Transcript reference volume _____ page _____.) (Copy of subpoena attached.)

3. A copy of the subpoena was served on [the witness] on _____, 198__.

4. I am advised and do verily believe that he will attend before the inquiry on the date and time specified in the subpoena.

5. The witness will be requested to give evidence on those matters specified in paragraph 2 of the request for subpoena and on the following issues:
[List the issues expected to be covered in evidence-in-chief.]

6. The witness will be requested to produce and comment upon those reports listed in paragraph 3 of the request for subpoena.

7. On behalf of [the participant] I do hereby confirm that the witness would not or could not provide a statement of evidence as provided for in the inquiry rules and that this statement of

intended evidence sets out as completely and accurately as I am able to determine the evidence of [witness] before the inquiry.

_____

COUNSEL/PARTICIPANT

Oath for Interpreters

Do you swear that you will well and truly and to the best of your ability interpret the evidence from the _____ language to the English language and from the English language to the _____ language, so help you God?

B-16

<u>Schematic for Hearing</u>

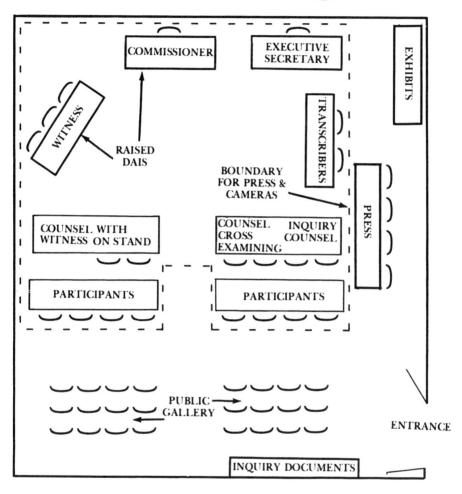

Checklist for Opening of Hearings

1. Call to order
2. Commissioner's opening statement
3. Introductions
   - Executive secretary
   - Inquiry counsel
   - Senior technical advisor
4. Describe facilities
   - Inquiry offices
   - Hearings
     Media rules
     Court reporters
     Library
   - Community hearings
   - Communication/regional offices
   - Filing submissions
   - Getting additional information
5. Exhibits (filed by inquiry counsel)
   - Order in council establishing inquiry
   - Commissioner's oath
   - Preliminary rulings
   - Notice of hearing
   - List of documents for each participant
   - Project application/government report, etc.
6. Opening statements
   - Inquiry counsel
   - Major participants
7. Call first witness

B-18

Checklist for Calling a Witness

Have executive secretary:
- Prepare list of witnesses scheduled;
- Provide filed statements of evidence;

1. Call participant/participant's counsel;
2. Participant calls witness;
3. Witness or panel of witnesses sworn by executive secretary;
4. Participant identifies witness for the record;
5. Give written statement, as filed, next exhibit number;
6. Record any changes or additions to filed statement;
7. Give any additional material next exhibit number;
8. Qualify witness as expert;
9. Have witness present evidence orally;
10. Call cross-examination in approved order;
11. Ask if participant requires re-examination;
12. Commissioner questions;
13. After the presentation is complete, thank witness for attending;
14. Have staff follow up any undertakings given by witness.

B-19

Oath of Evidence

Do you swear that the evidence you shall give to this inquiry shall be the truth, the whole truth, and nothing but the truth, so help you God?

OR

Do you solemnly promise and affirm that the evidence you shall give to this inquiry shall be the truth, the whole truth, and nothing but the truth.

Undertaking Index

Date	Transcript Reference	Party	Undertaking	Disposition
01.15.85	Vol. 19, p. 2093	Jones	List/suppliers	Exhibit 81
01.19.85	Vol. 23, p. 2371	Inquiry counsel	Cabinet minutes	Production refused, Vol. 27, p. 2819

Index